GAME DEVELOPMENT ESSENTIALS

MOBILE GAME DEVELOPMENT

Kimberly Unger

Jeannie Novak

DELMAR
CENGAGE Learning™

Australia • Brazil • Japan • Korea • Mexico • Singapore • Spain • United Kingdom • United States

DELMAR
CENGAGE Learning™

Game Development Essentials: Mobile Game Development
Kimberly Unger & Jeannie Novak

Vice President, Editorial: **Dave Garza**

Director of Learning Solutions:
Sandy Clark

Senior Acquisitions Editor: **Jim Gish**

Managing Editor: **Larry Main**

Associate Product Manager:
Meaghan Tomaso

Editorial Assistant: **Sarah Timm**

Vice President, Marketing:
Jennifer Baker

Marketing Director: **Deborah Yarnell**

Marketing Manager: **Erin Brennan**

Marketing Coordinator:
Erin DeAngelo

Senior Production Director:
Wendy Troeger

Senior Content Project Manager:
Glenn Castle

Senior Art Director: **Joy Kocsis**

Technology Project Manager:
Christopher Catalina

Cover Image *Zen Bound 2*, courtesy
of Secret Exit Ltd.

For product information and technology assistance, contact us at
Cengage Learning Customer & Sales Support, 1-800-354-9706
For permission to use material from this text or product,
submit all requests online at **www.cengage.com/permissions.**
Further permissions questions can be e-mailed to
permissionrequest@cengage.com

Library of Congress Control Number: 2011926286

ISBN-13: 978-1-4180-5265-2

ISBN-10: 1-4180-5265-5

Delmar
5 Maxwell Drive
Clifton Park, NY 12065-2919
USA

Cengage Learning is a leading provider of customized learning solutions with office locations around the globe, including Singapore, the United Kingdom, Australia, Mexico, Brazil, and Japan. Locate your local office at: **international.cengage.com/region**

Cengage Learning products are represented in Canada by Nelson Education, Ltd.

To learn more about Delmar, visit **www.cengage.com/delmar**

Purchase any of our products at your local college store or at our preferred online store **www.cengagebrain.com**

Notice to the Reader
Publisher does not warrant or guarantee any of the products described herein or perform any independent analysis in connection with any of the product information contained herein. Publisher does not assume, and expressly disclaims, any obligation to obtain and include information other than that provided to it by the manufacturer. The reader is expressly warned to consider and adopt all safety precautions that might be indicated by the activities described herein and to avoid all potential hazards. By following the instructions contained herein, the reader willingly assumes all risks in connection with such instructions. The publisher makes no representations or warranties of any kind, including but not limited to, the warranties of fitness for particular purpose or merchantability, nor are any such representations implied with respect to the material set forth herein, and the publisher takes no responsibility with respect to such material. The publisher shall not be liable for any special, consequential, or exemplary damages resulting, in whole or part, from the readers' use of, or reliance upon, this material.

Printed in Canada
1 2 3 4 5 6 7 14 13 12 11

CONTENTS

Part I: Foundation 1

Chapter 2   Mobile Hardware:
the physical framework 29

Chapter 6 Programming on the Go: ones and zeroes

Chapter 8 Publishing & Marketing: life after development 205

Introduction

Mobile Game Development:
small canvas, big ideas

You can't have innovation without constraint. The smaller and tighter the box, the more creative developers need to be to punch their way out. Mobile and handheld game designers are no exception. They embrace constraint—staring down the miniscule download sizes and teeny weeny memory cards with the gimlet eye of experience and an attitude that says, "I can break you with an ESC key and a couple of well-placed function calls."

Within the space of 10 short years, the mobile game industry—fueled by mad innovation and ever-increasing hardware capabilities—is well on its way to crossing the bridge between hardcore and casual. Smartphone owners who may have never thought of themselves as "gamers" have suddenly become a part of the wider audience. This not only opens the window to new types of games, but it allows us to find fresh eyes for gameplay styles long forgotten by the hardcore crowd.

This book is a starting point. Whether you're just dabbling on the fringes of mobile gaming—or you're interested in migrating from console development to mobile—we'll show you the roots of mobile game development and the core elements that lie beneath almost every mobile product.

Kimberly Unger
San Mateo, CA

Jeannie Novak
Santa Monica, CA

About the *Game Development Essentials* Series

The *Game Development Essentials* series was created to fulfill a need: to provide students and creative professionals alike with a complete education in all aspects of the game industry. As creative professionals continue to migrate to the game industry, and as game degree and certificate programs multiply in number, the books in this series will become even more essential to game education and career development.

Not limited to the education market, the *Game Development Essentials* series is also appropriate for the professional trade and consumer segments. Books in the series contain several unique features. All are in full-color and contain hundreds of images—including original illustrations, diagrams, game screenshots, and photos of industry professionals. They also contain a great deal of profiles, tips and case studies from professionals in the industry who are actively developing games. Starting with an overview of all aspects of the industry—*Game Development Essentials: An Introduction*—this series focuses on topics as varied as story & character development, interface design, artificial intelligence, gameplay mechanics, game simulation development, online game development, level design, audio, QA/testing, career guidance, and mobile game development.

Jeannie Novak
Lead Author & Series Editor

About *Game Development Essentials: Mobile Game Development*

This book provides an overview of the mobile game development process—complete with a historical framework, content creation strategies, production techniques, and future predictions.

This book contains the following unique features:

- ■ Key chapter questions that are clearly stated at the beginning of each chapter
- ■ Coverage that surveys the topics of mobile design, art, programming, production, distribution, and marketing
- ■ A wealth of case studies, quotations from leading professionals, and profiles of game developers that feature concise tips and techniques to help readers focus in on issues specific to mobile game development
- ■ Discussions that go beyond general mobile game development topics into emerging areas such as augmented reality, 3D, location-based apps, cloud computing, analytics, and social game development
- ■ An abundance of full-color screenshots, photos, diagrams, and illustrations throughout that expand on the concepts and techniques discussed in the book
- ■ Thought-provoking review exercises at the end of each chapter that help promote critical thinking and problem-solving skills (with annotated responses included in the Instructor Resources)

There are several general themes associated with this book that are emphasized throughout, including:

- ■ Differences between mobile platforms such as smartphones, tablets, and handheld devices
- ■ Distinction between mobile and more traditional game production phases, teams, and methodologies (e.g., console, computer)
- ■ Unique challenges, processes, and techniques associated with mobile design, art, and programming
- ■ New genres, gameplay styles, tools, and distribution models emerging out of mobile development
- ■ Widening player demographics and content features
- ■ Rise of a new indie development population due to low budget, accelerated production cycles, and diverse revenue models

Who Should Read This Book?

This book is not limited to the education market. If you found this book on a shelf at the bookstore and picked it up out of curiosity, this book is for you, too! The audience for this book includes students, industry professionals, and the general interest consumer market. The style is informal and accessible, with a concentration on theory and practice—geared toward both students and professionals.

Students that might benefit from this book include:

- College students in game development, interactive design, entertainment studies, communication, and emerging technologies programs
- Art, design and programming students who are taking game development courses
- Professional students in college-level programs who are taking game development overview courses
- First-year game development students at universities

The audience of industry professionals for this book include:

- Game industry professionals who are interested in entering mobile game development—either by joining existing mobile developers/publishers or starting their own studios
- Professionals such as producers, designers, artists, composers, sound designers, voice actors, and programmers in other arts and entertainment media—including film, television, and music—who are interested in migrating to the mobile game development industry

How Is This Book Organized?

This book consists of three parts—covering industry background, content creation, and production/business cycles.

Part I Foundation—Focuses on providing a historical and structural context to mobile game development. Chapters in this section include:

- **Chapter 1 Baby Steps: a brief history of mobile games**—provides a historical overview of mobile game development, from the feature phone era to the 3D-enabled smartphones of today

- **Chapter 2 Mobile Hardware: the physical framework**—evaluates mobile platforms, along with their associated software development kits

- **Chapter 3 Mobile Software: tools of the trade**—breaks down a wide variety of software tools used in mobile art, design, programming, and audio

Part II Function—Focuses on how mobile game developers create compelling content. Chapters in this section include:

- **Chapter 4 Mobile Design Differences: forget all you know**—explores design documentation, genres, and gameplay specific to mobile development

- **Chapter 5 Art for the Small Screen: painting angels on the head of a pin**—explains mobile art techniques, visual style, and dimensionality

- **Chapter 6 Programming on the Go: ones and zeroes**—surveys mobile operating systems, programming languages, and game engines

Part III Fruition—Focuses on production, distribution, marketing, and future predictions. Chapters in this section include:

- **Chapter 7 Going into Production: "avengers assemble!"**—outlines production cycles, roles and responsibilities, methodologies, and financing

- **Chapter 8 Publishing & Marketing: life after development**—highlights mobile publishing, marketing, distribution, and revenue models

- **Chapter 9 What's Next? a view of the mobile future**—analyzes trends, emerging technologies, theories, and predictions

The book also contains a **Resources** section—which includes lists of game communities, directories, libraries, tutorials, career resources, colleges & universities, development & post-production tools, organizations, news, reviews, research, events, related companies, books, and articles.

How to Use This Book

The sections that follow describe text elements found throughout the book and how they are intended to be used.

key chapter questions

Key chapter questions are learning objectives in the form of overview questions that start off each chapter. Readers should be able to answer the questions upon understanding the chapter material.

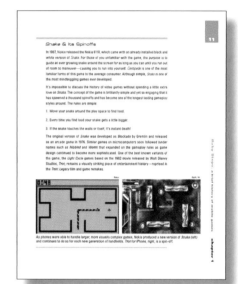

sidebars

Sidebars offer in-depth information on topics of interest—accompanied by associated images.

tips

Tips provide advice, inspiration, and techniques from industry professionals and educators.

quotes

Quotes contain short, insightful thoughts from industry professionals and educators.

notes

Notes contain thought-provoking ideas intended to help readers think critically about the book's topics.

case studies

Case studies contain anecdotes from industry professionals (accompanied by game screenshots) on their experiences developing specific game titles.

profiles

Profiles provide bios, photos and in-depth commentary from industry professionals and educators.

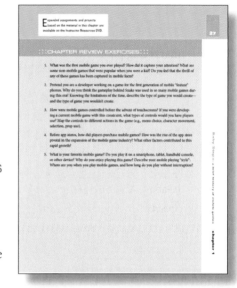

chapter review exercises

Chapter review exercises at the end of each chapter encourage readers to apply what they've learned. Annotations and answers are included in the Instructor Resources, available separately (see next page).

About the Companion DVD

The companion DVD contains the following media (or links to the most current versions of these media):

- Game engines: GameSalad Creator (GameSalad Inc.), Unity 3 (Unity Technologies), and 3DVIA Studio (Dassault Systemes)
- Modeling and animation software: 3ds Max 2012 and Maya 2012 (Autodesk)
- Mobile documentation and SDKs: PSP homebrew dev tools, KDE policies & licensing procedures, Creative Commons licenses, iOS SDK, Windows Phone SDK, Android SDK, Nokia SDK, BlackBerry SDK, LG SDK, and sample marketing plan
- Mobile apps and videos: *PewPew* (Jean-Francois Geyelin), *Trucks & Skulls* (Appy Entertainment), *FaceFighter* (Appy Entertainment), *TuneRunner* (Appy Entertainment), *Zombie Pizza* (Appy Entertainment), *Zen Bound 2* (Secret Exit Ltd.), *Train Conductor* (The Voxel Agents), *Train Conductor 2: USA* (The Voxel Agents), *Time Travel Treasure Hunt* (The Voxel Agents), *Pocket Legends* (Spacetime Studios), *180* (Headcase Games), *Ghost Ninja: Zombie Beatdown* (Gabagool Games), *Agiliste* (Bushi-Go, Inc.), *Parkade* (One Girl, One Laptop), *Speedx 3D* (HyperBees Ltd.), *Aces Cribbage* (Concrete Software, Inc.), *Aces Jewel Hunt* (Concrete Software, Inc.), and *Ash Lite* (SRRN Games)

About the Instructor Resources

The Instructor Resources (available separately on DVD) was developed to assist instructors in planning and implementing their instructional programs. It includes sample syllabi, study guides, test questions, assignments, projects, PowerPoint presentations, chapter outlines, chapter review exercise annotations, and other valuable instructional resources.

Order Number: 1-4180-5266-3

About the Authors

KU

Kimberly Unger designed her first game for the Apple IIe way back in the mid-'80s and has been working with storytelling either as a hobby or a profession ever since. She holds two degrees: English Literature & Writing from UC Davis, Illustration (with honors) from Art Center College of Design (ACCD). After graduating from ACCD, she was offered a teaching position—instructing students in 3D modeling and animation using Autodesk's Maya 1.0! She joined Starsphere Interactive soon afterward—juggling teaching and artist duties until the world of games won out and she joined the industry full-time. She next worked at Blue Planet Software on the newest versions of Tetris for the then next-gen consoles. When Blue Planet closed its doors in 2001, Kimberly went freelance—working as an independent for multiple studios, from small two-person teams up to console gaming powerhouses. Dozens of games have passed through her fingers since she began—mostly as an artist, sometimes as a producer. Kimberly is now taking advantage of her decades of experience as the Founder and Chief Executive Officer of Bushi-go, Inc.—a mobile game studio focusing on genre games delivered to mobile in an episodic format.

Photo credit: Mark Bennington

Jeannie Novak is the Lead Author & Series Editor of the widely acclaimed *Game Development Essentials* series (with over 15 published titles), co-author of *Play the Game: The Parent's Guide to Video Games*, and co-author of three pioneering books on the interactive entertainment industry—including *Creating Internet Entertainment*. She is also Co-Founder of Novy Unlimited and CEO of Kaleidospace, LLC (d/b/a Indiespace, founded in 1994)—where she provides services for corporations, educators, and creative professionals in games, music, film, education, and technology. Jeannie oversees one of the first web sites to promote and distribute interactive entertainment and a game education consulting division that focuses on curriculum development, instructional design, and professional development for higher education and secondary school.

As Online Program Director for the Game Art & Design and Media Arts & Animation programs at the Art Institute Online, Jeannie produced and designed an educational business simulation game that was built within the *Second Life* environment—leading a virtual team of more than 50 educators, students, and industry professionals. She was a game instructor and curriculum development expert at UCLA

Extension, Art Center College of Design, Academy of Entertainment & Technology at Santa Monica College, DeVry University, Westwood College, and ITT Technical Institute—and she has consulted for several educational institutions and developers such as UC Berkeley Center for New Media, Alelo Tactical Language & Culture, and GameSalad. Jeannie has also worked on projects funded by the National Science Foundation and Google for Lehigh Carbon Community College and the University of Southern California (USC) Information Sciences Institute.

An active member of the game industry, Jeannie has served as Vice Chair of the International Game Developers Association-Los Angeles chapter (IGDA-LA), executive team member at Women in Games International (WIGI), Game Conference Chair for ANIMIAMI, advisory board member at the Game Education Summit (GES), and session chair at SIGGRAPH. She has participated on the Online Gameplay selection committee for the Academy of Interactive Arts & Sciences' DICE awards since 2003 and has developed game workshops, panels, and breakout sessions in association with events and organizations such as the Penny Arcade Expo (PAX), Game Education Summit (GES), International Game Developers Association (IGDA), GDC Online (formerly GDC Austin), Macworld Expo, Digital Hollywood, USC's Teaching Learning & Technology Conference, and the Los Angeles Games Conference. Jeannie was chosen as one of the 100 most influential people in technology by MicroTimes magazine—and she has been profiled by CNN, *Billboard Magazine*, *Sundance Channel*, *Daily Variety*, and *The Los Angeles Times*.

Jeannie received an M.A. in Communication Management from USC's Annenberg School (where her thesis focused on using massively multiplayer online games as online distance learning applications) and a B.A. in Mass Communication/Business Administration from UCLA (where she graduated summa cum laude/Phi Beta Kappa and completed an honors thesis focusing on gender role relationships in toy commercials). A native of Southern California, Jeannie grew up in San Diego and currently resides in Santa Monica with her husband, Luis Levy. She is also an accomplished composer, recording artist, performer, and music instructor (piano/voice).

Acknowledgements

The authors would like to thank the following people for their hard work and dedication to this project:

Jim Gish (Senior Acquisitions Editor, Delmar/Cengage Learning), for making this series happen.

Meaghan Tomaso (Senior Product Manager, Delmar/Cengage Learning), for her management help during all phases of this project.

Glenn Castle (Senior Content Project Manager, Delmar/Cengage Learning), for his assistance during the production phase.

Chris Catalina (Technology Product Manager, Delmar/Cengage Learning), for his reliability and professionalism during the DVD QA phase.

Lisa Kincade (Content Reuse Specialist, Delmar/Cengage Learning), for her help ensuring that we've got our clearances covered.

Joy Kocsis (Senior Art Director, Cengage/Learning), for her help with the cover and DVD label approval process.

Sarah Timm (Editorial Assistant, Delmar/Cengage Learning), for her ongoing assistance throughout the series.

David Ladyman (Media Research & Permissions Specialist), for his superhuman efforts in clearing the media for this book.

IMGS, Inc., for all the diligent work and prompt response during the layout and compositing phase.

Cat Wendt, for coming to the rescue during the production phase.

Jason Bramble, for his help with DVD design, authoring, and implementation.

Per Olin, for his organized and aesthetically pleasing diagrams.

Ian Robert Vasquez, for his clever and inspired illustrations.

David Koontz (Publisher, Chilton), for starting it all by introducing Jeannie Novak to Jim Gish.

A big thanks also goes out to all the many people who contributed their thoughts and ideas to this book:

Ron Alpert (Headcase Games)

Scott Berfield (University of Washington Bothell Center for Serious Play)

Whitaker Blackall (Whitaker Blackall Music)

Sue Bohle (The Bohle Company)

Alex Bortoluzzi (Xoobis)

Aaron Calta (Race to the Moon; Royal Court Games)

Kimberly Carrasco (Tiny Tech Studios)

Sana N. Choudary (YetiZen)

Mark Chuberka (GameSalad)

Catherine Clinch (California State University Dominguez Hills)

Peter Drescher (Twittering Machine)

Quinn Dunki (One Girl, One Laptop Productions)

Jennifer Estaris (Total Immersion)

Scott Foe ("The Quentin Tarantino of Mobile")

Matt Forbeck (Full Moon Enterprises)

Caleb Garner (Part12 Studios)

Gary Gattis (Spacetime Studios)

Jacob Hawley (2K Games)

Jason Kay (Monkey Gods)

Jim Kiggens (Course Games)

Jamie Lendino (Sound For Games Interactive)

Luis Levy (Novy Unlimited)

Jason Loia (Digital Chocolate)

Ben Long (Noise Buffet)

Greg Lovett (Cushman & Wakefield)

Nathan Madsen (Madsen Studios)

Ed Magnin (Magnin & Associates)

Aaron Marks (On Your Mark Music Productions)

Terrence Masson (Northeastern University)

Lani Minella (AudioGodz)

Brett Nolan (AppAddict.net)

Paul O'Connor (Appy Entertainment)

Christopher P. Onstad (Mega Pickle Entertainment)

Chris Parsons (Muzzy Lane Software)

Cat Pinson (Icarus Studios)

James Portnow (Rainmaker Games; DigiPen Institute of Technology)

Neil Rennison (Tin Man Games)

Brian Robbins (Riptide Games)

Tom Salta (Persist Music)

Kevin D. Saunders (Alelo)

Jeff Scott (148Apps)

Bill Shribman (WGBH Educational Foundation)

Eric Speier (SMP; 5 Elements Entertainment)

Ed Stark (Vigil Games)

Adam Stewart (One Man Left Studios)

Drew Tolman (Beach Plum Media)

Chris Ulm (Appy Entertainment)

Emmanuel Valdez (Appy Entertainment)

Mary-Margaret Walker (Mary-Margaret Network)

Amanda Jean Wiswell (Zenimax Online Studios)

:::

Thanks to the following people for their tremendous help with media and in securing permissions:

Aujang Abadi (SRRN Games)

Ron Alpert (Headcase Games)

Fernando Blanco & Gary Gattis (Spacetime Studios)

Mark Chuberka (GameSalad Inc.)

Quinn Dunki (One Girl, One Laptop)

Jonathan Friedman (Assembla LLC)

Jean-François Geyelin

Tom Higgins (Unity Technologies ApS)

Raymond Hu (Core77, Inc.)

Simon Joslin (The Voxel Agents)

Jani Kahrama (Secret Exit Ltd.)

Tom Mleko (HyperBees Ltd.)

Daniel Odio (Socialize, Inc.)

Stephen Palley (Slide to Play, Inc.)

Shane Peterman & James Grove (ThinkGeek, Inc.)

John Roseborough (Freescale Semiconductor, Inc.)

Joao Diniz Sanches (Pocket Gamer)

Sebastian Santacroce (Gabagool Games)

Steven Sargent (Appy Entertainment, Inc.

Adam Stewart (One Man Left Studios)

Questions and Feedback

We welcome your questions and feedback. If you have suggestions that you think others would benefit from, please let us know and we will try to include them in the next edition.

To send us your questions and/or feedback, you can contact the publisher at:

DELMAR CENGAGE LEARNING
Executive Woods
5 Maxwell Drive
Clifton Park, NY 12065
Attn: Graphic Arts Team
(800) 998-7498

Or the lead author and series editor at:

Jeannie Novak
Founder & CEO
INDIESPACE
P.O. Box 5458
Santa Monica, CA 90409
jeannie@indiespace.com

DEDICATION

To my parents (who think that I think that they have no clue, but I know better), DrSpaus and the Three Things . . . and to DCE.

—*Kimberly Unger*

To Luis, who has joined me in nomadic bliss so that we can have big ideas together.

— *Jeannie Novak*

Part I:
Foundation

CHAPTER

1

Baby Steps

a brief history of
mobile games

Key Chapter Questions

- What is the definition of a *mobile game*?

- What are some *issues* that the mobile industry has faced during its history?

- What are some characteristics of *successful* games on early mobile platforms?

- What part do *smartphones* play in the mobile industry?

- How are the current generations of *smartphones and handheld devices* related?

If you had asked "Joe Average" off the street to tell you what a mobile game was just a few years ago, the answer might have been, "It's a game you play on your cell phone, right?" Joe would be correct—but with the broader market penetration of multiple-use phones over the past few years, mobile gaming has taken off and has extended into a whole new ball game. Traditional game publishers have mown through the playing field of mobile publishers, assimilating the most successful of those with the highest throughput and hitting what was previously a barely tapped market with a vengeance— bringing decades of experience and a wealth of skill and creativity to bear on what was previously considered a niche industry.

Where Did It All Begin?

It's impossible to discuss mobile games without going back to the roots of video games and the development of mobile devices. The original idea for *cellular phones* (telephones governed by a linked series of antenna towers or "cells" rather than the more standard transmission lines) was conceived back in 1947. At that time, it was posited to the Federal Communications Commission (FCC; the agency that oversees most types of broadcasting over the airwaves) that a large group of radio frequencies be set aside for this purpose. Unfortunately, the number of frequencies available was so small that only around 20 or so phones could work in any given area at once. This was *not* an easy service to sell.

Techie111 (Wikipedia)

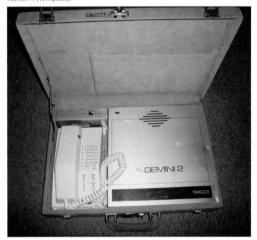

Early portable phones (Motorola Improved Mobile Telephone Service [IMTS], shown) still required a reliable source of power in order to function, which is why most were installed in automobiles.

In 1968, the FCC reconsidered and agreed to increase the number of frequencies reserved to allow for more mobile phones if AT&T and Bell Labs (which requested these frequencies) continued to develop and improve their technology. Even so, it wasn't until 1973 that the first call on a mobile "cellular" phone took place in the United States. By 1977, the first cellular systems were in place—and commercial cellular service had been approved for the US by 1982. Once cellular service was available to the general public, growth quickly outstripped the technology available—reaching over a million subscribers by the late '80s.

Technology for the Elite

Early cellular networks limited the number of calls on air at any given time to only 23—so while the hardware to make calls was expensive at the time, having cheaper hardware would still not have made cellular capability any more accessible. While the FCC was reluctant to increase the number of frequencies allocated, it opened the door to allowing alternate cellular technologies on the 800 band. This touched off an aggressive campaign by the manufacturers to develop new technologies and solutions to help solve the overcrowding issues—which led to the splitting of mobile into two classes of service: *analog* and *digital.*

Analog

Analog transmission allowed the broadcasters to tweak the radio signals so they can carry information such as voice or data. All analog services within the US were shut down beginning in the 2000s as the biggest carriers finally switched to wholly digital services. This caused some problems in areas where there was excellent analog (but no digital) coverage, but those issues were solved by the expansion of the digital networks. In particular, many alarm system and security companies had been using analog communications. Pre-shutdown examples of analog phones include the Audiovox MVX X502 and the Nokia 101. The analog process is very similar to that of FM radio: The signal is received and gets amplified and interpreted by the handheld; it is then sent to a speaker. One of the primary drawbacks of the analog system is the inefficiency of the transmission; analog signals are harder to compress than digital signals and thus require more bandwidth per communication. In addition, analog services are much less secure. For example, the epidemic of *cloning* (where a cellular account is duplicated on another phone, with the charges going back to the original account holder) cost the industry billions of dollars in the late 1990s. By 2008, most of the analog networks in the US were shut down by the major cellular carriers. While very small analog networks can still be found elsewhere in the world (e.g., Costa Rica), the technology is rapidly being phased out.

Redrum0486 (Wikipedia Commons)

Motorola DynaTAC 8000X

Digital

Most phones currently sold in the marketplace, from the Apple iPhone to the Motorola Razr, employ a *digital* service—where information is transmitted as a string of 1s and 0s. Unlike analog (which is used across all mobile handhelds that employ the service), digital is predominantly broken up into three subtypes (TDMA IS-136, CDMA IS-95, and GSM)—and phones built to work with one type of service are often not compatible with another. There are multiband phones such as the Nokia 6340i that are enabled to work on multiple networks in several countries, but these tend to be more specialized and higher priced units targeted at consumers who regularly travel between countries.

sieuquay (Photobucket)

Motorola V60T Color

TDMA IS-136

Several major US carriers such as AT&T once utilized *TDMA (time division multiple access) IS-136 (Interim Standard-136)*, but they have since switched over to the GSM standard. (See GSM section on next page.) For a period of time, dual-band phones, like the Siemens S46, offered customers the ability to access either TDMA or GSM. Much like analog before it, the TDMA capabilities were outstripped by the ever-increasing demands on mobile technology—such as streaming video, text messaging, and email. This bandwidth exists on both the 800 and 1900 bands and works by chopping the frequency band into individual time slots, then assigning a user a specific timeslot at regular intervals.

CDMA-2000

CDMA (code division multiple access) was developed by Qualcomm in the 1980s and became a standard in 1993; it was used predominantly in the US by Verizon Wireless, Alltell, Sprint PCS, and a number of other smaller providers. CDMA exists both on the 800 and the 1900 MHz bands and works by assigning digital codes to the voice signals within a broad spectrum. Currently, the CDMA standards are in the process of opening overseas (non-US) markets at close to the same rate that GSM networks (see next page) are penetrating the US and Asian markets. Both technologies provide a similar service, though historically CDMA is slightly faster—particularly where data (rather than voice) is concerned.

Soltys0 (Wikipedia Commons)   Sprint

The Nokia 51 (left) utilizes TDMA IS-136, while the Sprint
BlackBerry Curve (right) utilizes CDMA-2000.

GSM

GSM (global system for mobile communications) is based on an improved version of the TDMA technology. The engineers working on the GSM standard based it on a hybrid of the analog and digital technologies available. The GSM standard has been in use in the US since 1996, and systems utilizing it were initially the only ones that could provide voice, wireless, email, fax, and other data access.

Clemens PFEIFFER

Two 1991 GSM mobile phones with several AC adapters.

Newer, Better, Faster, Stronger

Thus far, a new standard for cellular communications has come to market around every 10 years or so—resulting in a consistent need to improve not only the network technology, but the user's equipment as well. The adaptation of new technologies is not instantaneous; there is no giant "kill switch" that will allow a carrier to shut down one system in favor of another overnight, so the creep forward appears much slower than it actually is—with smaller countries and carriers adopting these new services years later than their larger counterparts.

New Generations

You've probably heard of 3G and 4G networks, but do you know that "G" stands for "Generation"? Each generation reflects a dramatic technological shift in the way the information is transmitted to the handsets.

2G

The *second generation (2G)* of mobile phones made its European debut in 1991—followed by its introduction in the US within the next year. At around the same time, the technology took a great leap forward and we began to see the emergence of smaller and smaller handheld devices. SMS text messaging made its first appearance, rapidly becoming the communication method of choice for the youngest generation of mobile phone users. It was in the mid to late '90s that mobile games and applications first appeared on cell phones. This also heralds the rise of the *smartphone*—a mobile device that has the built-in capability not only to communicate, but to mimic the functionality of small computers by managing contacts and providing greater access to the Internet.

3G

As the demand for mobile access continued to grow, users of mobile services began to integrate data access functions such as Internet usage—and 2G technology simply couldn't keep up. In October of 2001, the first of the *third generation (3G)* systems were introduced in Japan by its predominant mobile phone operator (NTT DoCoMo) using the *W-CDMA (Wideband Code Division Multiple Access)* technology base. By the beginning of 2002, Europe and the US had launched their own competing 3G systems on the CDMA2000 using one of its 1x digital wireless standards known as *EV-DO (Evolution-Data Optimized)*.

Scared Poet (Wikipedia Commons)

The second generation of mobile phones had SMS text messaging capabilities (Motorola Razr, shown), which became one of the most popular forms of communication on mobile devices.

Courtesy of Apple Inc.

While smartphones of the previous generation had the ability to run limited applications, send text messages, and browse the web, the arrival of 3G (iPhone 3G, shown) expanded the tools and systems available to even casual mobile users.

4G

As mobile networks and features of mobile devices continued to expand, demand rose to meet and max out the capabilities of the 3G network. In the mid-2000s, mobile devices designed to allow laptop and netbook style computers access to mobile networks began to appear—pushing the 3G systems even faster toward maximum capacity. By 2009, it had become readily apparent that the 3G systems in place would not be able to meet the ever growing demand for mobile access. In 2010, the first of the *fourth generation (4G)* systems were brought online by Sprint in the US and by TeliaSonera in Scandinavia.

Sprint

While 4G networks came into play in the US and overseas, the hardware required to take full advantage of system capabilities was slower to reach the hands of the consumer (Samsung Epic 4G, shown).

How Many Gs Do You Need?

It wasn't until the advent of the third generation of networks in 2006 that the term "G" came into use as a service descriptor. "G" is not specific to a single cellular network, but rather it indicates a radical shift in the transmission technology and was applied retroactively to the previous generations (1G and 2G respectively).

What Makes a Game Mobile?

Mobile games are those played on non-traditional handheld consoles. Products such as cell phones, smartphones, palm computers, and media players (e.g., iPod Touch) all fall into this category. While this book covers the development aspects of other traditional console style handheld devices, this is because they have expanded over time from their original game-centric design to include text messaging, voice communications, and networking. Until 2008, however, the definition of mobile games excluded these handheld devices.

Most mobile games are downloaded through a provider's cellular service and played straight on the handheld. Others might be downloaded from a computer through a specially purchased USB cable or Bluetooth device. While smartphones with larger, "shiny" screens and million dollar advertising campaigns have captured the imaginations of many mobile phone users, the truth is that these devices represent only a small percentage of the overall mobile phone install base. The vast majority of mobile games are downloaded and played on simpler, less technologically advanced "feature" phones.

Mobile games first emerged in 1997 on "feature" phones (Nokia 3310, shown)—which functioned predominantly as phones, with a small LCD screen for simple tools such as reception bars, phone number display, and simple graphics.

Where Did It All Begin?

Game makers are an innovative bunch. Give them a piece of technology, and the first thing to pop into their minds will be, "How can I make a game out of this?" When mobile phones first went truly mobile—small enough to fit into a holster and requiring a battery weighing less than your average Rottweiler—building games for these devices became a reality rather than just a cool idea that was tossed back and forth by indie developers. There were a number of technological constraints that had to be addressed before mobile devices achieved enough market penetration to be viable for the software entrepreneur—but once those were met, the technology moved forward at a blinding pace.

:::::*Snake* & Its Variants

In 1997, Nokia released the Nokia 6110, which came with an already installed black and white version of *Snake*. For those of you unfamiliar with the game, the purpose is to guide an ever growing snake around the screen for as long as you can until you run out of room to maneuver—causing you to run into yourself. *Centipede* is one of the most familiar forms of this game to the average consumer. Although simple, *Snake* is one of the most mind-boggling games ever developed.

It's impossible to discuss the history of video games without spending a little extra love on *Snake*. The concept of the game is brilliantly simple and yet so engaging that it has spawned a thousand spinoffs and has become one of the longest lasting gameplay styles around. The rules are simple:

1. Move your snake around the play space to find food.

2. Every time you find food your snake gets a little bigger.

3. If the snake touches the walls or itself, it's instant death!

The original version of *Snake* was developed as *Blockade* by Gremlin and released as an arcade game in 1976. Similar games on microcomputers soon followed (under names such as *Nibbled* and *Worm*) that expanded on the gameplay rules as game design continued to become more sophisticated. One of the best known variants of the game, the *Light Cycle* games based on the 1982 movie released by Walt Disney Studios, *Tron*, remains a visually striking piece of entertainment history—reprised in the *Tron: Legacy* film and game remakes.

Nokia   Courtesy of Apple Inc.

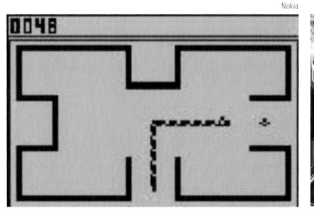 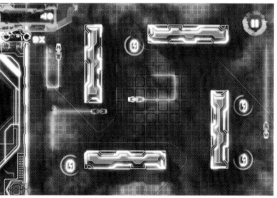

As phones were able to handle larger, more visually complex games, Nokia produced a new version of *Snake* (left) and continues to do so for each new generation of handhelds. *Tron* for iPhone (right) is a modern variant.

Baby Steps: a brief history of mobile games

chapter 1

Sony Ericsson

Though tiny and grainy images were standard on the first generation of color phones (Ericsson T68m, shown), manufacturers saw the potential and began to increase screen size and pixel depth.

Sanyo

The first few generations of camera phones (Sanyo SCP 5300, shown) had expanded the memory capacity to allow enough space to store photos.

Color Screens

The first break for mobile games came in 1998 when Siemens introduced the first color mobile screens. The advent of color opened up a whole new arena for mobile titles, allowing games to take advantage of more than just varying shades of grey. JavaOS was still the most common *operating system (OS)* used, and games were still around 5 KB in size—but with the extra memory that went along with a color screen, games finally had some room to grow. With the introduction of color screens, original content and updated versions of classic gameplay began to emerge. The most direct route to the consumer was still direct download from the carrier or by OEM (*original equipment manufacturer*; installed on the device when you get it). As more games became available to the consumer, the carriers began to formalize and more aggressively market their individual mobile stores and accompanying campaigns that pushed games, music, ringtones, and other applications directly to the user.

Camera Phones

The first big break after the release of *Snake* came when the *camera phone* was introduced in 2001—aided by the significant increase in the size of the screen, along with the massive jump in memory required to handle digital photography. While there were still many ports of existing games, web-based games started to make the jump as well—with classics such as *Bejeweled* finding a whole new audience while drawing existing fans to the mobile arena. Consumers could install multiple games on their handhelds and charge game purchases directly to their mobile accounts—rather than paying a third party or working with tricky and often confusing web downloads. Since camera phones needed access in order to print photos, the process continued to be streamlined so that consumers who were not as computer savvy could access games and other applications with relative ease.

PDAs

Personal digital assistants (PDAs) maintained a presence separate from mobile phones for years. Blessed with superior screen resolution and far more expansive memory, many games made the jump to PDA long before they became available on mobile. For example, *Serious Sam* was ported to the Palm OS in 2001 but didn't arrive elsewhere in mobile until 2010. However, most PDAs were primarily used in business applications—so while higher quality games were available, they didn't quite set the market on fire. Games were seen as a potential market that never quite reached its peak. Add to this the fact that each PDA (manufactured by Motorola, Palm, Nokia, and others) had different requirements, and the only way to get a game onto a PDA was by purchasing it online and downloading it to the device over a Bluetooth connection or a physical cable—thereby restricting a game players access to new material unless they were physically able to download it from the Internet over a desktop computer.

Special-Purpose Phones

Once camera phones proved to be popular, phone manufacturers began to diversify—developing different models of hardware based on their functions. Phones targeted at customers interested in downloading and listening to music, using camera functions or playing games became available to the consumer—each with specialized hardware and memory that would best suit the phone's primary task. Purchasing a phone that addressed a specific preference (e.g. high-resolution camera vs. high-quality sound) resulted in significant cost savings over purchasing a phone that could handle a broader range of tasks.

First-generation PDAs (Palm Pilot, shown) had a wide range of functionality that made them ideal for business use—but it took nearly 20 years for the PDA and mobile phone to merge into what is now known as the "smartphone."

The MP3 player phones (Samsung Uproar, shown) appeared on the market in 1997 and allowed music fans to download and play their music libraries on the go.

Baby Steps: a brief history of mobile games

chapter 1

Rise, Fall, Resurrection & Buyout

When it became clear that mobile gaming was not only here to stay but could actually turn a profit, publishers and developers began to flood the market. After all, there was a broad range of pre-existing content that could be re-released for mobile—and it seemed like a low-risk way to expand brand awareness without needing to develop completely new *intellectual property (IP)*. Many of the more traditional video game publishers were slow to enter the race; after all, the phone resolution was low and memory was small—and compared to a big, splashy AAA console title, there didn't seem much point to dedicating an internal team to the process. At the time, there were hundreds of small publishers and independent studios that wanted to get in on the action—and any number of them could be hired to develop a game on an outsourced basis. In fact, the market was initially so glutted with aspiring developers that the competition drove the price of development way down. The end result was the emergence of small teams that would break up after developing one title—with some team members being picked up by publishers or vanishing into obscurity.

The First Cycle

In 2002, the first run of mobile publishers lost their shirts. While games for mobile devices had a great deal of potential—and while there were oodles of people trying to get that first entry into what was being touted as a brave new world—the technology was still in its infancy. Equally important, the user base was often unaware that games were accessible from their mobile devices. The process of getting games onto those handsets was often convoluted for the average mobile user. It wasn't until the carriers began to commit direct support and advertising dollars that games on mobile devices really began to take off. The publishers that survived this first culling eventually went on to become the powerhouses in the industry—and one after another, they all had learned to apply the same lessons regarding depth and breadth of market penetration.

:::::The *Tetris* Phenomenon: No Platform is Safe

The Tetris Company has a single, simple goal for its flagship game: To have a presence on every platform in every country on the entire planet. Mobile phones are no exception. Variations of *Tetris* were some of the first games to appear on the thumb-sized black and white screens of the first generation of mobile phones. Since then, there have been several licensed, high-quality versions of the game for every new generation of mobile—along with a slew of sub-par knockoffs and copies with names such as *Tetrastic* or *Blockytris*—all hoping to cash in on the easy-to-learn, impossible-to-master gameplay that has made this game one of the longest enduring properties on the market. After 25 years, *Tetris* has managed to remain one of the most popular titles available on any game platform. In early 2010, it passed the 100 million download mark, officially making it the most downloaded game in mobile across all handsets, surpassing even *Snake* (but just barely).

Electronic Arts, Inc.

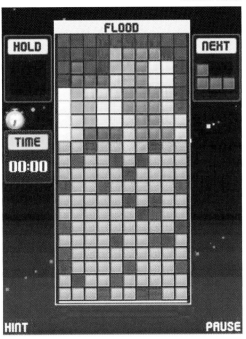

Tetris POP

The Tetris Company licensed its titular product on every phone imaginable—and as of this writing, the game is still one of the top sellers on the market today. This is a classic case of high-end outsourcing. While the Tetris Company has worked with and owned small development studios in the past, its primary business has been in licensing the game's IP for development by various publishers—including Electronic Arts. Most of the time, The Tetris Company has engaged in development in an advisory capacity rather than in a direct, hands-on fashion. This has allowed the company to maintain ownership of the IP and to continue encouraging development over the long term.

A Closer Look at the PDA

The first device with PDA functionality emerged in 1984 with the release of the Psion Organiser, which is often considered to be the first device to combine elements common to PDAs such as contacts, calendar, and notes. Even though the term "PDA" didn't arise until Apple's then CEO John Sculley coined it for use with the first Newton OS device (MessagePad 100) in 1993, the Psion is widely regarded as the father of this line of devices. Psion also created the Epoch OS, which was eventually combined with software advances and components from Nokia, Ericsson and Motorola to form the Symbian OS. Psion eventually sold all of its shares in Symbian to Nokia in 2004. For years, Symbian was the OS of choice for almost all PDA devices (and later, the first evolution of the smartphone). PDA developments ran parallel to that of the cellular phone—eventually including wireless networking and communication, Bluetooth, and the ability to sync data to a personal computer. With the Pilot, Palm took the lead in the PDA market—a lead the company maintained until consumer demand for an all-in-one unit that blended mobile access and PDA functionality required a new evolution of the device.

Boris Cornet (Wikipedia Commons)

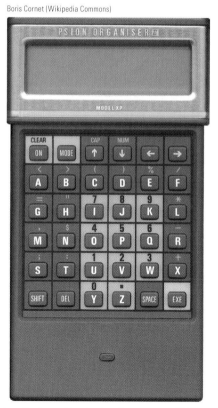

Early PDAs (Psion Organiser II, shown) had only a line or two of LCD screen, but the more complete keyboard made it much easier to enter complex data such as names and addresses.

As mentioned previously, the PDA's deepest market penetration was for business—yet it had much more potential as a game platform. Larger screen sizes, alternate forms of manipulation such as stylus control, and a more "classic" keyboard setup (rather than a flip-style phone keypad, for example) all made the PDA a seemingly perfect fit for mobile games. One advantage of PDAs was the prevalence of manufacturer-owned *application stores*. While these stores often focused on business applications, users were accustomed to going there first to find new software for their PDAs rather than trying to dig through more open marketplaces such as *carrier decks* (stores that are maintained and marketed by the carrier and are directly accessible from the phone itself). This experience of training the user base would prove to be an asset when the inevitable merge between cellular handhelds and PDAs came into play. PDAs maintained a presence apart from mobile phones until the late 1990s. Blessed with superior screen resolution and far more expansive memory, many games made the jump to PDAs long before they became available on cell phones.

The Emergence of the Smartphone

The PDA and the mobile phone were "kissing cousins" for around 10 years. Mobile phones often offered rolodex-like capabilities such as the ability to keep contact information at the user's fingertips, whereas the PDA offered the type of memory, screen sizes, and functionality that many users craved—but without the ability to download content or use the device as a phone, users were required to have two devices. Eventually, mobile phone manufacturers began to build *smartphones* that would allow users to replicate a number of the functions that the PDAs were already providing.

This jump to larger screens and expanded memory was pure gold to game developers, and the makers of mobile phones were well aware of this fact. There was another big development push right around this time as new developers were lured in by the promise of bigger and faster handhelds to work with, and the device manufactures were aggressively seeking game and application content to take advantage of their new hardware capabilities. It has been proven time and time again in this industry that a new and nifty piece of hardware that has no custom software available at release is going to have an extremely hard time getting off the ground. When smartphones first began to appear on the market, they suffered from a similar issue; smartphone manufacturers moved to correct this as quickly as possible by encouraging development.

PDA manufacturers were not about to be left out in the cold. Palm, Microsoft, and Blackberry all jumped into the mobile handheld market with cellular-enabled versions of their own PDA devices; however, bridging the gap between ease of use and depth of functionality proved to be more difficult than anyone suspected.

Diagram by Per Olin

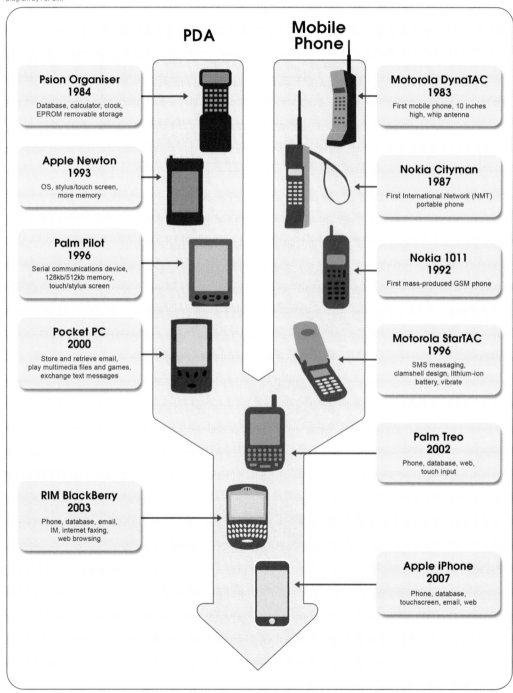

PDA

Mobile Phone

Psion Organiser 1984
Database, calculator, clock, EPROM removable storage

Motorola DynaTAC 1983
First mobile phone, 10 inches high, whip antenna

Apple Newton 1993
OS, stylus/touch screen, more memory

Nokia Cityman 1987
First International Network (NMT) portable phone

Palm Pilot 1996
Serial communications device, 128kb/512kb memory, touch/stylus screen

Nokia 1011 1992
First mass-produced GSM phone

Pocket PC 2000
Store and retrieve email, play multimedia files and games, exchange text messages

Motorola StarTAC 1996
SMS messaging, clamshell design, lithium-ion battery, vibrate

Palm Treo 2002
Phone, database, web, touch input

RIM BlackBerry 2003
Phone, database, email, IM, internet faxing, web browsing

Apple iPhone 2007
Phone, database, touchscreen, email, web

The Evolution of Mobile Gaming

By the end of 2005, the dust had settled on the first round of battle for mobile publication. The thousands of smaller one-shot publishers had either been assimilated by the larger publishers or had gone under—selling their IPs and closing up shop entirely. The big publishers had adopted a strategy of pushing as much content out onto the mobile networks as quickly as possible; in fact, many of the smaller studios were bought up based on their backlog of titles rather than their ability to generate new ones or *re-skins* (games with the art swapped out, resulting in a different aesthetic with the same gameplay and programming behind it) as quickly as the market demanded. The mobile market moved faster than any game market to date. A game could be expected to keep a "Top 25" spot on a carrier deck only for a matter of weeks; while having a clearly recognizable publisher name such as Jamdat or Digital Chocolate certainly served to make it easier for the consumer to find a mobile developer's titles, it did not necessarily add to the longevity of the games.

Mattel

Handheld Game Systems

It's impossible to look closely at the advent of mobile games without going a bit further into the past and tracing the roots of *handheld* games. Beginning in the 1980s, *LCD (liquid crystal display)* technology reached a point where small, single-purpose video games could be made available to the consumer. Initially, these were variations on football and other sports or watered-down versions of popular arcade titles such as *Missile Command* and *Galaga*. Despite their limitations, these handhelds were wildly popular—driving continued innovation and technologies that would eventually be copied in the PDA and mobile phone markets.

Early single-use handhelds from Mattel include *Football* (above) and *Sub Chase* (below)

Mattel

Single-Use Handhelds

The first generation of handheld games consisted of *single-use handhelds*. A static, painted-on screen and a series of LED lights were the only indicators the player received—from "character" movement to keeping score. Nevertheless, as proven by Mattel's popular *Football* handheld, consumers were eager to play games on portable systems rather than sticking to arcades and home consoles—even though the system limitations were far greater.

Single-use handheld games still maintain a presence in the marketplace, though they no longer hold a dominant position. Keychain games such as the massively popular *Tamagotchi* or the 2008 release of *My Meebas* by Mattel (which combined an evolution-style LCD game with the reward of releasing a plush version of the creature the player "raised" from the capsule attached to the game) have shown that even with the limitations of a monochromatic screen and simple 1-4 button gameplay, these products possess a longevity that bodes well for all game systems to come.

Tamagotchi was one of the most popular keychain games.

The Rise of the Cartridge

While Nintendo is often remembered as the leader of swappable game systems, the first handheld to feature multiple games that could be changed out via a cartridge was Milton Bradley's Microvision; handhelds were single-game only until its release in 1979. The Microvision ended up sacrificing depth of gameplay (such as it was at the time) for the ability to swap in multiple cartridges. Although the unit was a poor seller, it opened the door for more advanced cartridge-based handhelds to follow.

In 1989, Nintendo released the Game Boy—which utilized game cartridges and a now-familiar "D-pad" style directional controller, as well as two buttons that could be remapped by the game. For example, the "A" and "B" buttons might be mapped to "jump" and "shoot" in a side-scrolling platformer such as *Mario Bros.*, but they could be used as "boost" and "fire" in a top-down space shooter. The original Game Boy line sold over a million units and wasn't retired until around 1998, when the Game Boy Color was released.

Milton Bradley's Microvision was the first handheld to feature multiple games on cartridges.

Nintendo

Nintendo's first entries in the cartridge arena: Game Boy (left), Game Boy Advance (middle), & Game Boy Micro (right).

The same year the Game Boy was released, Atari came out with the Lynx—the first handheld game console with a color LCD display. Although both systems were commendable (and it was thought initially that the color display might be enough to give the Lynx an advantage in terms of market share), the Lynx never managed to garner the same broad appeal of the Game Boy.

Tjansen (Wikipedia Commons)　　　　　　　　　　Evan-Amos (Wikipedia Commons)

The Lynx (left), released in 1989, was the first handheld with a color LCD display. The Sega Game Gear (right), released in 1990, gave the Game Boy a run for its money—boasting a color LCD screen and a library of titles ripped from the then popular Sega Master System home console.

At this point in the history of the handheld console, the groundwork was put into place—with newer handhelds making inroads to processing power and memory—but these leaps were still largely incremental. For example, the Atari Lynx II (1991) was smaller and lighter—reflecting the use of smaller, faster processors—and the Game Boy Color (1998) boasted increased memory, a color screen, and improved battery life; these were improvements, but not innovations.

Atari　　　　　　　　　　　　　　Nintendo

The Lynx II (above), released in 1991, had faster processors and was smaller and lighter than the Lynx. The Game Boy Color (right), released in 1998, had increased memory, a color screen, and improved battery life relative to previous Game Boy systems.

Console Crossovers

In 2003, Nokia released what was widely considered the first "console crossover" product. The Nokia N-Gage was the first production attempt at developing an all-in-one device that not only targeted the game market but included the functionalities of the mobile phone as well. While the first-generation system sold almost three million units and provided easy access to games, the product designed to take market share away from Nintendo's Game Boy Advance (a pure gaming machine) failed to find its predicted runaway success; this was partially due to the cumbersome design—which made it necessary to remove the battery compartment in order to insert a game *and* engage in "sidetalking" because the speaker and microphone were positioned on the side edge of the phone.

The N-Gage was the first mobile phone that attempted to duplicate a full handheld console gaming experience. While Nokia ceased developing new games for the handheld by the end of 2010, the relative popularity and critical commentary that the N-Gage initially received helped open the door between the mobile and console industries.

Evan-Amos (Wikipedia Commons)

Nokia

The N-Gage (left), released in 2003, was the first mobile phone that attempted to duplicate a full console gaming experience. The N-Gage QD (right), released in 2004, beefed up the mobile phone components while dropping other features.

In 2004, Nokia followed with the release of the N-Gage QD—a device that removed or changed a number of the built-in components, such as the ability to play MP3s; the mobile phone aspect was now market-targeted. Rather than being able to access all three bands of GSM, the device now sold as a dual band product, with specific versions being developed for US or the European and Asian markets.

Right up against the release of the N-Gage QD, Sony unveiled the PSP (PlayStation Portable) as its entry into the handheld market. Unlike the N-Gage, the PSP focused strictly on games—though it did expand its features to include wireless Internet capabilities and the ability to browse the Web. The system originally shipped with *VoIP (voice over Internet Protocol,* the ability to make phone calls over the Internet).

Sony Computer Entertainment America   Sony Computer Entertainment America

The PlayStation Portable [PSP] (left), released in 2004, included wireless Internet capabilities. The PSPGo (right), released in 2009, had no cartridges—loading games from files downloaded directly from Sony.

The PSPGo, Sony's successor to the PSP, took the small handheld system one step closer to the smartphone market by eliminating the need for cartridges. The smaller and lighter game console was a download-only device, and games needed to be purchased through Sony's online store—much the same way that games are purchased for the iPhone through Apple's App Store (see next section).

The App Store

The consumers' ability to find games for their mobile devices continued to be problematic. When the PDAs entered the cellular market, they brought their device-specific *app stores*. Driven by a user base already accustomed to going to the manufacturer for applications to install on their devices rather than relying on the often massive carrier decks, app stores made it simple to find products that would run on the consumer's specific device. Handheld manufacturers, which had previously relied primarily on carrier placement, began to develop their own storehouses of games and applications—networking them with publisher web sites. As the ubiquitous all-in-one smartphone came to the forefront, the app store became an easier way for users to take full advantage of their handheld devices.

::::: Apple's App Store

It is worth noting that most device manufacturers and mobile carriers currently have their own version of an App Store, but none have put forth the massive marketing push that went along with Apple's App Store on the release of the iPhone. With a perceived single point of purchase for the consumer (not including sources for phones that have been legally "hacked" to allow for a broader range of content), Apple mostly fixed the purchase path for the average consumer—not only setting an idiot-proof standard but educating iOS users on how to load up on both paid and free apps.

Courtesy of Apple Inc.

Apple' App Store is the clear leader in application marketing, and the premier destination for all iPhone and iPad purchases.

The App Store might be thought of as a "walled garden"—a place carved out on the Internet where carriers, manufacturers or developers can promote products targeted at a single system or line of systems. Each carrier has its own store (e.g., Verizon's "Get it Now," Sony's PSN [PlayStation Network]); each of these storefronts is easily accessible from the user's mobile device and allows purchases to be charged directly to the user's account rather than going through a third party such as PayPal. Charging the fee through the carrier is one of the elements that separates an app store from a carrier deck. In the case of carrier decks, the charge shows up as a part of the phone bill—sometimes resulting in unpleasant surprises for users given to impulse purchasing!

The State of the Game

The mobile game industry has truly taken off. Huge, touch-enabled color screens and built-in app stores have turned the smartphone into a portable game console that may soon rival traditional handhelds such as the PlayStation Vita (PSVita) and the Nintendo 3DS—which are moving to cash in on the newfound user capabilities by offering Wi-Fi access, text messaging, email communications, and download-able content. Two key features that these handhelds do not (and may never) offer are business functionality and cellular bandwidth. While Sony has been moving toward a closer emulation of the lighter, more versatile devices, Nintendo has been pushing (as always) new and untested technologies such as 3D rather than trying to compete on even footing with established technology.

Sony Computer Entertainment America

PSVita

Samsung

Galaxy S II

Samsung

Galaxy Tab

Courtesy of Apple Inc.

iPhone 4

Courtesy of Apple Inc.

iPad 2

Nintendo

Nintendo 3DS

Baby Steps: a brief history of mobile games   chapter 1

As the smartphone, PDA, and handheld console markets complete for the hearts and minds of consumers, mobile technology continues to advance—churning out newer and better versions of the hardware, and resulting in some genuine leaps of brilliance along the way. In Chapter 2, we will take a look at the current state of mobile hardware and some of the capabilities and restrictions that must be kept in mind during mobile development.

:::CHAPTER REVIEW EXERCISES:::

1. What was the first mobile game you ever played? How did it capture your attention? What are some non-mobile games that were popular when you were a kid? Do you feel that the thrill of any of these games has been captured in mobile form?

2. Pretend you are a developer working on a game for the first generation of mobile "feature" phones. Why do you think the gameplay behind *Snake* was used in so many mobile games during this era? Knowing the limitations of the time, describe the type of game you would create—and the type of game you wouldn't create.

3. How were mobile games controlled before the advent of touchscreens? If you were developing a current mobile game with this constraint, what types of controls would you have players use? Map the controls to different actions in the game (e.g., menu choice, character movement, selection, prop use).

4. Before app stores, how did players purchase mobile games? How was the rise of the app store pivotal in the expansion of the mobile game industry? What other factors contributed to this rapid growth?

5. What is your favorite mobile game? Do you play it on a smartphone, tablet, handheld console, or other device? Why do you enjoy playing this game? Describe your mobile playing "style": Where are you when you play mobile games, and how long do you play without interruption?

Mobile Hardware

the physical framework

Key Chapter Questions

- What are the *basic components* for mobile and handheld hardware?

- How does *mobile* and *handheld* hardware differ?

- When is certain development hardware required?

- How does an *SDK* differ from a *devkit*?

- How do *handheld* and *console* kits differ?

"Industry standard" is the holy grail of hardware and associated software tools. Whether the tools relate to art, programming, networking or compression, the "industry standard" appellation means that a specific tool, or set of tools, is one of the most commonly used for a particular aspect of application development. This doesn't mean that you cannot use any of the other tools available (there is almost always more than one way to create an asset), but industry standard tools have been hammered on, tested, and retested—not only by the engineers who developed them, but by the community at large. Developers don't only work with tools that are well-written, but well-supported. As an added bonus, the development world is a generous place right now. There are books, tutorials, discussion forums, and a host of additional resources in the communities that focus on these tools.

Hardware Variety

When dealing with mobile devices, it's essential to consider the variation between manufacturers. The idea of a single set of hardware supported by one *operating system* (OS) is still new, and there is much debate on whether or not a tightly controlled system (e.g., Apple's iOS) is a better solution than a completely open, consumer-driven one (e.g., Google's Android). In most cases, you may work with multiple hardware configurations supporting a more limited number of operating systems. Consider Google's popular Android operating system—which is not only used to power a range of smartphones built by LG, Motorola, Samsung, HTC and others, but also to run a number of low-cost feature phones. At last count, Motorola alone supported 18 different smartphones—each with distinct hardware capabilities and all powered by the Android operating system. This means it will be necessary to test and debug a game for several devices (rather than just one) when developing for Android.

JPCSP freeware PSP emulator, with an image from *Hexyz Force*

Game development requires a range of actual, physical hardware to develop, test, and ultimately publish a product on any game system. Many manufacturers will provide a software *emulator* (a program run on a personal computer that is designed to mimic the functionality of a handheld unit) for testing purposes. Each of these systems—whether a game-focused handheld such as the Nintendo 3DS or PlayStation Vita (PSVita), or broader Android or Windows-based smartphones—require software allowing developers to build applications that work on their systems. On top of that, every system contains different processors and other options such as the ability to vibrate or Wi-Fi access (as opposed to cellular access). Emulators can only take you so far; once a game is running in a software simulation, building it to hardware strengths is the best way to make sure you've killed all the bugs and to ensure an engaging user experience.

Devkits

Devkit (development kit) is also referred to as an *SDK (software development kit)*, but the terms are intended to be separate. Simply put, a devkit involves a hardware component—which could be as simple as a dongle attached to the back of the computer or as complex as a suite of custom cards, PCs, monitors, cables, and more. "Devkit" and "SDK" both refer to the set of tools needed to develop software that works with a specific piece of hardware, or dovetails with specific sets of software. In many cases, you're working with software only, for example, if you want to develop a game that works with Facebook, your first step would be to download the Facebook SDK—no hardware required. Moving to more "proprietary" devices such as the 3DS or PSVita requires a much more comprehensive development kit—which includes developer-level access to the operating system and specific hardware and software that will allow you to access all of the system's capabilities.

Sun Microsystems, Inc.

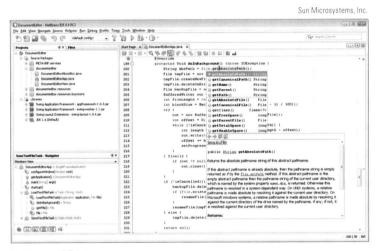

Netbeans IDE 6.9

Homebrew Development Kits

Homebrew games and applications not intended for formal publication and distribution may be created for a number of reasons—from hobbyists designing for a long-outdated system such as the original Nintendo Game Boy to developers wishing to impress peers with their programming chops on the console in question. Homebrew development kits are often the result of a great deal of hard work and passion on the part of independent developers. The issue with homebrew kits is that the end product will only work on other systems that have been similarly hacked. The developer still doesn't have access to the powerhouse of marketing and distribution that ideally goes along with being a licensed developer, and it is exceedingly rare that a homebrew-developed product sees the light of day as an official product.

Mobile and smartphone-style devices allow for a much more open system of development. Most phones are fully capable of being used as development tools with some small amount of modification. For example, Apple allows developers to software-provision iPhones so that they can be used to run applications that have not yet been approved to sell in the app store—a practice commonly known as *ad-hoc distribution*. With the proper permissions, developers can build out an application and test it on any phone that has been properly provisioned. Google's Android systems work in a similar fashion—but rather than requiring developers to mod their own phones for this purpose, licensed Android developers are given access to phones that have been unlocked specifically for the purpose of being used as development devices. One key technique, known as *flashing* (discussed in more detail later in this chapter), is the process of changing the firmware (OS) on a handset; this system may be used to change a phone from one carrier to another (or for less legal purposes such as cell phone cloning). Although these systems are available from the manufacturer, there is also a healthy third-party market; while developers may be required to create versions of software that will work with older systems, access to the hardware may be limited simply because it is being supported less vigorously than it was when new and top-of-the-line.

Genie Universal

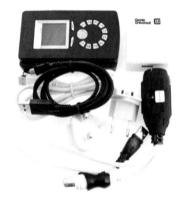

The Genie Universal Clip is a standalone service device that unlocks, flashes, and repairs Nokia phones (entire kit with battery, charger, adapter, cable, and SD card, shown).

SDKs can save you a lot of work, but that doesn't let you off the hook when optimizing and testing for every platform. Even the best tools don't allow you to be lazy.

Matt Forbeck
(Writer & Game Designer, Full Moon Enterprises)

I've had great experiences with SDKs; since I target the iOS platform specifically, I feel Apple has done a good job of providing a registered developer all the tools necessary for taking an initial concept to release.

Kimberly Carrasco
(Developer & Owner, Tiny Tech Studios)

Handheld Hardware Components

There are a number of physical hardware elements common to almost all handheld devices. While the appearance and location of these elements may vary depending on the device, the functionality is more or less the same in most cases—even with different manufacturers.

Screen

Older or more basic technology employs an *LCD (liquid crystal display)* screen capable of displaying black pixels on a neutral background. Some of these screens are back-lit; others, particularly on older or lower-priced "feature" phones, are not. The larger LCD screens are quite capable of delivering a solid user experience for many applications. Smartphones utilize larger displays up to 480 x 800 that are capable of delivering video and still images in full 24-bit color. Tablet devices such as the iPad and Galaxy Tab deliver a much larger screen resolution and physical screen size; however, these larger devices are directed more toward the netbook or laptop computer user and often do not possess the ability to make calls over a cel-lular network—but rather rely on third-party VoIP (voice over Internet Protocol) applications such as Skype to enable this capability.

T-Mobile

Some of today's most modern phones, including T-Mobile's myTouch 4G, still use LCD screens.

Screen Resolution

As newer technology emerges, screen resolution and clarity will continue to improve. For example, the original iPhone screen was larger than average for mobile devices at 320x240. The iPhone 4 continued to improve on this four years later with the introduction of the 920x640 pixel screen. In contrast, the tube-style NTSC televi-sion set that some of us grew up with has only 500 lines or so of "screen resolution" —made worse by muddy colors and reception issues..

Screen sizes for mobile devices vary wildly, even within the different devices offered by a single manufacturer. These different sizes and resolutions need to be taken into account when designing an application; this is covered in greater detail in Chapter 5.

Input Device

The most common *input device* for mobile units consists of manual keys or buttons. Mobile phones have the classic "phone" style keypad for input. These keypads often include additional buttons that can be re-assigned for use by applications. Dedicated game handhelds tend to have more minimalist button setups, reflecting the design of many console game controllers – which rely on four input buttons for most game functions. The more modern smartphones employ touchscreen technology, but much of the functionality mimics the physical keypad setup. The software supports gesture recognition, such as *multi-touch* (the pinching together of fingertips to scale an image up or down), but basic functions such as dialing a phone number are accomplished on an emulated keypad. The same applies to mobile devices that require the use of a stylus such as the Palm series of PDAs and Nintendo's 3DS. The touchscreens on these units do not *require* the stylus; they can be operated with a finger-touch, but the smaller screen size makes hitting any individual button accurately with a fingertip problematic at best.

D-pads (directional pads) and *thumbsticks* are currently only found on console handhelds and represent a classic solution to moving a character through a game environment. Not all games or apps use both devices, but most handheld console games use at least one of them. When working with a touchscreen device such as a smartphone or tablet, there is often a virtual version of a thumbstick or D-pad used to control game movement. Much of the innovation with touchscreen devices involves devising new forms of control for touch games in the absence of these types of controllers.

Make & Model	Accelerometer	Camera/ Video	GPS	HDMI Out	Light/ Proximity Sensor	Touchscreen
HTC EVO 3D	✔	✔ (3D camera/ video playback)	✔		✔	✔
HTC Thunderbolt	✔	✔	✔		✔	✔
LG G2 x	✔	✔	✔	✔	✔	✔
Motorola Atrix 4G	✔	✔	✔	✔	✔	✔
iPhone 4	✔	✔	✔		✔	✔

Smartphone Hardware Features

There are many different types of input controllers used on mobile phones. Some employ directional keypads, while others may use a trackball or something more akin to an analog joystick. These types of input devices might require some application redesign in order to compensate for the differences in control. A *Caterpillar-*style trackball game might not work as cleanly when used with a directional keypad, for example.

Sony Ericsson Mobile Communications AB   LG Electronics   Research in Motion Limited   LG Electronics

Mobile phones can have a broad range of input devices—including touchscreens, keyboards, trackballs, and D-pads. Phones pictured here include Sony Ericsson Xperia Play (D-pad), LG Vortex (touchscreen), BlackBerry Curve 3G (trackball, keyboard), and LG Cosmos (D-pad, keyboard).

Accelerometer

The *accelerometer* (component that determines the physical motion of the device such as tilting or shaking) found in high-end smartphones such as the iPhone 4 and Droid Bionic is simply another form of input device—and it's one that can be put to good use for games and other applications. The accelerometer not only allows the unit to tell when it is being moved quickly or shaken, but it follows the subtler action of tilting the phone as well. In standard iPhone applications, a simple tilt action can change the screen from a vertical to a horizontal format and back again. In more complex applications, the accelerometer can be tied to the GPS to pinpoint the user's location and heading on a map, steer a remote operated vehicle, or play a marble rolling game.

Sega

While accelerometer controlled games first showed up on traditional consoles such as the Wii (*Super Monkey Ball 3D,* shown), they're a natural match for mobile handhelds because the limited screen size makes complicated control schemes much more difficult to implement.

Gyroscope

The three-axis *gyroscope,* which helps to orient the position of the device (e.g., up, down, sideways), is an essential tool where many location based apps are concerned—particularly those that rely on real-world physical direction, such as Google Maps. The gyroscope is also used by many applications to determine when a phone has been flipped into portrait or landscape mode so the graphics can be updated accordingly.

Sanuk Games

Headcase Games

Twin Blades (left) is played in landscape mode, while, *180 Ultra* (right) is played in portrait mode.

Processor

The speed, power, and design of each mobile phone *processor* varies wildly from based on manufacturer and model. For example, Microsoft-enabled mobile devices currently use the ARM-developed (Advanced Reduced Instruction Set Computing

PeterJohnBishop (Wikipedia Commons)

Integrated Circuit (Atmel Diopsis 740 System)

[RISC] Machines) line of mobile processors, while Apple's iPhones use proprietary processors—also based on ARM technology. Other mobile handhelds sometimes use processors based on the MIPS architecture (developed by MIPS Technologies) or other RISC processor families, such as the Hitachi H. Currently, almost 90% of all mobile phones and portable gaming systems use ARM. Each line of processors varies with regard to graphics capabilities and speed, and comparisons between them are not as clear as those for PC CPUs. Units such as the PSVita and 3DS have proprietary processors that are designed specifically for their manufacturers, and their performance characteristics are significantly different from what you would find on a phone.

Memory

Many phones and handhelds utilize removable *memory* cards to provide additional storage for photos, videos, and applications. These cards are often the same found in cameras and other digital devices—and as such, they are often manufacturer-independent (e.g., a Samsung card could potentially be used in a Motorola phone). Smartphones currently have up to 64 GB of built-in memory, which should continue to increase over time. Phones released prior to 2005 have far less memory—rang-

ing from under 1-5 MB. It is not at all uncommon for there to be dramatic variations in memory, even within the various designs used by a single manufacturer; therefore, keeping the application size as small as possible, even on the larger multi-gigabyte phones, is essential.

Evan-Amos (Wikipedia Commons)

Smaller and smaller memory cards

Micro-USB Connector

In 2009, a large number of mobile manufacturers agreed to utilize a standardized *micro-USB (Universal Serial Bus) connector* for charging mobile handhelds—which allow a greater number of new phones to utilize a single standard charger. This also means that many more phones may be linked to a personal computer via USB—allowing them to be accessed and updated with little need for specialized hardware cables.

Brand	USB
Apple	proprietary
HTC	micro
LG	micro → mini
Motorola	micro → mini
Nintendo	proprietary mini
Nokia	mini
Samsung	micro
Sony	micro
Sony Ericsson	mini
Vodafone	mini

USB Types by Brand

ugi_giant (Photobucket)

Mini- and micro-USB connectors

SIM card (NTT DoCoMo
FOMA card chip)

Many carriers implement the use of the *SIM (Subscriber Identity Module) card* to identify a mobile unit on their GSM networks. Replacing the SIM card permits phones to be switched from one carrier to another, and it also allows users to replace their phones while still retaining any unique identifiers and phone numbers with a minimum of fuss. In the current generation of smartphones, swapping out the SIM card is a more advanced procedure. Often, a second-hand phone may be referred to by the seller as "unlocked"; this means that the SIM card has been swapped out. This "unlocked" state is riskier with newer smartphones and carries the possibility of the phone being *bricked* (rendered unusable, much like a very expensive brick) during the process.

Camera

The *camera* has become synonymous with cell phones over the last few years, and you would be hard-pressed to find *any* mobile phone that doesn't at least have a rudimentary camera built into it. The current generation of handheld consoles also has built-in camera and photo manipulation software. An interesting trend involves handheld and mobile games in which the player uses the device's camera to locate "invisible" creatures or game objects in the real world. Still in their infancy, games such as these involving *augmented reality* (*AR*)—combining virtual reality with real-world elements by viewing the physical world through a digital interface—will most likely continue to grow in popularity.

Nintendo

Sony Computer Entertainment America

Nintendo 3DS camera in use (left), and *inviZimals: The Lost Tribes* showing creature combat in augmented reality (right).

How Do Mobile Devices Differ?

Mobile devices vary wildly, even within the product lines of a single manufacturer. They are often designed with specific markets in mind and as such might include one or more additional features. Mobile devices can be divided into broad categories based on general feature sets, and each category can be further broken down into smaller and smaller subsets based on specific capabilities such as the inclusion of a camera or GPS. In essence, there *is* a phone for everyone—and this makes the need to target a specific market segment even more essential (e.g., 18-24 year-olds who download new ringtones every week, 12-14 year-olds whose parents insisted they own a GPS enabled "nanny" phone).

Feature Phones

Feature phones are the most basic types of mobile phones—built and designed for one primary purpose: making phone calls. Games and applications built for feature phones face the greatest number of restrictions, and in many cases the phones themselves are not able to download applications other than those provided by the carrier. Feature phones are usually capable of *SMS (Short Message Service)* mobile text communication, but they don't tend to have PDA-oriented features outside of maintaining a database of phone numbers entered or saved by the user; however, they often have lower-end camera capabilities.

LX600 Lotus (LG) feature phone (left) and Epic 4G (Samsung) smartphone (right)

By necessity, "feature" phones have a more limited, but much more established, set of parameters (e.g., known bugs, locked specifications). In contrast, smartphones are sometimes announced as having a certain set of specs and features, which change before the handheld hits the market (or vary from carrier to carrier).

Jady87 (Photobucket)

HP iPAQ PDA

PDAs

PDAs (*Personal Digital Assistants*) are handheld devices that often are not cellular capable—restricted to sending and receiving data over a wireless network, rather than accessing the cellular network directly. These devices often have superior screen size, higher resolution, and significantly more memory; many were the first mobile devices to enable touchscreen technology. One key advantage of PDA systems is the lack of a contract commitment; since they do not avail themselves of cellular networks, PDAs do not come with the minimum monthly cost that accompanies cellular phones and smartphones. PDAs often have a significant amount of office style functionality, such as the ability to read and review PDFs and PowerPoint presentations. Games developed for PDA systems are not subject to the file size restrictions associated with cellular or smartphones because they're downloaded over Wi-Fi or Bluetooth rather than cellular networks.

Smartphones

Smartphones came into the market in the 1990s when designers began combining the PDA functionality found in popular handhelds, such as the Palm line of products, with the capabilities associated with basic cellular phones. However, a top of the line phone from that time is now a middle-of-the-road gadget at best—and much of the unique functionality of smartphones has now become standard. Smartphones often offer dual connection capacity, with the ability to connect over a cellular network or through a Wi-Fi or Bluetooth network; this allows the user to upload or download much larger files without incurring excessive data costs. Smartphones and PDAs also share capabilities related to file creation and sharing, camera, audio, and video.

Courtesy of Apple Inc.   Samsung

iPhone 4 (left) and Galaxy S II (right)

Tablets

The market for *tablets* has exploded since the introduction of the iPad in 2009. While there have been a number of different touchscreen tablet and laptop/tablet hybrids in the past (e.g., the relatively successful Cintiq), the iPad was the first tablet device that coupled the deliberately limited functionality of smartphone computing and application design with the larger screen size desired by many consumers. Most of the major consumer electronics manufacturers have released or are preparing to release their own versions of these devices, helped along by the availability of operating systems that were originally designed for PDAs and smartphones. Google's open operating system, Android, Windows Phone 7, and the successful iOS from Apple are major players in the new generation of mobile computing.

Courtesy of Apple Inc. Samsung

iPad 2 (left) and Galaxy Tab (right)

Game-Centric Handhelds

Game-centric handhelds targeting the player market have long been dominated by only one or two competitors. As smartphones (iOS and Android-based, in particular) continue to target games, the line between console and phone is getting increasingly blurred. The two major contenders in game-oriented handhelds are the 3DS and PSVita. While both of these systems have Wi-Fi connectivity, only the PSVita is able to access cellular networks. These handheld units are larger, heavier, and more powerful than similar smartphones or PDAs, and they require specialized hardware and software for development that may only be acquired through a licensed agreement with the manufacturer. These development kits include "dev" versions of the handhelds that can be used to test the installation and performance of the game or app.

::::: Variations in the Mix

Each of the mobile handset manufacturers keeps track of models that are still in service, carriers that support each model, and operating systems and functionality that each model possesses. Even within a single manufacturer, there can be dozens of units that run the gamut from basic black and white LCD screen "candy bars" to the newest and most modern smartphones. Just as some carriers require developers to submit an application in order to be considered for their "decks," others may have different requirements that need to be met, such as functionality on a specific set of handhelds or a limited period of exclusivity. Within the developer resources for each manufacturer, a chart or similar layout should be available that will delineate the hierarchy of these units and manufacturer priorities.

Operating System	Recommended Development Unit
Android	Nexus S (replaces Nexus One)
BlackBerry (Android)	PlayBook
BlackBerry (Java ME)	BlackBerry Style
iOS	iPhone 4, iPad
LG Java	GD880 (Mini)
Nokia Symbian	N950
Windows Phone	HTC (with WP7)

Mobile Testing Devices

Mobile Operating Systems

Even though handheld devices are getting more complex, applications are developed on more traditional hardware systems. While the final application is small enough to download over a cellular network, the code libraries required to put it together utilize more space and sophisticated hardware. In addition, despite advances made in mobile keypads, typing a thousand lines of code with a pinky finger or stylus is a prohibitive task.

iOS

Apple's handheld and mobile devices are by far the most closed of the proprietary systems on the market. The hardware required to develop for the iPhone is fairly basic Mac hardware; a Mac Mini with an Intel processor, and Max OS X Snow Leopard will make it possible to run the necessary Xcode libraries. Every Macintosh computer comes with Xcode already installed, and it is available as a free download for developers looking to work with Apple product, so the tools to develop for iOS are free and easy to obtain.

Apple hardware (specifically Mac computers) is used predominantly to develop for Apple systems. While it is possible to find products that were initially programmed on a Mac for use on another operating system, such as Windows 7, they are few and far between. Historically, the PC has been the developer's tool of choice—but with a large number of programmers and developers flocking to develop for the iPhone, the experience base is widening and may cause a shift in the way the next generation of developers think. Specifically designed for mobile computing, the variant of OSX known as *iOS* is used in Apple's smartphone and tablet devices; applications developed for one device may easily be transferred to another as long as allowances are made for the variation in screen size.

Operating System	Processor	Memory	Disk Space
Mac OSX	Mac computer with Intel CPU (2.0 GHz quad-core)	4 GB	5 GB

Design Parameters for Mac iOS Versions

Courtesy of Apple Inc.

Courtesy of Apple Inc.

The iPad 2 screen is much larger than the iPhone screen (9.7" vs. 3.5" in diagonal), but its resolution is not much greater (1024 x 768, compared to the iPhone's 960 x 640)

The Benefits of iOS Development

A t the moment, iOS has the best marketing channel—and it allows us to reach the largest possible user base with the smallest investment in engineering. The iOS SDK is very strong, and it's a joy to work with. I like working with one system because it allows us to tailor our code to take best advantage of it, and we avoid the "lowest common denominator" problem that inevitably creeps into cross-platform efforts. The iOS ecosystem is also very homogeneous, which shortens our development time a lot.

Quinn Dunki (Chief Sarcasm Officer, One Girl, One Laptop Productions)

O ur current development is focused exclusively on the iPhone, iPod Touch, and iPad. We like to create universal apps that run natively on the iPhone, Retina (iPhone 4 and iPod Touch 4), and the iPad. It is a challenge as new, faster, and higher resolution models are released to make sure our games run acceptably on the oldest models, but still take advantage of the features of the new models.

Ed Magnin (Director of Development, Magnin & Associates)

T he benefits of developing solely for iOS platforms has meant that we've been working with a closed ecosystem. This has many advantages, one being that we only need to design for a limited number of hardware specifications.

Neil Rennison (Creative Director, Tin Man Games Pty. Ltd.)

Art & Sound: No Restrictions!

The development hardware and software restrictions apply predominantly to the developers handling the programming tasks. Art and sound assets can be created on any applicable system and brought over as needed.

Android

The *Android* OS was released under the Apache open source license; it was developed using a Linux kernel and as such may retain the greatest flexibility with regard to required development hardware. Versions of the SDK are available for Windows, Mac OSX (using an Intel processor), and Linux (i386).

Sprint Sprint

Android phones include the Samsung Replenish (left) and the Galaxy Prevail (right).

Operating System	Processor	Memory	Disk Space
Linux OS	2.0 GHz quad-core	4 GB	5 GB
Mac OSX	Mac computer with Intel CPU (2.0 GHz quad-core)	4 GB	5 GB
Windows OS	2.0 GHz quad-core 32-bit (x86) or 64-bit (x64)	4 GB	20 GB HD with at least 15 GB of available space

Design Parameters for Android SDK Versions

Developing Mobile Learning Games for Android

We are currently developing mobile learning games for Android. Our primary decision drivers for developing for Android include: the adoption velocity for Android; the wealth of training materials for Android development; and the low cost of entry to develop.

—*Jim Kiggens (Producer & Developer, Course Games)*

Developing for iOS & Android

We develop for iOS and Android, on smartphones and tablets. We started with iOS, since its development ecosystem along with the App Store is a terrific combination for developers. Android is slowly catching up, so we decided to support it and grow with the platform.

—*Alex Bortoluzzi (Chief Executive Officer, Xoobis)*

Jacob Hawley on Developing for Both iOS & Android Platforms :::::

JH

Jacob Hawley oversees all technical development and strategies for 2K Games, and he is also the key provider of solutions and strategies for the various IPs currently in development. Jacob's primary focus is the development of intellectual property and technology in and around the software industries. His game credits include such titles as *BioShock, Borderlands, Civilization, Medal of Honor,* and *EverQuest,* as well as many other games with MetaCritic scores above 85. Jacob's past positions include: Vice President of Engineering at Acacia Research Corporation; Enterprise Architect at Microsoft; Co-Founder and CEO of TKO Software; Vice-President of Engineering for ASML; Vice President of Engineering for Celoxica; and Director of Engineering at Creative Labs. He is also an active member in many industry associations – including the Academy of Interactive Arts and Sciences (AIAS), American Association for the Advancement of Science (AAAS), and Institute of Electrical & Electronics Engineers (IEEE).

Jacob Hawley
(Director of
Technology,
2K Games)

We develop for both the iOS and Android platforms. We were quick to adopt the iOS platform and begin building applications for it. To date, it is has been relatively easy for us to adapt our games to it. Android's changes and recent abandonment of previous versions has made it difficult to develop a stable pipeline for Android-based games. Nonetheless, with the nVidia Tegra chip, we see tremendous upside for the Android platform.

Ben Long on Developing for iOS vs. Android Systems :::::

BL

Ben Long's sonic signature has become a key element for top-grossing mobile game developers. In addition to mobile games, his music can be heard across every major television network including the *Stevie Wonder Biography* on A&E. Ben is a life-long gamer and has spoken at GDC China and SXSW Interactive. He is also the author of *The Insider's Guide to Music and Sound for Mobile Games.*

Ben Long
(Composer, Sound
Designer, Audio
Director & Author,
Noise Buffet)

I've been working on mobile games since the pre-iPhone era (a.k.a., the "dumbphone" era). This exposed me to fragmentation and the lack of audio standards pretty early on! Today, I prefer iOS not only because of its popularity, but ease of development. Android is now boasting more devices sold, but it also has the highest level of fragmentation—which means that a game will run great on one device and horribly on another. There are now QA/testing companies that specialize in ensuring the Android apps run across each device. For audio professionals, Android is great because it natively supports .OGG, which is superior to MP3 in every possible way. There are only a handful of iOS game engines supporting this format.

Java ME

Java ME or some variation thereof is used on a large percentage of existing mobile handhelds; however, due to steep variations in processor speed and overall functionality, it is still necessary to test applications on multiple emulators in addition to the actual handsets themselves prior to release.

Motorola

Phones using Java ME include the Motorola RAZR V3.

Operating System	Processor	Memory	Disk Space
Mac OSX	Mac computer with Intel CPU (2.0 GHz quad-core)	4 GB	5 GB
Windows OS	2.0 GHz quad-core 32-bit (x86) or 64-bit (x64)	4 GB	20 GB HD with at least 15 GB of available space

Design Parameters for Java ME SDK Versions

Windows Phone 7

There is tight integration across the board with almost all Windows products that makes Windows Phone 7 an attractive OS for companies targeting the business sector. Windows Phone 7 utilizes the .NET group of languages including .NET, C++, C# and VB.NET. Development kits for Windows Phone 7 will run only on Windows operating systems.

Sprint   Sprint

Phones with Windows Phone 7 include HTC Arrive (left) and LG Optimus 7 (right).

Operating System	Processor	Memory	Disk Space
Windows OS	2.0 GHz quad-core 32-bit (x86) or 64-bit (x64)	4 GB	20 GB HD with at least 15 GB of available space

Design Parameters for Windows Phone 7 SDK

KC

Kimberly Carrasco
(Developer & Owner,
Tiny Tech Studios)

Kimberly Carrasco was born and raised in Southern California. She graduated from California State University Fullerton in 2003 with a B.S. in Computer Science. Kimberly's enjoyment of the programming and design process led her to create Tiny Tech Studios—an indie iOS development studio that has released six apps since its launch in 2009.

I develop specifically for the iOS platform. I feel that the biggest advantage of targeting a specific platform is time. It's advantageous for a small development studio or even just a one-person development team to spend time and money on a well-polished release if the focus is solely on a specific mobile platform. The disadvantage is that the installed base is less than it would be when releasing on multiple platforms—and therefore, the chances of getting back your initial costs and making a profit are also less.

Sam Tepperman-Gelfant

Jennifer Estaris
(Experience/Game
Designer,
Total Immersion)

Jennifer Estaris worked in the software and newspaper industries before swerving over to grad school for creative writing, publishing video game-inspired fiction, and then re-swerving over to the game industry—working on casual, children, and massively multiplayer online games (MMOs) for all platforms at studios within Nickelodeon, Majesco, Atari, and Large Animal Games. An avid gamer, Jennifer is a member of the International Game Developers Association (IGDA) and the Academy of Interactive Arts & Sciences (AIAS) story panel—and she still writes game-inspired fiction for *Gamasutra*, *The Escapist*, and other fine publications.

The benefits of focusing on a specific platform include a more rapid cycle (get your game out there sooner!), the ability to take advantage of features that are system-specific—and most importantly, discard worries about compatibility and QA time (especially for Android). The disadvantage is reducing your reach. Less people are able to access your game, and they'll eventually come to expect it.

Brian Robbins is the Founder of Riptide Games, an iPhone and next-gen mobile game development studio based in Denver, Colorado. He has spent most of his career pushing the limits of emerging tech markets and is frequently evaluating new technologies for unique ways to entertain people. Brian has programmed over 100 games and still finds time to dig into coding whenever he gets a chance. In addition to running Riptide Games, Brian is a frequent speaker at industry conferences and is heavily involved in volunteering within the game industry—primarily through his work with the International Game Developers Association (IGDA). He currently serves as Chair of the IGDA's Board of Directors and as a Trustee for the IGDA Foundation. Brian has also chaired multiple Special Interest Groups and local chapters, and he was awarded the IGDA's MVP award in 2006 for his contributions.

Brian Robbins
(Founder,
Riptide Games, Inc.)

While we have done some minor development work on other platforms, the majority of our development efforts have been focused on iOS. This is largely due to the ease with which we can target all the iOS devices, coupled with the market that provides strong revenue potential. The main benefit that we see from doing this is being able to really get to know the platform and take advantage of everything it has to offer. Our biggest disadvantage, and my long-term concern, is that we are largely dependent on the iOS ecosystem and are looking for ways to diversify our revenue streams.

Developing for All Mobile Platforms

We develop for all mobile platforms: iOS, Android, Java, BREW, and others. Fragmentation has always plagued developers, but those that use technology to manage different platforms can dramatically increase coverage efficiently and maintain a high quality bar.

—*Jason Loia, Chief Operating Officer (Digital Chocolate)*

Handheld Operating Systems

Hardware considerations for handheld console products are significantly different from mobile phone devices. In the case of handheld console systems, there are hardware development kits and physical components that are required for formal game development on these different products; it's necessary to become a registered developer before gaining access to this equipment, which must be purchased or leased rather than being included in the "registered developer" package. The developer license is required to prove that the developer is a proper company—complete with a staff, office, and the finances in place to purchase the required equipment (with prior shipped titles a plus).

Nintendo 3DS

There have been several incarnations of the current Nintendo DS series handheld console, each of which has slightly different hardware and peripherals. Unlike handhelds that may share an OS across several different devices, the Nintendo hardware and software are predominantly proprietary. It's possible to purchase elements piecemeal when developing for Nintendo hardware. For example, small developers might just need one kit initially and enough of the hardware to push applications to one console in order to test the game properly. (As discussed in Chapter 3, emulators will only go so far.) Eventually, a developer may need more kits, upgraded hardware, and possibly even specialized hardware to test everything from camera functions to the accelerometer—to hardware add-ons such as joysticks, speakers or projectors.

Nintendo 3DS

Nintendo products are primarily coded in C++—but regardless of the language chosen, the code must eventually be *compiled* (condensed and translated into a working application) into a proprietary Nintendo format for use on the Nintendo line of handhelds. Part of Nintendo's development kit includes these compilers:

■ *Autostereoscopic 3.53" display at 800x240*: With 400 columns devoted to each eye, this compiler provides an effective viewing screen of 400x240 when using 3D. The top screen can also display 2D graphics, which allows for high-quality visuals.

■ *QVGA LCD screen at 320x240*: "Touchscreen" on the lower portion of the 3DS.Only the lower screen on the 3DS is touch-enabled. The LCD has been overlaid with a resistive touchscreen that can be operated by stylus or fingertip.

■ *2G of NAND flash memory*: The RAM can be expanded by using the Game Boy Advance slot.

It is interesting to note that the system was originally designed to render 2D to one screen at a time, rather than both. In the DSi model, rendering 2D to both screens at the same time can cause an unacceptable performance hit—but this is not an issue on the 3DS model.

Apples vs. Oranges

Some mobile and handheld devices are built to crunch numbers, and others are very heavy on their graphics capabilities. Many have been designed with an eye toward maximizing data and phone capabilities, while others view communications as secondary to PDA or computing functions.

System	CPU	GPU
3DS	266MHz ARM 11x2	DMP Pica 200
PSVita	ARM Cortex A9 quad-core	SGX543MP4+
iPhone 4	1GHz Apple A4 (ARM Cortex A8)	SGX535
iPad 2	1GHz Apple A5 (ARM Cortex A9)	SGX544MP2

Comparison of Technical Specifications Across Mobile Devices

:::::Wii U: The Console with a Twist

After Nintendo unveiled the Wii U prototype during E3 2011, there was a rush of excitement – but amidst all the "oohs" and "aahs," there was also some confusion. Was the Wii U a new console, a new controller or a portable system? The truth is that the Wii U is "all of the above"—sort of. The Wii U controller resembles a portable system—but it interacts with a new console base. The prototype version features a six-inch touchscreen, built-in microphone, speakers, gyroscope, accelerometer, rumble, and a camera that supports video chat. By acting as an overlay (trivia, sniper scope) or extension (golf tee) of the game being played on the television screen, the controller allows for *augmented reality* games (where graphics are superimposed over a real-world environment in real time). Cooperative and competitive play experiences are enhanced by having one player use the new controller while another uses the original Wii remote; if the players solely use the Wii U controller's screen and television screen, respectively, their experiences are completely different. Although the controller looks like a standalone portable system, it actually depends on the console base for processing. The controller's touchscreen either supplements or replicates the gameplay displayed on the television screen — and it allows a player to continue a game session by displaying the game even when the television is turned off. The system, which outputs in HD (a nice step up from the original Wii) is fully backwards compatible with the Wii and its associated peripherals.

Nintendo

Sony PlayStation Vita

The Playstation Portable series of handhelds has gone through a few iterations— some of which have provided major changes to the system (e.g., the removal of the optical drive), and some much more minor (e.g., an upgraded screen). Programmers for the PSP have mentioned that programming for it is very much like working with Sony's PlayStation 2 game console. Sony no longer supports the first generation of this line of portables in favor of the PlayStation Vita (PSVita). Unlike the Nintendo DS series (DS, DSi, 3DS), Sony's handheld has a single screen that is utilized for both display and use as a touchscreen. Coupled with the physical input devices (D-pad and thumbstick), this aligns with the idea that the

Sony Computer Entertainment America

PSVita

PSVita is essentially a portable PlayStation console and that any other functionalities—such as the potential ability to use Skype to make *VoIP* phone calls—are secondary to the device's primary function as a game console.

Handheld CPUs

The majority of the mobile and handheld devices on the market utilize a type of processor referred to as a RISC (Reduced Instruction Set Computing) processor. This type of processor was initially developed for the laptop market and functions on the idea that the simpler the instruction set, the faster the processor.

The original PSP used a single, proprietary MIPS-based CPU at 333Mhz. The internal memory could vary from 32 MB up through 64 MB, depending on the generation—and that memory can be allocated differently from unit to unit. The PSVita has upgraded from this to a quad-core ARM Cortex-A9 processor (which handles the majority of the computing functions) and has added a dedicated graphics processor, the SGX543MP4+.

Add-On Hardware

It seems that for every handheld or mobile console in existence, there are several studios that have developed hardware add-ons. Although the manufacturer might have sanctioned these bits of hardware, the company might not necessarily make it available; in all likelihood, it will be necessary to approach the developers directly to gain access to their SDKs and technology.

ThinkGeek.com

Emotiv Systems

Examples of hardware add-ons include the Joystick-IT joystick (developed by ThinkGeek; left) and the Epoc headset (developed by Emotiv; right).

Scott Berfield on the Benefits of Developing for Multiple Platforms :::::

SB

Scott Berfield
(Executive Producer,
University of
Washington Bothell
Center for Serious Play)

Scott Berfield has been a producer of games since the mid-'80s when he started out as a "Jack of All Trades" (yes—that was a real title!) at Mindscape in Northbrook, Illinois. Since then, Scott has shipped dozens of titles across all platforms; was directly involved in the launch of the Playstation, Xbox and Xbox 360 consoles; has taught Game Production at various schools; and acts as advisor to startup developers and consultant on mobile and downloadable game development.

I have worked on iOS, Android, and PlayBook apps. While diving deep into a specific system can bring rewards in the form of better performance fit for a platform, a small developer will ultimately be best served by generating as many products across as many platforms as possible. This pretty much requires the use of a system that can build for any target. To deal with the problems of generic results, you need to carefully design your UI [user interface] and various components to be tailored for the target platform. Game logic, graphical assets, and media can all be identical as long as you tailor the UI to the device. This way, you get the best of both worlds.

Emulators

An *emulator* is a software version of a hardware device that's designed to allow developers to create applications in a virtual environment and bang out the worst of the bugs before testing them out on a real-life piece of hardware. Emulators are designed to provide fully functioning virtual versions of the target hardware; all the buttons are in the same places, the screen size and resolution are matched up—and in some cases, even the performance of the processor is simulated. The added benefit, particularly in mobile, is that an emulator can be used to test a product on dozens, if not hundreds, of different phones. Mobile phone devices number in the thousands; even though there are "exemplary" systems (those that can be tested on that will represent a certain segment of the existing market), there are still many more hardware possibilities. Most development kits include emulators that allow developers to build and test their products, and these will most likely closely approximate the physical device. There are often third-party versions of emulators (official or unsanctioned), but these don't often contain the same intimate knowledge of the associated system hardware and OS.

Emulators are used to test an application in the absence of actual hardware for dedicated game handhelds as well—most notably Sony and Nintendo game consoles. Initial development is often done on a more general-purpose computer and tested on an emulator, which is more cost efficient than paying for a full hardware seat for each programmer working on the project. The out-of-pocket costs of development hardware for handheld consoles such as Nintendo's 3DS might be in the thousands of dollars—though this number continues to drop as companies fight for market share.

There is a software emulator available for nearly every phone on the market. This is the Android emulator that comes with Eclipse.

Testing Apps on Mobile Devices

After going to the trouble of building an application and testing it out using an emulator, it's time to test it on a real phone—preferably several of them. There are several testing methods, each of which varies based on manufacturer and generation.

Flashing

Flashing is the process making a change to the software that is installed on a mobile device. Once an application has been built and tested in an emulator, it's time to take that application out into the "real world" and test it out on the its associated device. When testing in-house, it's necessary to pick up physical phones and cables for each of the associated handsets. Interestingly enough, while there are many mobile devices available, the number of different USB cables associated with them is still fairly small. At one point, all of the manufacturers had different connection standards—but all models associated with a particular manufacturer were more or less standardized; for example, a cable for a Motorola flip phone would work on most other Motorola flip phones, but not on a Nokia phone. When working with licensed development software, the ability to flash a phone is built into the software; once a game is completed and compiled, the next logical step is to test it out on a real-life phone. Failing this, there are also a number of third-party programs that are designed to allow developers to flash any number of phones for the purpose of testing out the application.

Smartphones

Smartphones were designed from the outset to allow for the transfer of data; when they are plugged into a computer, they register very much along the lines of a hard-drive peripheral. However, the process of getting an application to properly function on the phone is often a little more complex than simply pushing it to the hard drive.

Apple

Once developers have gone through the *provisioning* process for an Apple product, it's possible to create a test version of the application that can be loaded locally into the iTunes store. Provisioning gives a product the permissions it needs to be run live on an iOS device. The provision only lasts a couple of months; once it expires, the app will no longer run on the device—and a new provisioning profile must be issued. From there, the application will load onto a provisioned phone and will run like any other application. Apple does not provide "unlocked" or dev iPhones to developers.

Jailbreaking

Let's be up front, shall we? *Jailbreaking* an Apple product voids the warranty and makes the guys and gals at the Genius Bar grumpy. However, if you're a new developer and working iteratively, you're going to burn through the hundred or so allowable provisions pretty quickly. Jailbreaking will allow you to load your game onto a handset as many times as you need without worrying about bumping up against the constraints of the Apple Developer Program.

Android

Android-based applications may be loaded onto a dev phone and tested from there. Registered developers may purchase unlocked dev phones through the Android Developers Program. Unregistered developers can use several other phones on the market as substitutions.

BlackBerry

BlackBerry applications may be loaded onto a dev phone and tested from there. BlackBerry developer and manufacturer Research in Motion (RIM) does not make dev phones available to BlackBerry developers; instead, RIM requires developers to flash the OS, which is standard operating procedure for mid-range phones.

Microsoft

Oddly enough, Microsoft has a fairly open configuration when it comes to testing applications on its mobile devices. Much like Apple, Microsoft requires products to be tested on an "in-service" model, rather than one that's been unlocked for development—but the tools provided allow developers to upload directly to the phone.

The Limits of Hardware

Many mobile devices use RISC processors based on architecture developed by companies such as ARM Holdings and MIPS; however, the processing speed, number of processors, and other hardware considerations such as *RAM (random-access memory)* or *VRAM (Video RAM)* availability give each mobile device a very different set of capabilities. Operating system considerations aside, any application design intended to be used across multiple devices (e.g., BlackBerry, iPhone, and Android) will need to incorporate strengths and weaknesses associated with each set of hardware.

:::

In Chapter 3, we'll move on to elements needed to program and develop apps for each of the operating systems discussed in this chapter. Keep in mind that each device will have hardware requirements that may limit the end product, and that having the same operating system on multiple devices does not necessarily mean that the app will work well on each device.

Expanded assignments and projects based on the material in this chapter are available on the Instructor Resources DVD.

:::CHAPTER REVIEW EXERCISES:::

1. Create an original idea for a mobile game. Is your game appropriate for smartphones, tablets, and handheld devices—or a subset of these platforms? Why? Consider hardware components of each type of device (including input devices) in your answer.

2. What are the benefits and disadvantages of developing a game for a single device vs. multiple devices? If you were somehow required to develop the game idea you created in Exercise 1 for all three types of platforms (smartphones, tablets, and handheld devices), how would you ensure that the game would be ideal for each of them?

3. Experiment with games that make creative use of a camera, accelerometer or gyroscope. Choose one of these features and discuss how you would expand on the original game idea you created in Exercise 1 to effectively utilize this feature.

4. Play a game that was created exclusively for one platform and discuss how it could be developed for additional platforms. What types of components within the game would need to be modified in order to make the game successful on all platforms?

5. What type of smartphone do you have? Do you prefer to play games using Android or iOS devices? Why? What are the benefits and disadvantages to developing a game for iOS, Android or both operating systems?

Mobile Software

tools of the trade

Key Chapter Questions

- What types of *software* tools are often used in mobile development?

- Is *specialized* software required to deliver an app to the consumer?

- Can a *single software tool* be used with different mobile operating systems?

- What *industry standard* tools are used for mobile development?

- How do *smartphone*-based tools differ from *handheld* tools?

The most powerful tools in a mobile game developer's arsenal are the people who help develop the application. However, what are the tools required for the actual development process? Will it be necessary to purchase Visual Studio suites for every computer? Is Photoshop really the only way to go when it comes to image manipulation? During the *pre-production* phase, the initial period when the design and concept documents are created, it will be necessary to consider different software tools needed for the development process. A number of these tools may be available for free from the manufacturers or developers; others may have been developed by outside vendors and will need to be purchased or licensed. For every paid option available, there are at least a few free ones—but it will be necessary to carefully weigh their advantages and disadvantages.

Tool Categories

Software tools for application development fall into two primary categories: graphics and programming. In some cases, it will be necessary to utilize tools that bridge the gap between the two in order to produce a final product, but they will predominantly focus on one aspect or the other.

Graphics

Photoshop and Illustrator are the "big dogs" when it comes to 2D art for video games, but are these *graphics* tools the best of the bunch for creating mobile games in particular? Before choosing any graphics tool, consider the visual style associated with the game. For example, will it be photo-realistic—or cartoony? While it's possible to shoehorn distinct art styles onto different programs, it is often more efficient to choose a piece of software (and an artist who is well-versed in it) that best supports the intended look and feel of the game.

Photoshop

Photoshop is an all around graphics toolkit. While it was originally designed for photographic manipulation, it has since evolved into an entire creative suite of applications designed not only to handle asset creation for any type of project, but to allow the smooth transfer of asset creation across each program in the suite. This means that it's possible take an image from Illustrator to Photoshop to ImageReady and back again without having to constantly import and export—saving time and image quality.

Put a Limit on Those Processing Steps!

Be sure to limit the number of processing steps an image goes through on export. Taking an image through five different programs risks loss of image clarity and increases the chances that something will go wrong—such as an undesirable palette shift.

As a standalone art tool, any version of Photoshop can do most of what's needed for mobile games. Going beyond standard painting tools, Photoshop has the ability to compress files, add or remove *transparency* (invisible pixels, essential for creating 2D animated sequences called *sprites*)—and save or export to any number of formats that are standard for games, such as .png or .bmp. Photoshop is brilliant for *pixel-painting*—working with images in bitmap form to achieve those nice clean edges that work well for sprites. However, Photoshop doesn't historically do as well with *vector-based* art—the mathematically-created graphics that are easy to scale up and down, much like you see in web applications. Photoshop was originally *raster-based* (it draws images pixel-by-pixel), which means that its default tools and toolset can scale images up and down—but it takes a great deal of hand-retouching and time to achieve an acceptable end result. The more recent versions of the software also contain vector graphics capabilities, but the pixel-based tools are still where the program's true strengths lie. Combine this with the fact that so many games are being developed for mobile and web platforms (where vector graphics are the norm), and Photoshop can drop to a second- or third-place contender—not due to any inherent flaw in the program, but simply because it's not the right tool for the job.

The pixel-level manipulation available in raster-based tools for graphics creation and manipulation (such as Photoshop) can make it a simpler task to keep clean, aliased edges on sprites.

Illustrator

Raster artists might take a bit of time to get used to *Illustrator*, which leans more toward graphics and cartoons. Illustrator started out as a predominantly print-based program; the necessities of scaling advertisement images, text, and other elements up and down to accommodate different sizes from a single base graphic made it an invaluable tool in the advertising industry. What it does not do so well is export finished images in a well-compressed format suitable for mobile. Illustrator may be used with mobile applications designed to work with vector graphics—or another program will be required to compress and export images into a file that Photoshop and DeBabelizer can use.

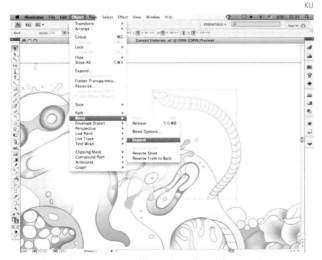

Vector graphics software such as Illustrator allows the user to create smooth, Boolean-based graphics that can be cleanly rescaled for use in a number of different screen sizes—from the very large to the very small.

DeBabelizer

Often called "Debab" for short, *DeBabelizer* is one of the most powerful professional art tools available for manipulating and *compressing* (decreasing file size by removing unnecessary or redundant information) single images or applying the exact same series of manipulations to a large batch of files (such as an animation sequence). Photoshop also manipulates and compresses images, but much simpler manipulation and tighter compression operations are possible with DeBabelizer. However, DeBabelizer is not well-suited to creating an image from scratch.

Programs such as DeBabelizer Pro have targeted image manipulation and compression rather than creation—allowing them to focus on better and tighter compression algorithms.

DeBabelizer vs. Photoshop: Compression .png Files

Interestingly, DeBabelizer has possibly the best image compression for most formats with the exception of .png. Photoshop .png files, as of this writing, consistently have fewer kilobytes.

Flash

Flash applications cannot run on an iPhone, but they can be run on both Windows and Android handhelds. However, Flash as an image creation tool has been vastly underrated. Flash couples the vector-based graphics possible in Illustrator with the ability to *keyframe* (break a movement down into individual frames of animation) full animated sequences—providing a lot of image creation flexibility. Much like Illustrator, however, Flash doesn't handle the export and compression of images very well. Therefore, Flash is best coupled with software such as DeBabelizer for best effect.

While Apple has attempted to eliminate any use of Flash on its iPhone and iPad units, Adobe has remained undaunted. Turning its R&D funds toward moving all Flash export tools to Android, Adobe has made it possible for developers to create games in Flash and then export them to Android systems. This effort has allowed many existing Flash games to make the jump from web to mobile with far less effort.

only_vie90 (PhotoBucket)

Flash is predominantly used to build web-based applications, but it is this very functionality with an eye toward small file sizes that makes it such a powerful tool for game image creation.

Inkscape

Inkscape is not as well-known as Illustrator, and it's an *open source* program (the underlying programming is open and available to everyone with the will to contribute)—which means that it's a low-cost alternative to a commercial program such as Illustrator. It is designed predominantly for web media, but it can export to pretty much all of the necessary formats. Like Illustrator and Flash, however, it still does not easily provide clean, well-compressed images for mobile use. One of the key issues with any of the free or open source alternatives is that it's more difficult to find someone who is experienced in their use. This adds extra time and cost in the form of training game artists to work with these tools—time and cost that will probably end up being more than double the cost of acquiring standard image software.

DiSmeCha, Inkscape.org

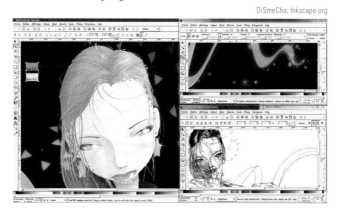

Inkscape is a powerful vector graphics tool that can serve as a low-cost alternative to Illustrator, but finding game artists with experience in its use may prove to be problematic.

Mobile Software: tools of the trade   chapter 3

GIMP

GIMP could be thought of as "the program that would not die." One of the longest running open source image manipulation programs around, and containing many features similar to Photoshop, GIMP (GNU Image Manipulation Program) continues to maintain the reputation of being a solid tool as long as its users are able to work with a minimum of support. Missing functions can be written in by the users—but again, as with Inkscape, it might be difficult to find others who are familiar with the program.

Griatch Art, GIMP.org

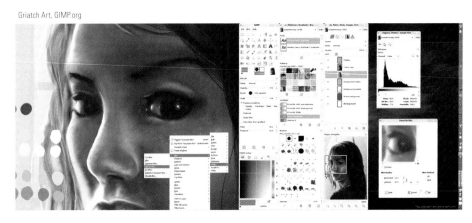

GIMP is a powerful open source editing tool that possesses many features similar to Photoshop.

Interface Builder

Interface Builder (included with the documentation and downloads for iPhone and iPad development tools) is one of those programs that blurs the boundary between graphics and programming tools; it allows you to put together a working interface for an iPhone app in a drag-and-drop fashion, with much of the function preconfigured. A clunky or poorly designed user interface is a key element that can drive a player away from any application; having a tool specially engineered to handle this aspect of development is essential, and it helps make this part of the process simpler for programmer and artist.

Courtesy of Apple Inc.

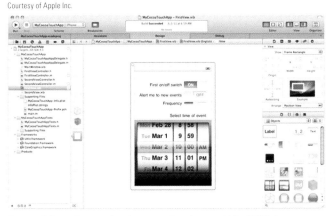

Some of the software development development kits (SDKs) may include customized tools such as Interface Builder that will help streamline the development process.

Expression Blend

Microsoft provides a copy of *Expression Blend*, available as a free download from its developer site as part of the SDK. It's a user interface tool designed to be used with for Windows Phone applications. Closely tied to Silverlight, Expression Blend serves a broader purpose than just mobile apps; it can be used for desktop and web applications as well. It has a similar high concept to Apple's Interface Builder in that it allows designers to create and test their user experiences without repeatedly going back and forth with the programmers.

Not all software development kits (SDKs) needed for mobile development come with toolsets as comprehensive as those provided by smartphone manufacturers (Microsoft's Expression Blend, shown).

Maya & 3ds Max

Now that mobile and handheld games have reached 3D capability, programs such as *Maya* and *3ds Max* are finding a broader reach—allowing developers to build and animate for 3D environments, but also to *pre-render* (render out as a movie) and swiftly iterate 2D backdrops and characters with any desired *perspective* or *point-of-view* (*POV*). Maya and 3ds Max are industry standard tools for console and PC games, but there is a smattering of other lower-cost 3D programs such as Milkshape or Blender for mobile development. Many of these lower cost 3D tools are effective—but like most non-standard tools, there are several issues familiar to production artists (e.g., inability to export to the desired format). The lower cost tools tend to be starting points for many artists who wish to self-train in 3D—and as such, many of them move on to 3ds Max or Maya once they can do so. The end result is a lot more "up and coming" talent for low-cost tools rather than experienced talent.

Autodesk, Inc

Autodesk, Inc

While each of the 3D programs used for game development have their own particular quirks, they all revolve around very similarly designed user interfaces based originally on traditional architectural rendering processes (Maya and 3ds Max, shown).

When it comes to successfully exporting images into the correct format with the proper level of quality, the end result is most important—not what it took to get there. Larger studios may have a preference—requiring Tool A or Tool B in order to keep the source files within the studio or due to restrictions with the in-house production pipeline. Familiarity with industry standard tools is essential—but open source options can serve independent developers quite well.

Art Software for Mobile Development

The usual standards apply: Photoshop, 3ds Max, Maya, After Effects, and so forth for the visuals, to say the least. Dealing with "more limited" gameplay experiences means we can lean back on older, well-established techiques from previous generations of console and PC gaming, rather than having to completely figure things out from the top-down once again production-wise.

—Ron Alpert (Co-Founder, Headase Games)

We use Flash for certain projects, Photoshop for 2D. I like Zoe as a sprite sheet exporter for Flash. Our 3D tools depend on who we hire for a given project, but I'm personally a fan of MilkShape 3D as a tool for basic modeling, animation, and conversion.

—Caleb Garner (Game Producer, Part12 Studios)

We have a more mature art department with experience on PC and console games, so we use 3ds Max to create the 3D models that go into our games. We export our models to Collada and then use our own tools to convert them to install in our games. While there are many commercial engines available for the iPhone, we have more control over how our tools work by developing them in-house—and we don't have to share revenue or credit with others.

—Ed Magnin (Director of Development, Magnin & Associates)

I've been doing a lot of our artwork in Illustrator because I like the flexibility of working resolution-independent—especially with all of the jumping back and forth we've been doing between iPhone, retina size, and iPad recently (we're attempting a universal app). For that situation, we've been setting up Smart Object files in Photoshop, which we run scripts on to generate the assets we need at various sizes.

—Adam Stewart (Co-Owner, One Man Left Studios)

Emmanuel Valdez on Generating 2D Animation for Mobile :::::

EV

An 18-year veteran of the video game industry, Emmanuel Valdez is currently the Project Director, animation director, and co-founder of Appy Entertainment, a mobile entertainment game publisher. At Appy, he contributed work on all the apps shipped including *Trucks & Skulls*, *FaceFighter*, *Tune Runner*, *Zombie Pizza*, and *Candy Rush*. Prior to Appy, Emmanuel co-founded independent game developer High Moon Studios and was Game Director of *The Bourne Conspiracy* and co-creator of the vampire western FPS *Darkwatch*. Emmanuel was also the creator of *Ready 2 Rumble Boxing* and *Ready 2 Rumble Boxing: Round 2* for Midway Home Entertainment. His other video game credits include *B.I.O. Freaks*, *ESPN Extreme Games*, *NFL Gameday*, and *ESPN Baseball Tonight*. Emmanuel also worked at Sammy Studios, Sony Computer Entertainment, and Park Place Productions.

Emmanuel Valdez
(Project Director & Co-Founder, Appy Entertainment, Inc.)

At Appy, we have a unique set of tools for generating 2D animation for our games. Our very first app we had in development allowed users to edit and manipulate video taken with a mobile device's camera. We incorporated Apple Final Cut Pro into our production pipeline as a tool for generating video clips for stock footage and assorted transitions. When that app was canceled, we continued to use Final Cut Pro to create 2D character and FX animations. It's not an ideal tool for creating animation for several reasons—primarily that it was not designed to produce animation content required in our games. The XML exporter needed extensive post processing to extract the data needed to have the animations run in our game engine. Iterations were slow because of the extra time needed to render video for previews. The lack of a hierarchical character rig setup made it impossible for our animator to produce quality character animations. We later discovered that an application included in our Final Cut Pro suite of tools, Motion, was the perfect 2D animation tool. Motion is an animation tool used for generating title animations and motion graphics. It gave us the ability to quickly generate 2D animation by empowering our animator with curve editors, fine manipulation controls, and a comprehensive hierarchical character rig setup for a forward kinematic solution. We also improved the conversion of Motion data to our game engine animation data process for quick iteration.

Programming

The tools required to program for mobile games are determined first by the pre-ferred platform (PC vs. Mac). This might sound like reverse intuition—but when you are working with code, the specifics of the end platform (e.g., inherent bugs) may cause issues. This is particularly true in mobile development, where versions of a game may need to be built to work on thousands of different phones.. For example, it's possible to use certain programming tools to program for Android devices, PSVita, and PS3.

> We use a wide range of tools—including Photoshop, Final Cut Pro, Ruby, and Ruby On Rails. We also have a proprietary tool chain and editing system used to build our games.
>
> —Chris Ulm (Chief Executive Officer, Appy Entertainment, Inc)

Eclipse

Eclipse is an open source software development environment built on the Equinox *OSGi* (a dynamic module system built for Java) runtime. It began predominantly as a Java *integrated development environment* (*IDE*) (a suite of tools that often consists of a source code editor, compiler and/or interpreter, build automation tools, and a debugger)—but with a broad range of support, it now covers a broad spectrum of programming needs (including mobile).

Contributing to the Eclipse Software Community

Even though Eclipse is open source, there are still some licensing requirements. The Eclipse software community welcomes feedback and contributions—and if you come up with a way to improve the product, they would love to hear about it. Visit http://eclipse.org for more information.

The Eclipse Foundation

Most of the integrated development environments (IDEs) within software development tools such as Eclipse follow a similar layout and format, so jumping from one to the other when switching projects is possible.

Xcode

Xcode is an IDE developed specifically to work with Apple's operating systems—on both mobile and Mac. It allows the management of multiple devices and will handle all of the certificates and installation of an app onto the iPhone. It is tightly integrated with Apple's Cocoa and Cocoa Touch *application programming interfaces (APIs)*. Xcode comes already installed on most recent Macs and is available as a free download for all iOS developers.

Currently, there is no Apple-sanctioned version of Xcode available for Windows—although there are workarounds (such as creating a drive partition and installing OSX) that have been developed by a few enterprising souls using VMWare (a virtualization software). However, using workarounds will reportedly void the Xcode warranty, so it's necessary to carefully consider whether the cost of the repair is going to be worth shoehorning the software to work on a PC rather than a Mac.

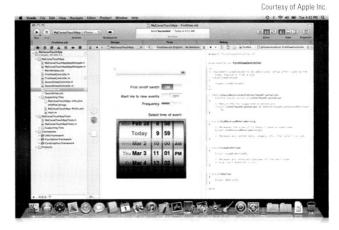

Courtesy of Apple Inc.

Xcode requires a somewhat different process than developing with a PC-based integrated development environment (IDE)—despite the outward similarities in the development environment.

> We use Xcode for writing and compiling; Photoshop, Apple Motion, and GIMP for art production; and many in-house tools written in various scripting languages.
>
> —*Quinn Dunki (Chief Sarcasm Officer, One Girl, One Laptop Productions)*

Java ME

Java ME (Java Platform, Micro Edition) is an open solution designed to give users a broad range of options and tools for development. Sun Microsystems compiled all the different elements, from the *connected device configuration (CDC)*, *connected limited device configuration (CLDC)*, and all of the Java *stacks* (data structures) into a single download. Included are a custom emulator and a real gem of information: the built-in *wireless universal resource file (WURFL)* database search engine that provides the mobile device specifications for over 8,000 mobile devices. The entire SDK can be downloaded for free from Sun's Java ME development site.

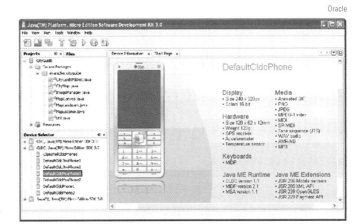

Oracle

Java ME (formerly known as J2ME) is a Java platform designed for embedded devices, such as mobile feature phones.

NetBeans

One of the drawbacks to working with IDEs for Java ME is that not all of them can be used with each individual SDK (e.g., Motorola vs. HTC vs. LG). *NetBeans* is one of the IDEs of choice for Java ME, precisely because it covers a very broad range of devices and manufacturers. A nice feature is that it too includes a custom tool for interface design—Visual Mobile Designer, much like to tools provided by Apple and Microsoft. The development environment contains many of the same fundamental elements found in Visual Studio or Xcode and includes the ability to develop mobile games with a visual editor designed to work with the Mobile Information Device Protocol (MIDP) 2.0 Game API. The Mobile Game Editor is another tool that enables artists and programmers to work concurrently rather than requiring assets to be passed back and forth.

> **W**e are currently developing mobile learning games for Android using the Java SDK, Android SDK, Eclipse, and Unity. For us, this suite of tools is affordable, accessible, and scalable.
>
> —*Jim Kiggens (Producer & Developer, Course Games)*

NetBeans, Inc.

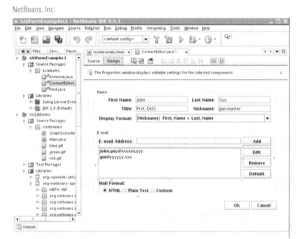

NetBeans allows developers to create apps in languages other than JavaME—such as C, C++, PHP, Ruby, and Groovy—although JavaME is the most useful for mobile development.

GrapeCity

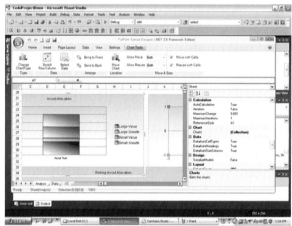

Despite cosmetic similarities in the interface setup of the integrated development environments (IDEs), each has its own unique set of tools and challenges for the programmer (Visual Studio 2010, shown).

Visual Studio

Similar to Eclipse, Microsoft's *Visual Studio* is an IDE that can be used to program for multiple systems—from the Xbox 360 to the Windows Phone mobile platform. Visual Studio has the added advantage of supporting many programming languages through a language service format that allows the debugger and code editor to be adapted to the needs of a specific client or project. In addition, it provides "Express" versions of the software that are already tailored to Visual Basic and Visual C# at low to no cost—making them ideal for mobile development, which already runs on a very tight budget.

chapter 3

Debuggers

Not all SDKs come with *debuggers*, but most of those listed in this chapter do in fact have their own. The debugger is the program or plugin (depending how it's set up) that reads through the code and tells indicates the location of the mistakes so that a programmer doesn't have to go through the code line by line. Most debuggers also allow developers to handle high-end functions such as running a program step by step to check the progress of the program through each line—stopping the program at will either by setting up breakpoints or looking for specific events. Some debuggers have the ability to modify the state of the program while it is running, rather than merely observe it. In many cases, it's possible to skip a section or start the program up again after it finds an error. The presence or absence of a debugger can be a key sticking point when deciding on an IDE. Keep in mind that a debugger can change the behavior of a program—most often regarding how fast or slow it handles its internal timing. Once the program is run without a debugger, its performance may increase dramatically.

> We use the Unity game engine, which makes multi-platform deployment much easier. Without it, we would have to create our own engine and adapt it to every platform we target.
>
> —Alex Bortoluzzi
> (Chief Executive Officer, Xoobis)

> We use our proprietary C++ technology, the Spacetime Engine, to author our games. It is integrated with 3ds Max. We also use Photoshop to create textures, and Perforce as our source control.
>
> —Gary Gattis (Chief Executive Officer, Spacetime Studios)

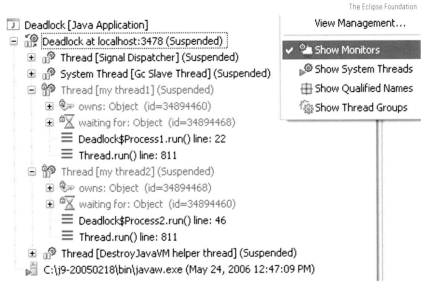

A debugger can run a program line by line, showing where the errors occur and how they affect the program (Eclipse, shown).

DSi & 3DS Software

For a fee, Nintendo provides a complete development kit for its DSi and 3DS handheld consoles. In order to work with these handheld systems, it's possible to utilize Eclipse or another development environment for programming—but sooner or later, it will be necessary to employ *CodeWarrior* in order to compile everything into a language that the Nintendo DSi can run. The majority of the software needed—varying forms of libraries for the *ARM* (the microprocessor that controls the DSi)—is custom-built programming created by Nintendo specifically for its line of handhelds. The various development pieces (hardware or software) can be ordered "a la carte" as needed; developers pay only for the elements required by the project. For example, if a game isn't going to take advantage of the DSi's networking capabilities, then it's not necessary to purchase the software designed to work with those functions. By going with this "a la carte" method, the developer is able to minimize the costs involved and can focus on the specifics of the game rather than worrying about code bloat or ensuring that unwanted functions have been written out of the product. Nintendo has proprietary formats for graphics and other non-programming elements, but the initial development for most of these takes place in readily accessible programs such as Photoshop or Maya—and the final result is exported to something "Nintendo-friendly" during the last or next-to-last stage of production.

Freescale Semiconductor, Inc.

CodeWarrior Development Studio is an IDE that provides a framework designed to accelerate the development of applications used on handheld devices.

Cat Pinson on Developing Proprietary Tools :::::

CP

Cat Pinson's career in game development began as a QA tester for educational games. She soon acquired a position as QA tester at Icarus Studios to work on their MMO *Fallen Earth*. Cat was quickly promoted to Lead Tester for *Dexter: The Game*. After releasing *Fallen Earth*, its expansion *Bloodsport*, and *Dexter*, she left the U.S. to work at CCP Iceland as a QA Tester for *EVE Online: Incursion*. Cat is now back in the States with her game designer husband, tech-loving toddler, and a very corpulent cat.

I've found that proprietary tools can be excellent; they're tailored to your goals, tend to have fewer unnecessary features, and may wind up costing less than purchasing a software package. On the other hand, proprietary tools must be developed and maintained. If there is no team specifically focused on these tasks, developers that are actively producing client-facing products will often postpone them, lower their priority, or not maintain them at all. Any of these scenarios can easily become a bit of a train wreck.

Cat Pinson
(Lead Quality
Assurance Tester,
Icarus Studios)

PSVita Software

Historically, developing for the handheld console market has been only slightly less prohibitive than full console development with regard to cost. (For example, Sony provided a complete development kit for its PSP handheld consoles for a substantial fee.) The PSVita has made a significant change in this practice. With the cost of development kits for the PSVita averaging about the same as Unity, Sony is opening the floodgates to a host of small development houses who previously were unable to even consider developing for a handheld console. In addition, it's been rumored that Sony has allowed early access to development kits for members of the "homebrew" community as well. It's well known that having a stable of quality titles across all genres is essential to the successful launch of any game console, and Sony seems to be taking the lessons of the past to heart.

Development kits provided by hardware manufacturers can contain both hardware and software components, as well as equipment specifically designed to allow programmers deeper access to the systems (PSP devkit shown).

Audio Software for Mobile Development

I use Logic Pro to produce all my music and sound effects. I am in the process of expanding my VST collection, but I primarily use Logic's built-in instruments, as well as the Jam Packs. Logic is extremely powerful, and I still have so much to learn about it.

—*Whitaker Blackall (Composer & Sound Designer, Whitaker Blackall Music)*

I am able to do pretty much anything using my ProTools project studio, Twittering Machine. The MacBook Pro is the nerve center for audio production, and it is networked to the iMac used for code development. I rely on Waves plugins (sound design), Peak and Audacity (audio editing), Xcode for C++, and Eclipse for Java (programming). I also maintain a range of hardware synthesizers and microphones.

—*Peter Drescher (Sound Designer, Twittering Machine)*

For mobile audio asset creation, I've used everything from Nokia Composer for old monophonic MIDI conversions, to BREW emulators and general MIDI synthesizers. Especially for older feature phones, assets must be delivered in the appropriate low bit rate formats. Thankfully, this is fading as much more powerful iPhone and Android platforms take over. I'm working on an iPhone game now; the extra memory feels like such a luxury, after working with some of those older devices!

—*Jamie Lendino (Composer & Sound Designer, Sound For Games Interactive)*

For audio, the tools are typically the same, which is the beauty of creating music and sound effects for mobile game. Whether the final format is a digital audio file or MIDI, audio content can be created with familiar tools and allow the creativity to really flow!

—*Aaron Marks (Composer & Sound Designer, On Your Mark Music Productions)*

Nathan Madsen on Digital Audio Workstations for iOS :::::

NM

Nathan Madsen is the owner and founder of Madsen Studios LLC, a full production audio house. Since 2005, Madsen Studios LLC has provided audio solutions for over 140 projects in indie films, live stage, Anime, commercials, DVDs, Sony PSP, Nintendo DS, PC, Internet, iPhone, iPod, iPad, and on Android and Windows Phone 7 platforms. In addition to audio production, Nathan enjoys lecturing on campuses and panels about the game industry, writing articles about his craft, and meeting other game developers passionate about the industry and technology.

Nathan Madsen
(Composer & Sound
Designer,
Madsen Studios LLC)

When creating audio for the Apple line of devices (iPhone, iPod, iPad, etc.), I use a collection of DAWs (digital audio workstations): Pro Tools 9, Logic Pro 9, and Reason 5/Record 1.5. At the initial creation stage, it matters less (to me) which DAW is used; I'm more concerned with which one will help me quickly and effectively write the style of music/sound effect needed. More often than not, I use the Rewire technique to combine DAWs together as well. Once the content is created, I then use Peak Pro XT to edit the files and make sure both the level and the data size of each audio segment are appropriate; I do this through trimming and exporting the audio with lower sampling and/or bit rates. I always require video footage of the game to work with; sometimes new clients can push back on this concept—thinking that I can just guess on the sound's pacing and timing. A quick discussion about whether they want the sounds to be estimates or exact fits usually convinces them! For me, all the DAWs offer good things; it's more a matter of personal preference and workflow. With the exception of Reason/Record, all of the other DAWs support working to video—and I especially enjoy how Logic allows for multiple renders at the same time.

Do-It-Yourself

A number of companies offer a *do-it-yourself* (*DIY*) setup that involves a framework into which developers can slot artwork. These companies will publish your application to the app store for a flat or monthly hosting fee. Many of these setups are basic—consisting of a few social media feeds delivering custom information—but some provide a more comprehensive package. DIY services might be worth the time and cost savings for simple applications. Be aware that developers are often required to share a revenue stream, or at fork over upfront and monthly hosting fees to keep the application available through the app store.

Drag & Drop

In addition to Unity, there are a number of other engines targeting *drag-and-drop* development. Developers import the art, assign the function, and "ta-da—you have a game!" One of the forerunners in this area is GameSalad, a cleverly built 2D engine that gives designers and artists the ability to build game functions (e.g., spaceships that can shoot) without needing to create the underlying programming from scratch. Game engines require that you carefully consider what the game needs and whether or not it can be built using a "template." (See next page for a discussion of pushbutton development.). There are a number of "cookie cutter" games out there (e.g., multiple variants on the "Match Three" game type)—but stellar art, particularly on the iPhone and Android, can help set the game apart from the others.

GameSalad Inc.

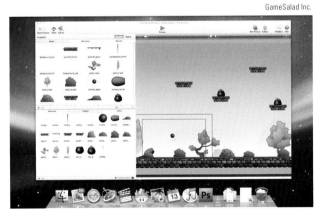

GameSalad Creator is an authoring tool aimed primarily at non-programmers, allowing them to create games using a drag-and-drop technique.

Drag-and-drop game development tools exist for nearly every platform and all do their best to streamline the development process as much as humanly possible. However, every game is different—and not all are going to fit within what these tools can do—so check carefully before committing to a tool that might not necessarily work.

Pushbutton

Pushbutton development involves a template or tool that allows developers to plug in their own artwork and—whammo!—they're off to the races. This gives developers a very fast turnaround time, but it is extremely limiting. Developers are required to work only with the template (no custom changes outside the art allowed) and will end up with a very simple, cookie cutter application. Unlike drag and drop development, which requires some programmatic modification and can be customized as much as the designers skills will allow, pushbutton is a wholly closed box system with no access to the code and additional fees changed for any modifications.

Many pushbutton application products are more focused on working with pre-existing blog content and RSS feeds than on developing custom application functionality (AppMakr, shown).

Industry Standard or Developer's Choice?

The number of development tools on the market is extensive, which can lead to "developer's choice" as long as the software can export art that can be used in the end product. Major studios (e.g., EA, Glu) expect employees to work with industry standard programs such as Photoshop rather than open source software like GIMP for a number of reasons—incuding the fact that the work is often handed off to another developer. Small studios sometimes work with industry standard tools, since it's easier to find qualified artists who are familiar with them. For programming, the choices are simpler: Initial programming for most handheld systems can be executed in one or two standard IDEs, then compiled through a custom compiler provided with the hardware manufacturer's SDK. In any case, it's necessary to decide which development tools will be used ahead of time so that the software can be optimized for the greatest number of mobile units.

As we move into Chapter 4, we'll take a deeper look at how mobile game design must undergo a critical change due to technical limitations inherent in the devices themselves. Gone are the multi-layered gameplay systems, lengthy play sessions, and complex control schemes that are considered "top of the line" on console and computer games. Restrictions involved in mobile development take the design process back to a simpler time when the pixel was king.

Expanded assignments and projects based on the material in this chapter are available on the Instructor Resources DVD.

:::CHAPTER REVIEW EXERCISES:::

1. Choose two of the graphics tools discussed in this chapter and use them to create a "look and feel" for an original game idea. Consider color scheme, typography, and general user interface layout. Which of these tools gave you better results, and why?

2. Build a draft user interface or simple title screen for your original game idea using Interface Builder (iOS) or XML Layout Editor (Eclipse). Prior to development, create a sketch of the title screen or series of frames (storyboard) showing any interface variants. Indicate the function of each active interface component.

3. Choose one of the audio tools discussed in this chapter and create a set of sound effects and/or ambient audio to accompany your original game idea. How will you use audio as an interface element?

4. Code the "Hello, World!" app using Xcode (http://developer.apple.com/xcode)—following this tutorial: http://developer.apple.com/library/ios/#documentation/Xcode/Conceptual/iphone_development/100-iOS_Development_Quick_Start/development_quick_start.html#//apple_ref/doc/uid/TP40007959-CH3-SW9. Alternatively, use Eclipse to build an installable version of "Hello, World!"

5. Experiment with the Unity engine and compare it to drag-and-drop development using GameSalad Creator and pushbutton development using AppMakr. Consider how you would use these tools to refine and polish the draft interface or title screen you created in Exercise 2. Which of these programs is more user-friendly? Which provides you with more options?

Part II:
Function

Mobile Design Differences

forget all you know

Key Chapter Questions

■ How can early *scale* and *scope* decisions affect the end product?

■ How can choice of *platform* influence game design?

■ How do shortened *play sessions* make a difference in a game?

■ How can built-in *peripherals* add value to a mobile game?

■ What game *genres* translate well to mobile platforms?

The precepts of game design apply across all types of games, from high-end life simulations and traditional tabletop games to the many variations of rock-paper-scissors. A mobile game product is cut much closer to the bone than most. There is no padding—not as much room for fancy visuals and soul-throbbing music. There is no room for forgiveness if the interface is "muddy" or the keys that control the character are too close together. The player will simply move on and find another game.

Smaller Doesn't Mean Easier

It is a common misperception that designing for mobile is "easier"—that somehow the limitations of scale, scope, and screen size put the designer in a neat little box and help keep production delays at bay. In the interest of pushing the envelope of producing games—even relatively miniscule ones by current standards of game design—it is arguably the designer's job to bump up against those constraints as much as possible without breaking the project as a whole. Working within such a tiny box can prove to be a challenge—especially if one has already designed large-scale projects. Knowing where to cut and what to trim while still maintaining a coherent game structure and that ever ephemeral "fun" factor is a design skill that has to be learned and perfected over time.

There are a number of elements to take into consideration during the mobile game design process. Some of these game elements will affect how the initial design is laid out, and others should be considered when expanding upon an already existing design.

Many of you may be familiar with the concept of the *game design document* (GDD). In traditional PC and console games, the GDD is the final word in the game's content. The GDD is often an exhaustive stack of paper that includes not only descriptions of gameplay, user interface (UI) design, and other key elements—sometimes even a complete technical outline. In PC and console design, it's not uncommon for these documents to exceed 100 pages—and in the case of a product that will take millions of dollars and years to develop, that isn't such a bad thing.

In mobile, however, the standard product cycle is 3-6 months. Everything in the cycle is dramatically—even brutally—shortened. The GDD as we know it is dead—well, for mobile at any rate! Instead, mobile game developers often create a collection of mini-docs—each one of which describes an important function of the game, fits into an accelerated production schedule, and can be completed as its own task.

Nimble, Lean & Mean

There are more than a few production philosophies out there that fall under the umbrella of what is known as *Agile* development—including *Kanban, Scrum,* and *Lean* production styles—each of which works in its own way as a framework for mobile. All of these methodologies, which will be discussed in Chapter 8, break a design down into small, manageable chunks. (Scrum calls these chunks "stories," while Kanban refers to them as "cards.") Each of these chunks should detail a functional piece of a game. Examples might include "game posts to player's Twitter account after player completes Level One" or "bird explodes when hit." Some of these chunks might be essential, such as the development of gameplay physics; others might be "shiny" like unique particle effects.

Vision Statement

The *vision statement* (or *design overview*) often consists of the game's *high concept* and a brief overview of the gameplay. In mobile game design, this section of the design tends to be simpler—with a sharper eye toward gameplay rather than world-building or even the storyline. This is not to suggest that story and world-building are not important in mobile games, but the very nature of mobile games means that the player will not be as forgiving of issues with gameplay mechanics (e.g., how buttons function, ease of use). If a game isn't easy to pick up and simple to play, the player will move on to the next game; with 99 cents as a common price point, many players are willing to find something new rather than spend the extra time fighting with the controls.

A simple way to handle the vision statement is to boil the game down to a single sentence or phrase (e.g., "*Diner Dash* meets *Iron Man*" or "Bob the Monkey, a thousand typewriters, one big hammer"). Any element you expect to add to the game needs to be checked against the vision statement; if it doesn't fit or help make that statement a reality, it should be added to a "wish list" and revisited at a later date—or removed completely.

- *Must Have:* Elements that are essential to the game.
- *Want:* Elements that would be good to have in the game—but not having them won't kill it.
- *Wish:* "Blue sky" elements that will make the game super shiny—but will only be included if there's time and money to spare after items from the above categories have been incorporated.

In mobile games, there is some leeway; due to the built-in ability to update applications, elements on the wish list can be added weeks or months after the game initially ships—so keeping them around is always a good idea.

Diagram by Per Olin

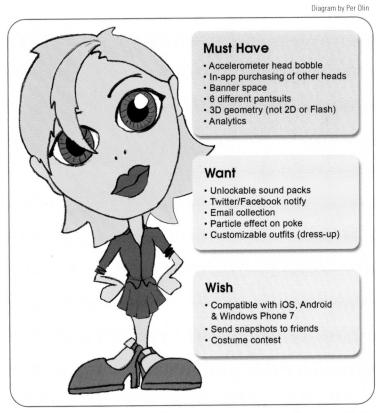

Must Have
- Accelerometer head bobble
- In-app purchasing of other heads
- Banner space
- 6 different pantsuits
- 3D geometry (not 2D or Flash)
- Analytics

Want
- Unlockable sound packs
- Twitter/Facebook notify
- Email collection
- Particle effect on poke
- Customizable outfits (dress-up)

Wish
- Compatible with iOS, Android & Windows Phone 7
- Send snapshots to friends
- Costume contest

"Must have," "want," and "wish" lists for hypothetical game, *Bobblehead Betty.*

One of the most talked about concepts in software development, the *killer app*, is bigger than a category such as "games" or even a single product; it's one that causes the related hardware to fly off the shelves—like *Halo: Combat Evolved* did for the Xbox and *Quake* did for PCs. The term "app" is very broad—referring to any piece of software rather than a specific class. In essence, a game is an app; it's just a very specific type—one that requires an entirely different perspective when it goes to market than one focusing on business or lifestyle. As such, games are judged by a somewhat different set of metrics than the latest word-processing or note-taking application. Apps come in all shapes and sizes—from the simplest *Hangman* game to complex, custom-written medical file sharing software.

Genres

When it comes to mobile devices, games and applications are often lumped into several, fairly broad categories. Let's take a look at the most common mobile game *genres* and the relationship between genre and platform choice.

Adventure

Although the *adventure* genre has dropped in popularity on computer and console platforms, it has found a new place on smartphone, tablet, and handheld devices alike. The traditional point-and-click interface can easily be mimicked on all portable devices—and the reflective, puzzle-solving gameplay component is a natural fit.

Fire Maple Games

The adventure genre has found a new home on mobile devices (*The Secret of Grisly Manor*, shown).

Arcade

Almost every "classic" arcade game from *Pong* to *Pac-Man* has been brought over to the mobile platform, with re-imaginings of the genre and its associated gameplay. Games that are part of the *arcade* genre (often included as a subset of the *action* genre) work particularly well on mobile devices because they were originally developed during a "simpler" time in game development history; hence, they require less complicated control schemes and smaller screen real estate.

Namco Networks

Originally created with an eye toward file size restrictions and shorter play sessions, arcade games such as *Pac-Man* are a natural match for mobile.

Retro Mobile

I don't specialize in any particular genre, but I think that older game styles from the '80s tend to translate really well to mobile. Home computers from that era were slow, with low memory and low resolution, so the games reflected that. A lot of really great game styles were invented to fit those constraints. Most of them are just as fun now as they were then, and we can polish them up a lot with modern rendering hardware.

—Quinn Dunki (Chief Sarcasm Officer, One Girl, One Laptop Productions)

Casino

Poker games have had a wild run in the mobile space for a while and still remain one of the more popular styles in the *casino* genre. Most card, dice, and other tabletop games (e.g., roulette, keno) that can be found in traditional casinos are part of this genre. Casino games of all types work well on mobile platforms, since they're usually 2D and not resource-intensive; they're particularly strong on smartphones and tablets due to touch interfaces. Other real-world tabletop games that are not found in casinos (e.g., checkers, chess, mah jong, backgammon) also do well on mobile devices for the same reasons.

Scary Robot Productions

Casino games (e.g. card games, checkers, chess, etc.) were some of the first to make the jump to mobile because they rely much more heavily on programming skill than beautiful visuals (*Poker with Bob*, shown).

Fighting

Games in the *fighting* genre are not particularly effective on mobile devices. It takes a lot of precision for players to execute special moves, which must be "dumbed down" on mobile devices. Directional control is also a problem, even on tablets. Fighting games tend to work best on handhelds with hardware D-pads. The PSVita's dual analog setup—while touch-based versus actual harware analog sticks—make fighting games more feasible on the handheld platform.

Square Enix

Fighting games such as *Dissidia 012 Final Fantasy* tend to work best on handhelds with hardware D-pads.

Music & Rhythm

Fueled by the success of franchises such as *Rock Band* and *Dance Dance Revolution*, games involving *music and rhythm* grew in popularity on traditional console systems. However, sales began to dwindle in recent years due in part to the general "fad effect," cumbersome hardware peripherals, and players that became weary of being "nickled and dimed" through premium content. Due to the physical hardware controls (e.g., buttons, stylus) associated with handheld devices, music and rhythm games are not as appealing on these platforms; the need for tactile control, which more closely emulates the process of playing an instrument, is essential for the player experience. However, just as console-based music and rhythm games utilize controls like dance pads and drumsticks/pads, the feeling of one's fingers against a touchscreen could be thought of as more visceral and physical—even primal!

Appy Entertainment, Inc.   YayPlay

Mobile platforms may breathe new life into the music and rhythm genre (*Tunerunner* [left] and *Touch Dance 2 for iPad* [right]).

Platformer

Games that are part of the *platformer* genre (also often a subset of the *action* genre) involve controlling a primary character that jumps over obstacles and onto various "platforms" while moving quickly across the screen. Platformers work particularly well on mobile devices such as smartphones utilizing a one-button control.

Semi Secret Software, LLC

One-button controlled platformers such as *Canabalt* work particularly well on mobile devices.

Puzzle

Wildly popular, especially on the previous generation of mobile devices, *puzzle* games are often among the simplest to pick up—yet they provide many sessions of satisfying gameplay. Due to their relatively straightforward design and limited "pick up and play" sessions, puzzle games work quite well across all mobile platforms in single-player mode. Synchronous, real-time online multiplayer puzzle games are quite common on smartphones—with upwards of 20 players simultaneously unscrambling words and answering trivia questions. Asynchronous, turn-based games such as *Scrabble* and *Words With Friends* have grown in popularity on both tablets and smartphone devices due to gameplay that allows players to have several instances of two-player games running simultaneously, where a turn can be taken at each player's leisure.

Zynga

SouthEnd Interactive AB

Word and puzzle games such as *Words With Friends* (left) and *Ilomilo* (right) are well-suited for handheld screens.

Tilting Games & New Mobile Genres

We specialize in tilting games apparently, since that's all we've released to date. We're working on that, though. I don't know that we've focused on "translating genres." That implies retrofitting existing gaming conventions from the other platforms, forcing them to work on an alien device. We start prototypes focusing on what the device can do and where we can take that, not necessarily how we can force Game X, which would be better served on another platform, to work on an iPhone. So working with the device and seeing where that takes us, instead of trying to force it to be an Xbox.

—Adam Stewart (Co-Owner, One Man Left Studios)

Role-Playing

The *role-playing game* (*RPG*) genre is a natural fit for mobile. Often designed to allow players to drop out at any point and pick up again where they left off, RPGs are appropriate for long-form games and storylines. Tablets are particularly well-suited for RPGs—since a comparatively larger screen is more ideal for the greater complexity of an RPG interface and environments; an onscreen D-pad or point-and-click interface is also sufficient to control the player character, since movement is not a main RPG gameplay element. Visual interfaces on smartphones and handhelds can be a little more challenging due to smaller real estate, which makes it difficult to read numerical stats during combat.

Square Enix

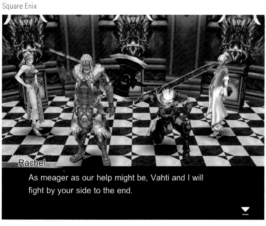

SRRN Games

Role-playing games with scrolling (*Chaos Rings Omega*, left) or tiled (*Ash*, right) backgrounds are a natural fit for mobile hardware.

:::::MMORPGs Break Free From the PC

Massively multiplayer online role-playing games (*MMORPGs*) are experiencing a resurgence due to the rise of mobile devices—particularly smartphones. As cell phones became more pervasive in the early 2000s, hardcore players expressed a need to check their stats when they weren't near their desktops; today, players have the ability to do just this through mobile apps that act as *extensions* to traditional MMOs. Better yet, they may find themselves playing fully-functional MMOs on their mobile devices—allowing them to take a break from their "primary" PC MMOs. Historically, handhelds have been slow to enter the MMO fray due to the lack of an always-on connection to the Internet—which Sony is trying to address with the PSVita.

Spacetime Studios

Gameloft

Pocket Legends and *Order & Chaos* attempt to replicate the *World of Warcraft* look and feel on mobile.

Shooter

First-person shooters (*FPSs*) work well on mobile devices because the player doesn't have to worry about camera control. Although a virtual D-pad is needed, not much precision is required; aiming can be accomplished by swiping the screen. *Third-person shooters*, on the other hand, are not very common across all mobile devices; this is generally due to the camera control issue, which makes movement and navigation challenging.

Gameloft

Gameloft

First-person shooters such as *N.O.V.A. 2* (left) work well on mobile devices, while third-person shooters such as *9mm* (right) are not very common due to the camera control issue.

⋮⋮⋮⋮⋮ The Action-Adventure Hybrid

Digital Chocolate, Inc.

Jack, make your way through the lobby and reception area. You should find an elevator at the northeast corner of the building.

OK

The *action-adventure* "hybrid" genre combines the eye-hand coordination of quick movements associated with action sub-genres such as fighting, platformer, racing, and shooter with the puzzle-solving and point-and-click interface elements of adventure games. In mobile devices, camera control and jump mechanics are concerns. The fixed camera helps, but there's still a jumping problem due to directional control issues with the platform. A good configuration for mobile action-adventure games incorporates a 2D view and one-button control system. Handheld devices containing hardware D-pads/sticks provide the best solution.

Action/adventure titles such as *24* tend to require quick thinking and faster reflexes.

Sports & Racing

Arcade-style *racing* and *sports* genres play well on mobile devices. For example, just accelerating and braking are often the only actions required in an arcade-style racing game—and players can easily touch the screen to brake on smartphones and tablets. However, it's more difficult to pull off a *simulation*-style racing or sports game on a mobile device due to the fine control of acceleration and braking required; turning the screen around is not a perfect solution to this problem. In this case, tablets can work a little better due to onscreen buttons that are larger and more visible—and a handheld can often be the best solution due to the physical buttons.

Electronic Arts, Inc.

X2 Games

Arcade-style racing games such as *Need for Speed Shift* (left) work well on mobile devices, while simulation-based sports games such as *First Touch Soccer* (right) may push the envelope when it comes to mobile control schemes.

Diagram by Per Olin

Platform	Screen Real Estate	Controls
Handheld	Adequate	Physical hardware/stylus (DS series only)
Smartphone	Adequate	Touch
Tablet	Optimal	Touch

Platform Trade-Offs Affecting Genre Choice

In Search of the 3DS "Killer Genre"

Immersive gameplay can benefit the most from 3D display technology. Arcade-style action games, vehicle simulations (with airplanes and race cars)—any game relying on a first-person perspective—are well-suited for 3D. When a rumor circulated about the impending announcement of *Metroid 3D* in early 2011, fans filled forums with posts anticipating the true 3DS killer app—and they were very disappointed once the rumor failed to be upgraded to "fact." This—and the buzz around *Conduit 3DS*—show that FPSs might lead to the first 3D killer app. Nintendo and its pioneering 3D console depend on it.

Nintendo

The best genre choices for stereoscopic 3D handhelds such as the Nintendo 3DS appear to be fast-paced, immersive games like *Mario Kart 7*.

I believe the best games are those you can come back at anytime and that don't take too much of your time on a play session: Something cool, quick, and fun for those times when you're idle and ready for some gameplay action.

—*Alex Bortoluzzi (Chief Executive Officer, Xoobis)*

I often work with games that place a strong emphasis on story elements, although that's not always the case. With mobile platforms, it's best if the story is part and parcel with the game rather than involving huge chunks of tiny, hard-to-read text.

—*Matt Forbeck (Writer & Game Designer, Full Moon Enterprises)*

Strategy

Strategy games are often ports of larger scale PC or console properties. However, more original IP games in this genre are beginning to emerge. Interestingly, strategy games have never taken off on console systems—primarily due to controls. (The joystick model doesn't allow for fine selection ability and commands, which are much easier to handle through a PC's mouse-keyboard combination.) *Real-time strategy (RTS)* games work particularly well on tablet devices. The relatively larger screen real estate gives players a wider view of the game space—allowing for more detailed movements, intricate resource management tasks, and stats visibility. The touch-enabled interface allows players to touch any button on the screen to issue a command, draw to select, and swipe to move the screen (landscape) around. An RTS sub-genre that's popular on mobile devices and PCs is known as *tower defense*—which involves attempting to stop enemies from crossing a map by building towers that shoot at them as they pass.

PopCap Games

Digital Chocolate, Inc.

Strategy games are often simpler than what might be found on a console or a PC, but that doesn't make them any less challenging. (*Diamond Islands* [left]; *Plants vs. Zombies* [right]).

It's not as important to have fine control in *turn-based strategy* games, which work even better on mobile than RTSs across the board. Allowing time for reflection gives players the ability to avoid snap decisions or a high degree of precision—which is in alignment with mobile device controls.

Turn-Based Strategy Games on Mobile Devices

Since my particular product line is a turn-based strategy game, the chief restriction with any mobile version is the screen size—which limits the detail players can be offered. This makes tablets more friendly to this type of game than, say, smart-phones. Really though, any game genre can be used on mobile platforms—as long the designer understands the advantages and limits of the particular device.

—*Chris Parsons (Product Manager, Muzzy Lane Software)*

Mobile Games for Kids

There are several mobile games on the market such as *Where's Mommy?* and *Monkey Preschool Lunchbox* that are developed for very young children and focus on early education concepts. Tablets work quite well for these games, since the screens are larger and touch-enabled—allowing toddlers' less dexterous fingers to more easily point and select items onscreen. Games developed for this age group do best when modeled after the traditional point-and-click adventure game interface style. Older kids who are still too young for smartphones might have access to personal media players such as the iPod Touch—which shares the screen size and general design with the iPhone (and other smartphones) but lacks traditional smartphone features such as a cellular signal and data connectivity.

Pitashi! Mobile Imagination

Children's games such as *Where's Mommy?* translate well to mobile devices because they are often simpler when it comes to interface requirements.

The game's primary genre is chosen during the design pre-production process. Sometimes this is a clear-cut decision; at others, it's a bit on the fuzzy side. Many mobile games are promoted as cross-genre hybrids; fast moving plate-spinner style games that once would have been slotted under the "puzzle" genre might also show up under "action-adventure." This kind of genre bending opens up new possibilities in marketing and advertising games that might be able to find audiences in several different categories. It is interesting to note, however, that a number of these games fit very solidly within a single genre—and the cross-promotion seems to be more of a marketing effort than a result of any true genre-breaking elements within the game itself. Different carriers may even split these game types up into even more genres and sub-genres. For example, Verizon Wireless splits its "casino" category into "casino," "card," and "dice" headings.

Mobile Learning Games

We specialize in mobile learning games. Access to and permission to use mobile devices in the classroom are still obstacles. Also, faculty in general have a low level of mobile learning literacy. The state of mobile learning games for the classroom today is very reminiscent of the use of the web in the classroom in 1995.

—*Jim Kiggens (Producer & Developer, Course Games)*

Bill Shribman on Creating Mobile Games for Children :::::

BS

Bill Shribman
(Senior Executive
Producer,
WGBH Educational
Foundation)

Bill Shribman is responsible for all interactive media for kids within the WGBH Educational Foundation, including national PBS sites for *Arthur*, *Between the Lions*, *Zoom*, *Postcards from Buster*, *Curious George*, *Design Squad*, *Martha Speaks*, and *Fetch*—which have won several awards, including the first Prix Jeunesse given to a web site. Bill is the creator of several original broadband projects including the *Fin, Fur and Feather Bureau of Investigation*, *The Greens*, and a photographic news service for PBS KIDS called Beeswax. He has written and produced content for web, audio podcast, CD-ROM, interactive television, kiosk, radio, and television—and he is currently working on interactive content for emerging platforms including PSP, iPhone, interactive whiteboard, Wii, and surface tables. Bill has received Emmy nominations for his television and online work.

I focus on creating educational games for young children. Since learning goals effectively become part of each game's SDK, baked in from the start, mobile devices (phones passed back from an adult; kid-owned devices like iPods; shared devices like tablets) offer a range of affordances. Portability and mobility are the most obvious, so we have focused game development on games that can be played anywhere, or location specific ones that benefit from the user being somewhere untethered: math games to play at the supermarket, or augmented reality games that can be played with markers scattered around a gymnasium, for example. Many devices' gestural inputs also give us access to kids who may find keyboards and trackpads daunting: our work with kids with autism is very exciting when mapped to tablets, for example. And clearly, there's an emerging market around mobile games that has not existed in the kids' space online besides a few breakout successes with subscription services—so mobile offers lower barriers to new producers wanting to create sustainable production models.

Where Does Your Game Fit In?

Carrier distribution tends to categorize a little more tightly, which means that a developer is often required to list a game under a single genre rather than being allowed to cross-market it in several genres. As of yet, the app store model does not have any such limitations.

Story Elements in Mobile Design

No matter what platform you're developing for, there is one consideration that has to come before all others. A game must have one or more compelling characters that become immersed in an interesting sequence of events that challege your characters and force them to grow. Finally, there has to be a way for the player(s) to experience a satisfying—aka, happy—ending. It doesn't matter if you're designing an MMORPG or a simple little exercise about angry birds. The key to success in all game design is to begin and end with a good story.

—Catherine Clinch (Adjunct Professor, Department of Mediated Instruction & Distance Learning, California State University Dominguez Hills)

We specialize mainly in interactive fiction, which takes the form of "choose your own adventure" style gamebooks presented as interactive e-books. We feel these kinds of genres are particularly well-suited to the new tablet platforms, in particular the iPad. We can present the book as a real book, with users able to turn the pages. Technically, we can save the reader time by automatically skipping the chosen pages when presented with the options. We also have dice-rolling mechanics in the books, so realistic dice can actually bounce across the pages as you shake the iPad.

—Neil Rennison (Creative Director, Tin Man Games Pty. Ltd.)

Terrence Masson on Narrative & Story Structure in Mobile Games:::::

TM

With 20 years of production experience, Terrence Masson's work includes feature films (*Star Wars*), games (*SimCity 4*) and award-winning animated shorts (*Bunkie & Booboo*). He also single-handedly developed the computer graphics (CG) pipeline for South Park. Terrence consults with major production studios on creative development; is a member of the Producers Guild of America and the Visual Effects Society; and has been active in SIGGRAPH since 1988—as 2006 Computer Animation Festival Chair and as SIGGRAPH 2010 Conference Chair.

In our Creative Industries Game Design program at Northeastern University, we focus on "gameification" in our Interactive Media curriculum—using story structure and narrative to drive user experiences, even in relatively mundane areas of content. All game genres benefit from this approach, of course—with particular attention paid to mobile platforms due to small screen size and relatively short attention/use periods on those platforms. (I just finished co-teaching our two-semester Senior Capstone class with Brian Sullivan (of *Age of Empires* fame), and part of our team focused on a mobile web game as a distribution platform. The students were very new to game design—so while coding and art were relatively straightforward, the "make it fun and interesting" part was a huge challenge. They learned a ton!

Terrence Masson (Director of Creative Industries, Northeastern University)

Game Mechanics

Game mechanics, the way in which the game functions, is of paramount importance in game design for any platform—from console to computer to mobile. Each genre comes with its own baggage—a series of expectations on how the game is played, the rules involved, and the controls needed to make the game playable. There might be some crossover in large-scale titles; for example, *BioShock* is classified as an FPS—but the hack puzzles employed when the player is trying to gain access to equipment follow the game mechanics of a specific type of puzzle game. The game does not try to impose the FPS mechanics on the puzzle game, nor does it try to impose the puzzle game mechanics on the shooter. The game mechanics stay true to their relevant game types.

Players have a tendency to gravitate toward genres and play styles that are familiar to them. Knowing what to expect, they're more comfortable spending their impulse money on something they know they'll like. Betray the player by switching around the game mechanics that have been standard for a certain genre (or worse, by actively promoting a game in the wrong genre), and a developer can run the risk of revenue loss and a hit to its reputation.

It is worth noting that gameplay mechanics are not entirely tied to the game controls, particularly in mobile. There's a greater opportunity to mix things up simply because there are so many different smartphones available. For example, the FPS genre allows the player to walk (forward, backward, left, right), jump, and shoot. The diverse nature of mobile devices, however, means that it's often necessary to "mix it up" a bit with regard to the physical aspects of the game controls: Should the trackball on the BlackBerry Curve be used to control a player's movements? How about the accelerometer? Should every single number key on the keypad control weapons and inventory? Can the game be played with just one hand (or one finger)? The direct link between the physical controls and the gameplay mechanics is an important area to review prior to development.

> I cannot afford to specialize. In the fragmented and crowded market for mobile apps, you only get to specialize once you have a huge hit. Until then, you need to cast your seeds widely and see what grows.
>
> —Scott Berfield (Executive Producer, University of Washington Bothell Center for Serious Play)

> We enjoy developing games in a wide variety of genres. Rather than adapting games to the iPhone, we try to think of things that would be fun to do on the iPhone and then develop a game around them.
>
> —Ed Magnin (Director of Development, Magnin & Associates)

:::::The Same . . . But Different

There are many games that appear to be knock-offs or clones of one another—but when you get deeper into their gameplay, it becomes clear that there are subtle differences that make them appeal to entirely different types of players. The accompanying images show two games that incorporate a very similar basic game concept but still retain enough differences to appeal to distinct audiences. The game mechanics in *Bejeweled* and *Bubble Ducky* both involve "Match 3" gameplay: matching up items into vertical or horizontal rows of at least three. Both games require the player to swap two items that are side by side in order

PopCap Games, Inc.

Digital Chocolate, Inc.

The game mechanics in *Bejeweled* (left) and *Bubble Ducky* (right) both involve "Match 3" gameplay.

to successfully create a match. Although the programmers will handle these two games in a very similar fashion, the artists have a mandate to create clear differences in visual style. Designers could further differentiate these games through *specials* (game pieces that have different effects on the way the game is played): What happens if a player lines up four items? What about unique objects such as *bombs* or *wildcards* (game pieces with random effects)? These finer details can really lock in the difference between one game and another.

Prototyping

No game designer is worried about a game being too much fun, way too innovative, or too pretty. Instead, developers worry that it's going to be as dull as paste, bland—something the reviewers will ignore. This is not an insoluble problem; in fact designers have been tackling this issue since game pieces were carved out of twigs and rocks and colored with berry juice. This is where game *prototyping* comes into play—in which an early version of a game is created and tested to verify whether the gameplay and game mechanics you've chosen to work with are going to be any fun at all.

There are almost as many ways to handle prototyping as there are game genres in existence. A simple (and oddly fun) way to go through this phase is to create a *paper prototype*: Draw out a *playing field* (a physical mockup of the game screen); grab a bunch of coins, teabags or action figures; and try to play through your game. Paper prototyping works particularly well in puzzle and sandbox games. For point-and-click adventure titles, try storyboarding scenes and different pathways to success or failure. It's not necessary to utilize artistic detail; boxes and stick figures will suffice.

Kyle Gabler

Kyle Gabler

As a part of the Experimental Gameplay Project, four students developed over 50 games within the space of a single month using "quick and dirty" prototyping techniques (*Super Tummy Bubble* prototype [left] and final game [right], shown).

Ideally, a game should be prototyped before it is taken to a publisher or other funding source for backing—but time is often tight, opportunities arise, and a developer might assume that the genre has been playtested enough. Then the game hits *alpha* (fully functional, but with bugs and ugly graphics), and it's about as boring as watching toenails grow! This is what alpha is for: the point at which a game is structurally complete and a developer can start pounding on it with a will to figure out what breaks easily, where the story needs more strength, whose weapon is horribly overpowered—and why was it a good idea to include *that* particular sound effect?

With mobile games, prototyping is especially necessary when considering how a level will flow and how actions will naturally follow one another to lead the player to the conclusion of the game. Mobile players by definition don't have a lot of time to devote to gameplay at any one sitting, so forward motion through the game is essential—even if it sometimes feels like there's a bit of a "cheat" going on. For example, if players die too many times in a level during the popular Xbox Live game *'Splosion Man*, they are given the option of skipping the level and proceeding onward; granted, the player character is required to wear a pink tutu until the player completes a level from that point on, but the flow of the game isn't interrupted! If players come up against a puzzle that gives them too much trouble, they can still continue onward through the game. This way, you avoid losing your players if they just can't get that one double-jump timed just right.

Twisted Pixel Games, LLC

If players die too many times in a level during *'Splosion Man*, they are given the option of skipping the level—but the player character must then wear a pink tutu until the next level is complete!

Multiplayer

While it's a runaway hit in the console and computer markets, the *multiplayer mode* has been slow to take hold in mobile games. It has been suggested that this is due in part to the inherently shorter play sessions that go along with mobile gaming—but it's impossible to ignore the ongoing issues with networking devices together in a reliable and easy to use fashion. Early attempts at multiplayer utilized infrared connectivity—but any interruption of the IR (infrared) beam connecting the two devices would cause a disruption in the game. Bluetooth allows for a more reliable method of connecting devices, but the time constraints still exist. Unless players carefully pre-plan their game sessions, the odds of bumping up against another player who is also ready to play are miniscule.

Mobile MMOs

We have taken the traditional PC MMO and broken it down into its fundamental components. Mobile users typically look for a meaningful experience in 3-5 minutes. We then chain those short sessions together to allow the users to play for as long as they like. By doing this, we have created a new mobile game genre, the "pick-up-and-play 3D MMO"; it allows thousands of people to play together, all over the world—over Wi-Fi, 3G, 4G, and even Edge networks.

—*Gary Gattis (Chief Executive Officer, Spacetime Studios)*

"Pick Up & Play"

"Pick up and play" games will often have the most broad success, if they can be successful in communicating to the player the basic rules/hook of the game within the first 30 seconds or so. Basically, "you touch stuff and good things happen" should be a golden rule—much more so than on any of the previously established platforms.

—*Ron Alpert (Co-Founder, Headcase Games)*

Player Market

Mobile players come in all shapes and sizes—and a good percentage of them aren't "gamers" in the classic sense but fall into the more general umbrella of "casual" gamer. Consider not only the *demographics* (e.g., age, gender) of the target audience, but *psychographics* (e.g., lifestyle) as well. For a title focusing on cooking, does a 42-year-old soccer mom want to see photorealistic food, or will something in a cartoon style be more appealing? Many budding designers tend to isolate themselves from the current crop of titles in an effort to avoid the "me too" effect, but games are not created in a vacuum; there's a greater risk of having this happen through isolation. Only by adding new experiences and references, mixing things up, and pushing the boundaries of what works and what's new and nifty will a developer set itself apart from the rest.

Mobile games attract players who might not otherwise consider themselves gamers. With mobile's short play sessions, ease of use, and ubiquitous availability at the touch of a button, people who might not have considered video games as a pastime before are trying out all kinds of new game experiences. Mix in casual gamers who are used to web-based social games and hardcore gamers who spend hours at a time in front of consoles and computers—and there's a broad mix of experiences and tastes to address. Mobile gamers represent a class onto themselves; whatever other types of systems or consoles they may use, they become mobile gamers once they leave their homes—restricted to short play sessions while waiting to pick up the kids, riding the bus, or hanging out between classes. A survey conducted by Information Solutions Group showed that over 60% of all respondents played games while waiting for appointments and 52% played games during *work hours*. (The survey did not ask specifically whether respondents were playing while at work.) Gameplay times are short, with 62% of respondents saying they played less than 15 minutes a session. Regardless of gameplay habits while at home with a console or computer, the nature of mobile gaming instills similar play patterns across the board.

Casual Games: The Life of the Mobile Party

Arcade and casual-friendly games are huge right now for many reasons (e.g., global accessibility, not terribly hard to develop). At the same time, there's so much competition—but it's the safest bet right now. (Niche development can be costly and harder to market for smaller developers.) A smart, forward-thinking designer can look back at years of established "action+reflex" games and try to retool them to take special advantage of the abilities now prevalent (e.g., touchscreen, online)—and this brings a new richness to old standbys when applied appropriately.

—*Ron Alpert (Co-Founder, Headcase Games)*

I specialize in the casual game genre, with a preference for games with story. I haven't encountered that many restrictions other than content—but then again, my content fits the target demographic. The best games for mobile include quick puzzlers and entertainment/comedy—nothing with too much tension.

—*Jennifer Estaris (Experience/Game Designer, Total Immersion)*

I work on every conceivable genre, with the majority falling under the "casual" category. This genre translates well to mobile due to the quick and accessible nature. Also, many non-gamers are more likely to try out a casual game since they're great time-killers. Social integration is obviously working for developers, and the casual market is where it's at. As the device power increases, so will the complexity and quality of mobile games.

—*Ben Long (Composer, Sound Designer, Audio Director & Author, Noise Buffet)*

Kevin Saunders on Factors Affecting Mobile Design :::::

Kevin D. Saunders programmed his first game, a port of Intellivision's *Astrosmash*, on a ZX81 when he was six. His interest in programming (and games) continued through college, where he worked on artificial intelligence systems. Kevin has 13 years of experience in video game design and production--working with companies such as Electronic Arts, Obsidian Entertainment, Westwood Studios, LucasArts, Sega, and Atari. He has been credited on 11 titles and has been a key contributor to seven; all titles have an average review score of 81%. Kevin is Creative Director at Alelo—directing projects such as a multiplayer online language learning RPG and a mixed-reality system used in Marine training. Prior to Alelo, he was Lead Designer and Producer of *Shattered Galaxy*, the winner of the 2001 Independent Games Festival and GameSpot's Most Innovative Game and Best Multiplayer Strategy Game. Kevin has Bachelor of Science and Master of Engineering degrees from Cornell University.

KS

Kevin D. Saunders
(Creative Director,
Alelo)

Game design for mobile devices is most affected by three factors:

1) The way in which people use their mobile devices for entertainment differs from how they use console systems, computers, or even handhelds. Mobile games are ideally easy to start, interrupt, and resume—requiring a minimal time commitment from the player.

2) Mobile devices have unique interfaces (e.g., touch screens, accelerometers, few hardware controls, smaller screen sizes), which require new conventions to be followed—while also providing new possibilities for gameplay.

3) With the vast quantity of mobile content available—and the challenges of marketing mobile games effectively—factors such as a recognizable license, art style, and even the game's title become more influential to a game's success. (This point could be dismissed as not really being about game design—but if a design goal is to maximize entertainment value, I would argue that the ability to reach the target audience should be a consideration and could dictate other aspects of the design.)

While it is true that the demographics of mobile device users (and thus potential mobile players) is different from computer and console game players, I do not think this means that mobile games must necessarily target a broader audience. There is room for complexity and sophistication within the realm of mobile games, and hardcore gamers have mobile devices as well. It is true, however, that the importance of principles such as usability and simplicity in design become more prominent in mobile games. Even hardcore gamers approach mobile games differently than they would console games; the situations in which they play such a game, their mindsets, and their expectations are all different.

Jason Loia, Brett Nolan & Ed Stark on Player-Centric Mobile Development:::::

JL

Jason Loia
(Chief Operating
Officer,
Digital Chocolate)

Jason Loia is COO at Digital Chocolate, a leading online and mobile social game developer and publisher founded by Trip Hawkins that has rapidly emerged as a leader in new digital media and social games. Best known for *Millionaire City*, *MMA Pro Fighter*, *Rollercoaster Rush*, and *Tower Bloxx*, Digital Chocolate led all software companies in App Store downloads in 2009—and in 2010, it was the fastest-growing developer of Facebook social games with virtual goods. Focused on original brands and technology for a wide variety of platforms, the company has made over 100 different award-winning games and works with 200 leading web and mobile channel partners in 80 countries. Digital Chocolate has operations in San Mateo, Helsinki, Barcelona, Bangalore, and Mexicali. Prior to Digital Chocolate, Jason helped found one of the first mobile game studios in the US. Jason holds and MSEE from Stanford and an MBA from Harvard.

Unlike PC or console gamers, mobile gamers demand a short, dedicated burst of entertainment adrenaline—usually associated with filling time between activities. They'll generally tolerate lower game depth and ramp-up time for a quicker "jump-in and-play" experience—so the game design has to address this shorter, more "bursty" game session. Since it's not appointment-based gaming with friends, the tempo of the game must be able to allow a player to jump right back in spontaneously throughout the day.

BN

Brett Nolan
(Founder & Editor-in-
Chief, AppAddict.net)

Brett Nolan is a software engineer, gadget geek, gamer, husband, and father of two little girls. In 1997, he graduated with a degree in Computer Science from Hamilton College and went on to earn a Masters in Software Engineering from Brandeis University. By day, Brett has worked as QA Engineer for several high-profile tech companies. As a child, he was an avid gamer starting with the Atari 2600—followed by the Colecovision, Apple][e, Apple //c, Sega Master System, Nintendo, and Game Boy (with a bit of a hiatus until the emergence of the Dreamcast and today's modern consoles). In 2009, Brett purchased his first iPod Touch—and his love of mobile gaming was rejuvenated. Soon afterward (in his spare time), he founded AppAddict.net—an iOS-centric news and review site. It has been experience that has allowed Brett to meet some truly amazing and interesting people. He has gotten to see a whole new side of this exciting and massive, yet tight-knit development community.

I've found that the best mobile games are those that offer players a satisfying (and complete) experience in 2-5 minute chunks. Graphics and actual gameplay aside, this is what makes games such as *Angry Birds* and *Canabalt* so successful. When waiting at the doctor's office or on hold on the phone, we tend to get stressed and annoyed—feeling like our time is being wasted. If you can complete a level or two, or up your best time in a survival run, you feel like you accomplished something in what would have otherwise been wasted time. Sure it's not necessarily life-changing—but this tiny victory, this sense of accomplishment and purpose, can instantly improve a person's mood and demeanor.

Ed Stark is a game designer, author, and creative director currently working in the field of video game MMO development after nearly 20 years in the tabletop game industry. While at West End Games and TSR/Wizards, Ed wrote several novels and short stories as well as dozens of tabletop RPG products. As Creative Director for the *Dungeons & Dragons* game line at Wizards of the Coast, he oversaw the design and development of *D&D* Third Edition and v.3.5. Ed also worked closely with the developers of numerous *D&D* computer games—including *Neverwinter Nights*, *Baldur's Gate*, *Demon Stone*, and others. After Wizards of the Coast, Ed worked as Designer at Red 5 Studios on the *Firefall* team-based shooter. From there he moved to Vigil Games, where he became the primary story developer and writer for *Warhammer 40,000: Dark Millennium Online*—an MMO currently being developed for the *WH40K* universe.

Ed Stark
(Senior Designer,
Vigil Games
[a division of THQ, Inc.])

In my opinion, smartphone game designers need to take into account the way people play smartphone games. Most want a quick, easy-to-access experience—something they can play while waiting in line or preparing to do something else. The game can still have long-term goals, but it should have very short reward cycles. Players should feel that they've had the opportunity to accomplish something every few minutes—and have a sense of completion. Ideally, this sense of completion opens up a new challenge—perhaps one that can be shared with friends playing the same game on connected networks.

Key Mobile Design Considerations

1. How does the game take advantage of the touchscreen?

2. What is the length and complexity of the experience?

3. What is the business model underpinning the game (IAP? Ad supported? Free to play? Multiplayer/community? Check-in based?)

—*Chris Ulm (Chief Executive Officer, Appy Entertainment)*

Short Play Sessions

Remember that you don't want to retrain your audience or remind them where they left off every time they have five minutes. If you choose to create a larger story-driven game, give the players a simple way to remember what has happened—since you have no idea what their play schedule is like.

—*James Portnow (Chief Executive Officer, Rainmaker Games; Professor, DigiPen Institute of Technology)*

> They used to be called casual games, but now you're seeing all kinds of formerly "hard-core gamer" titles on smartphones—just shrunk down in scope so that you can play for minutes at a time, instead of hours.
>
> —*Jamie Lendino (Composer & Sound Designer, Sound For Games Interactive)*

> As with any game, you need to consider how and where it will be played. Then you can figure out how to make playing the game as easy as possible, even if the game itself is challenging.
>
> —*Matt Forbeck (Writer & Game Designer, Full Moon Enterprises)*

Gameplay

Gameplay focuses on how the game should be played—step by step in some cases. Mobile games should focus very clearly on this element—not only on how players move in different directions, but how they execute such moves given a device that is designed with phone and text type functionalities in mind rather than the ergonomics that make a controller easier to operate.

Pick Up & Play

Mobile games address a fast-moving mindset. Even hardcore gamers expect a different experience—a much shorter learning curve—from mobile games. The *pick up and play* component needs to be present—where the game is immediately playable, allowing the player to just drop in and go. Marrying a game to a clear genre type and following the established canon that goes along with that genre, particularly where the controls are concerned, will go a long way. If every shooter on the market uses a virtual joystick to move the player through the scene, then completely scrapping that mechanic in favor of an accelerometer-based movement style is going to require spending additional time retraining the player—time that might be better spent on actual gameplay than on a training level. It's necessary to weigh the risk of engagement time. Players should be drawn into a game in under a few minutes; changing basic "understood" control mapping and other standard elements necessitates a compelling way to introduce these modifications to the player.

Concrete Software, Inc.

Games such as *3D Lawn Darts* use a "pick up and play" gameplay style that is conducive to short play sessions.

"Easy to play; hard to master" has become the golden catchphrase in mobile. Players are often drawn to games that challenge them without requiring a long, upfront time commitments or complex control systems.

Shorter Play Sessions

By their very nature, mobile games are short-form. Average play sessions measure in minutes, in contrast to the hours required for most games played on a console or computer. Games tend to be played while users are waiting in line for takeout orders or riding the subway to work in the mornings. The limited time available in one sitting lends itself to games with *shorter play sessions*—and indeed, the top sellers on mobile devices are consistently games in the more casual stripe (e.g., bubble-poppers or box-droppers such as *Tetris* or *Potion Motion*). Mobile players are, by their very nature, more opportunistic and willing to snap up a five-star rated game that's just gone on sale. Don't forget that a player will have to drop out of the game at *any* moment to respond to a phone call or text message. How should this possibility be handled? Longer play sessions with *checkpoints* (where the game is automatically saved without player intervention), such as those used in console shooter games, are not as viable in mobile games as having shorter levels or automatic saves during interruptions so that the player can drop back in at any time.

Utopian Games

Games with shorter play sessions such as *DropZone* are ideal for the mobile market.

Screen Size

Dealing with very small screens (especially compared to the theater-sized flat-screen monstrosities available at most local television retailers) has a dramatic effect on gameplay. Some games, such as most in the puzzle genre, will naturally scale down—but for games that normally cover a large area of play, there will be some challenges. RPGs and RTS games are often hit the hardest simply because they require large maps and innovative thinking in order to display all the information required.

Kairosoft Co., Ltd

Tycoon-style gameplay in games such as *Game Dev Story* is a natural fit for smaller screen sizes.

::::: Turnkey "Fog of War"

RPG and RTS maps are often huge in relation to the actual screen size of their associated platforms—whether mobile, computer, or console—but this issue is actually to the benefit of the gameplay on mobile devices. The screen acts as a "window" into the game world—requiring players to scroll around and maneuver their points of view in order to see everything they need to see. This also allows for game actions to occur off screen without any program resources devoted to the graphical representation of these actions. In console titles, the *fog of war* effect is often brought into play—where players cannot "see" what is going on in a certain area until characters or troops are activated in that area. Having a smaller screen size allows for a physical version of this effect to be utilized without the need to program it directly.

KU

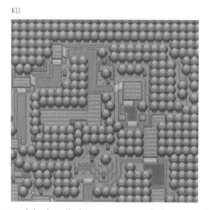

The screen of the handheld serves as a window onto the game's map rather than showing it all at once.

Game Visuals

While both 2D and 3D options are available on most smartphones, 2D is the only option available for any older devices. When creating visual aspects of a game, how would you cross the 2D-3D divide? If the initial version of the game is developed in full, glorious 3D, consider how to translate this visually for other platforms. Will animations and backgrounds be pre-rendered? Will the visual style change completely? Give special consideration to the characters. For mobile, the focus needs to be on clearly recognizable elements on a small and occasionally even black and white screen. One of the reasons the "bobblehead" or "chibi" look for mobile game characters is so popular is that it allows for a clearly recognizable face on a character that is often around 34 pixels tall. In Chapter 5, we will touch on how to maximize a character's design to make it stand out against the background art even when working with characters small enough to dance on the head of a pin.

Halfbrick

The "chibi" look in games such as in *Monster Dash* is popular because it allows for clearly recognizable faces on very small characters.

Varying Controls

The *controls* on most smartphone models differ from one another—whether they consist of trackballs, number keys, side buttons, or arrays of menu buttons at the top or bottom of the keypad. Ideally, one control scheme should be developed that can be adjusted to a limited degree for each unique device the game will be delivered on—but drastic differences are sometimes needed. Is the game suited for "one-button" gameplay? Some games, such as *Beach Mini Golf 3D*, require the player to press a single button multiple times as the gauge on the power-bar slides up and down; these control schemes are easy to port to many different smartphones. A game developed to be used with an accelerometer and touchscreen, however, will require a re-design of the controls and possibly even the gameplay as it is ported to smartphones that don't have such features built in.

Digital Chocolate, Inc.

Many mobile games, including *Beach Mini Golf 3D*, use "one-button" gameplay to control a slider-bar rather than more complex keypress controls.

Mobile Audio Design

It is important to listen to your compositions and sound effects on the device itself. Quite often, what sounds great in headphones or studio monitors does not sound very good coming out of the mobile device's speakers. Since most people will be hearing your audio from tiny speakers, it is important to mix your productions to sound good in all scenarios.

—*Whitaker Blackall (Composer & Sound Designer, Whitaker Blackall Music)*

On the audio side, we must take the small size of the phone's speaker into consideration. It's even worse than on a Nintendo DS or Sony PSP. Any gamer who cares about the audio will listen through headphones—but we need to make sure that kick drums, explosions, bass guitars, and other low-end instruments still have enough mid-range and higher frequencies to cut through.

—*Jamie Lendino (Composer & Sound Designer, Sound For Games Interactive)*

While I don't specialize in a certain genre of games, I have quite a bit of experience writing music and creating audio for fun/casual/cutesy games on the iPhone/iPod/iPad. From an audio stance, there aren't many restrictions to this particular genre of mobile games—just to mobile games in general. Most of the time, mobile games cannot support highly interactive audio like a console device can—and many times, clients want great sounding audio with very small data space and/or usage. For this reason, and for the reason that many players can only play a game quickly (e.g., in an elevator, during a lunch break), many games that do well are casual ones allowing the player to get in, play, and get out very quickly.

—*Nathan Madsen (Composer & Sound Designer, Madsen Studios LLC)*

Lani Manella, Peter Drescher, & Aaron Marks on Mobile Audio Constraints :::::

LM

Lani Minella
(Master Creator,
AudioGodz Inc)

Lani Minella has voiced more than 450 computer and video games, as well as television and anime series. She is famous for her role as Rouge the Bat (in *Sonic The Hedgehog* games). She has also had roles in the: *Baldur's Gate*, *Clive Barker's Undying*, *Diablo*, *Diablo II*, *Duke Nukem 3D*, *EverQuest: The Legacy of Ykesha*, *Half-Life*, *Leisure Suit Larry: Magna Cum Laude*, *Sonic Adventure 2*, *Sonic Heroes*, *Sonic Battle*, *SoulCalibur III*, *StarCraft*, *Unreal*, *Unreal Tournament 2003/2004*, *WarCraft III: Reign of Chaos/The Frozen Throne*, *World of Warcraft*, and the *Nancy Drew* series. Since 1992, her company, AudioGodz, has provided voice acting, directing, casting, and writing for games. As a one-stop shop, AudioGodz also utilizes sound designers and composers to provide all things audio.

Size is still the main issue with any mobile app, so decisions have to be made regarding balance between graphics and voiceover (VO)—which cannot exceed 20 MB in some cases (and there are different formats for different devices). There are FMODs which enable better utilization of space. As far as VO recording is concerned, with size limitations there won't be as much spoken word with more focus on emotes for the various attacks, victories, and losses. In this respect, we are more limited—but it's not impossible to showcase dialogue in small segments. EQ and compressing the sound to be good over small phone speakers might also be a difference, since many people don't wear headphones while playing mobile games. The same rules should apply such as (e.g., putting as much action in the words as possible), especially since the screens are even smaller than other platforms, and there are still plenty of games that need automated dialogue replacement (ADR—or "looping") in a language different from the original.

PD

Peter Drescher
(Sound Designer,
Twittering Machine)

Peter "pdx" Drescher is an interactive audio veteran and published authority on game audio technology. He produces music, sound effects, and voiceovers for multimedia software and mobile devices. A former Audio Director at Microsoft, Peter was assimilated into that position by the acquisition of Danger, Inc. (makers of the T-Mobile Sidekick)—where he was Principal Sound Designer. In the past, Peter has been a road dog bluesman piano player, computer programmer, and circus performer. Currently, he works out of his ProTools project studio, Twittering Machine.

Until recently, mobile game audio has consisted of a few beeps and some MIDI music. This was necessary due to extreme technical constraints on file size and CPU. However, bandwidth bottlenecks have expanded dramatically, and high fidelity mobile audio is now commonplace. FMOD audio middleware (a game audio engine used predominantly on XBOX/PS3 console games) has now been released for iOS and Android, providing a cross-platform method for producing sophisticated interactive soundtracks. Even so, while emulators are helpful for development, the only thing that really matters for mobile audio is how it sounds on the actual device—through audio hardware and tiny speakers.

The biggest constraint to producing audio for mobile games is the horrible sound quality of cell phone speakers. They distort, they're not loud enough, and they have *no* bass response whatsoever. Thus, when creating background music for levels, the user will only hear the melody and the snare drum—not the bass line or the kick drum. Explosion sound effects are also problematic; you'll hear all of the crackle and hiss, but none of the boom. Of course, since most phones are also media players, users frequently use headphones—which eliminates the issue to some degree (but even then, care must be taken to ensure that mobile game soundtracks don't distort the speakers when the headphones are not in use).

AM

Aaron Marks is not only an outspoken advocate of great audio in games but an accomplished composer, sound designer, field recordist, voiceover artist, and owner of On Your Mark Music Productions. Aaron is also the author of *The Complete Guide to Game Audio* and lead author of *Game Audio Development* (part of the *Game Development Essentials* series), a member of the audio production faculty at the Art Institute of California - San Diego teaching the art of field recording and sound for interactive media. Aaron has music, sound design, field recording, and voiceover credits on over 120 game titles for the Xbox and Xbox 360, PlayStation 2 and 3, Wii, Dreamcast, CD/DVD-ROM, touchscreen arcade games, iPhone/iPad, Class II video slot machines, Class III mechanical and video slot machines, coin-op/arcade, and online and terminal-based video casino games. Through the years, Aaron has written for *Game Developer Magazine*, *Gamasutra.com*, *Music4Games.net* and the Society of Composers and Lyrists. He wrote an accredited college course on game audio for the Art Institute Online, is a member of the AES Technical Committee for Games, was an AES Game Audio Workshop chairman, was on the launch committee for the Game Audio Network Guild (G.A.N.G.), and is a popular guest speaker and lecturer at game-related conferences and academic functions.

Aaron Marks
(Composer & Sound Designer,
On Your Mark Music Productions)

Storage space, processor capabilities, and download sizes can be quite limiting when putting a mobile game together. Audio and graphics are the largest competing file types, adding to the complexity of creating audio without severely impacting everything else. The best way around this with audio is to make use of compressed audio formats such as .mp3 and to stretch the music coverage through the use of loops. Often, I have to limit file sizes even further by downsampling to 22 kHz and using only mono files instead of stereo. There's a delicate balance between file size and audio fidelity, but going about it smartly will ensure that you still get the most bang for the buck!

Eric Speier on Size Limitations & Mobile Audio Design :::::

ES

Eric Speier
(Owner & Composer,
SMP; Founding
Managing Partner,
5 Elements
Entertainment)

At mobile game development company 5 Elements Entertainment, Eric is helping to put the final touches on the company's next mobile game—which follows on the heels of their recent success, *TxT Fighter*. Published by Trade West Digital and Chillingo (publisher of *Angry Birds*), *TxT Fighter* is a classic brawler that uses texting as its fighting mechanism. At SMP, Eric Speier composes music for television, film, and games—and he's scoring the upcoming primetime Fox animated series, *Napoleon Dynamite*. Slated to be released in January 2012, the series—based on the cult movie hit—stars all of the original actors, with involvement from creators Jared and Jerusha Hess and *The Simpsons*' veteran executive producer/writer, Mike Scully. Eric's studios are in Santa Monica, California.

Size is key in mobile audio development. Smartphone carriers have a cellular network limit on the size of apps that can be downloaded over their cellular networks. That size limit is not enforced when downloading from Wi-Fi, but many apps are purchased on impulse—and if they exceed that size limit (e.g., 20 MB for AT&T, 30 MB for Verizon), people will stop the order and often forget to buy it later when they are on Wi-Fi or at their computers. Due to this, developers often try to keep their app sizes below this restriction.

Another approach to keeping the file size down in music is to use MIDI files or mods playing a custom synth engine. You can then create a sound palette and play many separate pieces taking up very little space using the same sound set. This approach was used often in the early days of computer and console music. The disadvantage is that the sounds are not as detailed or varied as they would be if you used music created with live players, detailed sample collections, or a combination of both.

That said, there are certainly games where developers and publishers decide not to observe the cell phone network's bandwidth limit. I've seen this happen when a title is already a widely known property and the publisher is certain that people will buy it regardless. We did this with *TxT Fighter* to show what a developer could do with high-end smartphones. When a decision like this is made, you can go ahead and create and sculpt the game's sound and music—much like what is done for a PC or console game.

I've worked on everything from AAA console games to Facebook games, to DS, PSP and iPhone. Fortunately, the tools to create the music stay the same for me for the most part. It's just a question of file format and compression.

—*Tom Salta (Composer, Persist Music)*

Social Components

Mobile games often make good use of social components; nearly every title out there has some sort of *leaderboard* technology in place—a way for players to post high scores and accomplishments, and contact and interact with other players. With a huge number of players actively engaged with social networking services such as Facebook and Twitter, it is becoming more common to use free development kits provided by some services to link a game directly to them—allowing developers to post game scores and stats directly to their social networking profiles. This has an added benefit of serving as automatic "word of mouth" promotion. When players post scores and other information to their social network profiles, they get the word out about the game and encourage their friends to try the game out for themselves.

Firemint

Games such as *Flight Control* contain leaderboards—allowing players to post high scores and accomplishments.

Technical Issues

There are many *technical issues* that affect mobile gameplay design. Consider the fact that there are well over 3,000 different types of phones using CDMA (code division multiple access) networks that are still in service; add to this the thousands of makes and models of phones that use GSM (Global System for Mobile Communications) networks, and there's a massive base of platforms to work from. While the initial design might be created with an eye toward the newest mobile devices on the market, keep in mind that several of the major mobile networks require developers to provide versions of their games for multiple smartphones for the benefit of distributing via their built-in networks (carrier decks). This means that in order to maximize a product, the game and associated gameplay must be scalable—from two-tone screens and code-generated graphics all the way up to vector graphics and 3D animation—for every mobile device that a particular carrier supports. From the outset, consider the fact that multiple GDDs and versions of your product might need to be created to accommodate the different platforms on which the game will be distributed.

Ultimately, consider working with a platform that can be deployed on as many devices as possible. Each mobile manufacturer will have its own OS in place, and attention should be focused on where these intersect. There are currently several commonly used platforms that will allow a game or application to run on devices build by multiple hardware manufacturers, and there are higher-end smartphone operating systems that support a single manufacturer's devices. Operating systems and their associated programming languages are listed below.

Operating System	Programming Language
Android	Java
BlackBerry	Java
BREW	C
Java ME	Java
.NET Compact Framework	C#, VB, .NET, Basic4ppc
Palm	C, C++, Pascal
Symbian	C, C++
Windows Phone	C, C++

Operating Systems Programming Languages

Development Environments

When it comes to choosing a mobile *development environment*, look closely at your company's vision or primary business model. Will the game be pushed to as many platforms as possible? Will the company develop for a smaller market of high-end phones? Most of the major carriers have a long list of smartphones they want a game to run on, and many of them use different code platforms such as Symbian or Java ME. It's essential for programmers to identify how the design process should flow from one platform to the next. Java currently holds the greatest market penetration; well over 50% of all mobile units on the market can run Java ME apps, which account for more than 350 million users worldwide—so it would make sense to design for these phones first. However, even within this breadth of access, there will be differences depending on the mobile device model.

- **Java ME:** The *Java ME* ("Micro Edition") development environment is the most common currently in the market, and it can be programmed using Java. http://java.sun.com/javame/index.jsp
- **Symbian:** Many of the higher-end mobile devices utilize *Symbian*, but none of the mid- or low-range units do. Games can be programmed for Symbian in either C or C++. http://developer.symbian.org/

- **BREW:** Created by Qualcomm and originally developed for CDMA mobile phones, BREW (*Binary Runtime Environment for Wireless*) is used in some feature phones. Software for BREW can be developed in C or C++. From there, the programming is compiled down into native code for the phone—which can provide a big boost in performance. http://brew.qualcomm.com/brew/en/developer/overview.html

- **Windows Phone:** Microsoft's *Windows Phone* is similar to the version developed for use on PDA devices and desktop applications using the .NET framework. Any of the .NET main languages can be used—including C and C++. http://developer.windowsphone.com/Default.aspx

- **Android:** Applications for Android are often developed in Java. Android consists of a kernel based on Linux—with middleware, libraries, and application programming interfaces (APIs) written in C. http://developer.android.com/index.html

Download Size

Decades ago, there was a cool calculator watch that everyone just had to have. A mobile game needs to fit on that watch—or as close as possible. Most feature phone games and applications need to be in kilobytes—but smartphones can move up into the megabytes, and each phone has its own specifics with regard to memory and download size. The rules get thrown out the window when dealing with the largest mobile units, but there are still requirements to be met; depending on the carrier, a cap (e.g., 20 MB, 30 MB) may be placed on 3G/4G downloads. Games or apps larger than 10 MB must be downloaded over a computer network—a step that may alienate some casual, "spur of the moment" players. Hardcore players, on the other hand, are more likely to plan ahead for their game purchases and may put up with the extra effort required to manually download a game over a network.

Headcase Games

Chair Entertainment Group, LLC

Puzzle games such as *180* (left) tend to be small in size, while the action/role-playing hybrid *Infinity Blade* (right) requires a lengthy download.

Game Engines

Game engines are recent entries into the mobile scene and are used primarily for Android and iPhone devices. Engines such as Unity and GameSalad provide ready-made platforms on which entire games may be developed and deployed. Unity has always specialized in 3D game development, while GameSalad Creator was designed to create 2D games. Unity requires developers to purchase a *seat* (a license to use the engine on no more than two development computers, with the ability to develop an unlimited number of games). The basic version of GameSalad Creator is free, while the professional version (which includes additional features such as leaderboards, promotional links, and priority tech support) is $499 per year. It is worth noting that licensing agreements change all the time depending on the popularity of the game engine and the games that have been developed with it.

Unity Technologies

Game engines such as Unity come as a complete development package—including sample code, games, emulators, and an editor.

A game engine is the core set of programming that a game can be built around. Engines often come with tools for rapid prototyping and samples of games that have already been produced so that a developer has something to start with. This is not to say there is no programming required when you are using most engines—with the exception of GameSalad Creator, which attracts non-programmers with its use of visual editors and a "drag-and-drop" feature. Many games do require some customization, if not the occasional complete re-design of an effect or a *shader* (collection of rendering elements all packaged together; e.g., texture, glow effect, bump map, transparency) type. The decision to use a game engine as opposed to coding the game from scratch is not one to be taken lightly. If the game is built from the ground up, the developer will have a greater degree of control over elements that get included; for example, if the game engine contains code for dynamic lighting (which isn't needed for the game), it's just taking up space that could be used for other features.

::::: *Dexter: The Game*:
Design Hurdles

Marc Ecko Entertainment

When testing the *Dexter* game for iPhone, memory usage was the biggest issue. If the memory usage was too great, the game would just crash (and possibly the device as well). The programmers had to constantly change code, and the artist had to use lower poly models to combat this. The other major issue involved saving the game. We had to make sure that if a player got a phone call while playing, they wouldn't lose a lot of progress from not having saved it. We also had to take into account that players would probably play in small chunks of time and need to save often. The design of the game itself had to work well with short play sessions, making the game accessible and easy to pick up again. *Dexter* is an adventure game in which the player must solve various cases and make choices as to how they should end. A journal was added so that players could easily see their progress and what they needed to do next. We also had voiceovers that would help guide the player in certain levels of the game.

—Amanda Jean Wiswell (QA Tester, ZeniMax Online Studios)

Built-In Hardware

Mobile devices have unique build-in hardware components that open themselves to exciting new possibilities where games are concerned. These components include a global positioning system, accelerometers, vibrate setting, touchscreen, and camera/video.

Vibrate Setting

While the option to set a smartphone to *vibrate* seems to have been around almost as long as the devices themselves, applications have only recently taken advantage of this feature—using the built-in vibrate mechanism much like the "rumble" feature found in console controllers, and allowing designers to give some physical feedback in response to the player's actions.

Able Pear Software

Games such as *Fridgemags* utilize the vibrate setting as a gameplay element.

Global Positioning System

A *global positioning system* (*GPS*) receiver is integrated into almost all mobile phones—allowing them to access location and time information anywhere on Earth through the US government's *global navigation satellite system* (*GNSS*). GPS receivers allow users to participate in location-based social networking services such as foursquare and augmented reality games and apps such as *Paranormal Activity: Sanctuary* and *Layar*. Here's an example of how "location-based" content can work: A movie tie-in game could access a mobile device's GPS to determine which theatre the user is near—along with the date and time—and whammo: the user receives access to exclusive downloadable content related only to that particular screening while waiting in line to see the film. GPS has also been used widely in social games and events—notably in Tony Hawk's Twitter Hunts, where the famed skateboarder uses Twitter to broadcast clues about hidden items all over the US. The downside is that some carriers require that the player is provided with the option of not using the location-based functionality—so consider alternate gameplay for those players who aren't comfortable allowing access to their physical locations.

Ogmento

Paranormal Activity: Sanctuary is a location-based, massively multiplayer augmented reality game where the player's real-world setting becomes the front line of a supernatural conflict.

Layar

Layar is a mobile augmented reality app that displays digital information about the real world into a smartphone's field of vision.

Leveraging the Strengths of Mobile Hardware

Designing for mobile requires thinking differently than when developing a PC or console game. It's a different medium altogether, and this needs to be taken into consideration. My publisher once said: "One finger, tap, maybe hold." That's all the complexity of the most compelling games in the mobile arena right now. As for peripherals, the beauty of mobile gaming is its simplicity. When you add accessories, the simplicity is gone. I want a device that I take out of my pocket, play some good game on it, and put it back in my pocket—without big set-ups and extra stuff.

—*Alex Bortoluzzi (Chief Executive Officer, Xoobis)*

Every console presents an opportunity to create something unique. It's up to the creator to embrace each console's strengths, and to be mindful of its weaknesses. What makes a great experience on one platform isn't necessarily going to translate well to another. For example, since mobile platforms are currently focused on touchscreen interfaces and devoid of dedicated buttons, it's better to create games that don't require precise button combinations or twitch-style reactions. Instead, try to look for things the device does well. What interface motions come most natural when using the device? Make this a focus, and your audience will appreciate it.

—*Aaron Calta (Creative Director, Race to the Moon LLC; Producer, Royal Court Games LLC)*

I think mobile game design is similar to other platforms in the sense that you have to leverage its strengths. For mobile, this means things like always-on networking, microphones, gyroscopes, vibration, and quick startup. From a usage standpoint, mobile games tend to get played often—but for short sessions (less than five minutes). People use them to kill time while standing in line at a movie, or sitting at a bus stop. For tablets, I think the balance may shift the other way. Sitting on the couch for a couple of hours to play a tablet game is perfectly reasonable, whereas most people would not do this with their phones.

—*Quinn Dunki (Chief Sarcasm Officer, One Girl, One Laptop Productions)*

We try to take advantage of the accelerometer, multi-touch screen, and pinching gestures—attempting to keep buttons and controls to a minimum. For example, we often use a landscape view for gameplay and then allow a top-down view to pause the game and view the map. In other games, it may be appropriate to also support a top-down mode, like we did in our *Skittleball* game.

—*Ed Magnin (Director of Development, Magnin & Associates)*

Electronic Arts, Inc.

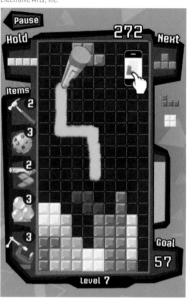

Tetris makes excellent use of smartphone touchscreens.

Touchscreen

A *touchscreen* (touch sensitive screen used in lieu of a keypad or buttons) is found on high-end smartphones and mobile devices. It opens a broad range of options to the designer in terms of gameplay and player control and has paved the way for new and innovative gameplay styles.. In many cases, it has been as much a question of figuring out just how simple the controls can be when controlling a game (*Tetris*)—and in others, it has involved the development of a whole new set of controls (*Infinity Blade*). Many games use a mockup of traditional controls (e.g., virtual joystick) rather than developing new control memes. The field is wide open in terms of designing and developing new sets of controls for games and applications using the touchscreen.

Accelerometer

Only a limited number of smartphones have a built-in *accelerometer*—which enables the device to determine whether it is being moved, tilted, shaken, stirred, or any number of other physical actions. Accelerometers are used in a broad array of applications—from triggering a refresh of a web page to steering racing boats. They offer a truly unique opportunity for game designers to build a product that moves beyond button mashing and finger-twitching.

Sega

Super Monkey Ball uses an accelerometer-based control scheme—allowing players to control momentum by tilting the device back and forth.

Camera & Video

The majority of mobile devices contain built-in cameras that allow users to snap pictures and take videos on the go, or download images from their computer or email service. Game designers have been experimenting with ways to use these photos and videos as part of the gameplay experience, with some limited success.

NBC Universal, Inc.   Skype Limited

In addition to a still camera feature (*Cylon Detector*, left), many smartphones also have video capabilities (*Skype*, right).

There are a number of apps that work by using photo manipulation. For example, SyFy Channel's *Cylon Detector* takes a pre-existing photo (e.g., from a Facebook page, the web, or images saved on the camera) and allows you to run a pseudo-test on it to determine if you are, in fact, a Cylon (from the hit series *Battlestar Galactica*). It then applies a cutout image over your photo, effectively mapping your face onto a character from the show. Other applications allow users to manipulate photos in a number of different ways (e.g., drawing on top of them, placing cutout heads on in-game characters, adding captions and other elements—and squashing, stretching or smearing the image).

A New Twist on an Old Design

In many ways, designing games for mobile devices is just like designing for console systems. There are key design decisions to make, with the goal of giving players an experience they will want to repeat. However, designing for mobile games is also a completely different experience. The restrictions are excruciatingly tight—involving limited file size, memory, play sessions, and screen real estate.

::

In this chapter, we have looked at many key elements that can make a big change in the way a developer might handle the initial prototype for a mobile game. The following chapter will provide a closer look at a game's visual design—incorporating a few old-school tricks that have found new life in the highly challenging space of mobile and handheld development.

Expanded assignments and projects based on the material in this chapter are available on the Instructor Resources DVD.

:::CHAPTER REVIEW EXERCISES:::

1. Create a vision statement for your original game idea. Include a high concept and a brief gameplay overview. Boil the game down to a simple sentence or phrase. Do your game elements and vision statement correspond to one another? (Keep refining your statement until they do!)

2. Build a list of design elements you'd like to include in your game. Now categorize your elements by assigning them to one of the following lists:

   - Must Have: Essential elements that *must* be included

   - Want: Elements that would be good to include (but not having them won't destroy the game)

   - Wish: "Blue sky" elements that should only be included if there's time and money to spare—and only after the "must haves" and "wants" are handled

   Did you categorize your elements correctly? How many elements are in each list? Now refine your "must have" list by confirming that every single element on it is truly essential; if not, move any non-essential elements to "want" or "wish." Now imagine that no additional elements can be included. Will your game suffer? If so, look at the "want" list and move any essential elements from "want" to "must have." Refine your "must have" list again until you're satisfied that you have all the design elements you need.

3. Play three mobile games from different genres. Compare at least three design features of each game (e.g., interface design, gameplay, story, level structure, save-game, navigation, controls). Focus on design rather than art features (e.g., interface functionality—not visual style). Now choose one of the games you played and play two additional games from that same genre. Determine whether certain design features seem to be associated with that genre, and discuss why this might be the case.

4. New "unofficial" mobile genres (e.g., tilting, touch) have been created based on mobile hardware features. Choose two of these features (e.g., vibrate, GPS, accelerometer, touchscreen, camera/video capabilities) and create your own new genre that incorporates them into gameplay. Provide a quick design overview of an original game that is a "good fit" for this new genre.

5. Create a paper prototype for your original game idea:

   - Draw a playing field that incorporates layout and navigation elements used in your game.

   - Place "characters" (represented by miniatures, coins, teabags, action figures, or any other suitable markers) into your playing field.

   - Play through your game.

   It might be necessary to storyboard parts of the game. For example, point-and-click adventure titles might require scenes with pathways to success and failure. However, artistic detail isn't needed!

CHAPTER

5

Art for the Small Screen

painting angels on the head of a pin

Key Chapter Questions

- What are some key *restrictions* placed on art for mobile devices?

- How can *screen size* and *resolution* affect a game's visual design?

- What *art asset requirements* are associated with different mobile devices?

- What are some effective *character design* techniques used by mobile game artists?

- What are the benefits and disadvantages of *2D* vs. *3D* for a mobile game?

You might think that art crammed onto a screen smaller than your hand is not much to speak of—but with a bit of innovation and some practical tips and tricks, the art in a mobile game can turn out to be quite dynamic and engaging. With the advent of more screen real estate, greater color depth, and expanded memory with an eye toward capturing video and photos, mobile devices are fully capable of delivering a visually delightful game experience.

Art for Mobile

Art for mobile games derives from the same "old school" roots as art for more modern PC and console titles. Back when games were being pushed to mobile, scale and scope restrictions made the days of the Atari 2600 look positively epic by comparison. Two-color LCD screens the size of a thumb, memory restrictions, load requirements: These problems had been solved before, but they represented brand new ways of thinking to the current crop of game developers. The visuals, much like early classic games, were often generated programmatically rather than developed by an artist. In fact, many of the early mobile titles were direct knock-offs of classics such as *Caterpillar* and *Tetris*—games already associated with tight restrictions that served as examples of "what to do" as this new market began to take off. As mobile games grew more powerful (with photo and video capabilities, music, and larger and more dynamic color screens), they were able to grow and adapt with equal speed—rapidly expanding into 3D and including social features such as leaderboards and player matching.

THQ   Capcom

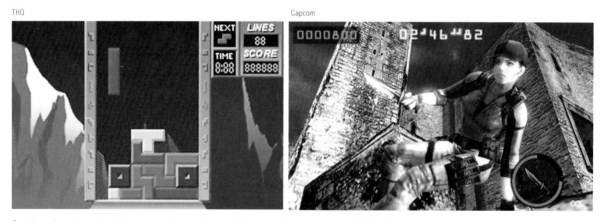

Quality of art has clearly improved from older mobile games (*Tetris Worlds*, left, for GBA) to newer games (*Resident Evil: The Mercenaries*, right, for 3DS).

There is a tendency, particularly among those who are technologically inclined, to focus on the new and nifty—to focus only on the highest end systems available. With thousands of mobile units in the marketplace that are either older or equipped with different features, there are many potential customers that developers would ignore if they only paid attention to the newest devices. Considering the fact that many carriers still want that depth of coverage, developers ignoring these other devices are looking at a sea of lost potential. The advent of app stores that focus on a single technology and manufacturer has made it easy to pay attention to that one device. However, it is worth noting that the publishers (the companies that are making considerable profit on mobile games) still maintain a focus on carrier decks and creating versions of games that are playable on many different devices—not just the shiny new toys.

Standard Software

A good copy of Photoshop can go a long way in game design; it has become the ubiquitous "do everything" program that nearly every game artist uses on a regular basis. However, while Photoshop may be superior for the task of creating and editing images for mobile, Equilibrium's DeBabelizer has the upper hand when it comes to file compression. For example, a file saved out of Photoshop as a .png can often be a kilobyte or two larger than a .png file saved out of DeBabelizer—and when it comes to mobile, every kilobyte counts!

For 3D, both Maya and 3ds Max will do the trick—since most programs and programmers are familiar with how they handle the data, and importing/exporting Max or Maya files to game engines or custom coded games is standard practice. There are less expensive options available as well—such as MilkShape, which is a popular tool among indie developers.

Equilibrium   Mete Ciragan, chUmbaLum sOft

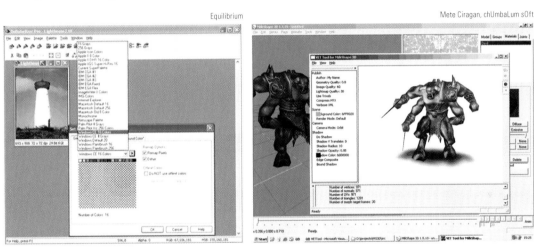

The 2D art tool, DeBabelizer (left), is superior to Photoshop when it comes to file compression—while MilkShape (right) is an affordable alternative to the 3D standards, 3ds Max and Maya.

Screen Sizes & Resolution Issues

For mobile phones, there is no official overall standard when it comes to screen size—but as the industry has matured, manufacturers have begun to adopt similar parameters. However, screens associated with older devices are smaller with more variety and less standardization. On phones that are still more "phone" than PDA (which are still the most common units available), the current standard is around 176 x 220 with 12 pixels of that height being taken up by phone-centric elements (e.g., battery, signal)—leaving an effective screen space of 176 x 208. The newest generation of 3G and 4G mobile devices such as iOS- and Android-based phones and tablets not only possess larger screen resolutions (anywhere from 320 x 240 to1024 x 768), but this entire space is available for development. Take a look at the different styles of mobile devices shown in the images on the next page for a comparison of screen sizes.

LG   Samsung   Courtesy of Apple Inc.   Samsung   Nintendo   Kyocera   Sony Computer Entertainment America

Mobile devices come in many different sizes. Devices shown here include the LG LX400 (top left), Samsung Replenish (top center left), Apple iPhone 4 (top center right), Samsung Galaxy Tab (top right), 3DS (center), Kyocera Echo (lower left), and Sony PlayStation Vita (lower right).

> **A**rt certainly needs to be smaller and readable at high pixel densities. One of the reasons we like iOS is the quality of the displays on Apple devices. We can make small art that still really pops with detail.
>
> —*Quinn Dunki (Chief Sarcasm Officer; One Girl, One Laptop Productions)*

Even with the larger resolution, there are still extra considerations when it comes to the art and design aspects of a mobile title. In AAA console titles, it's all about the hyper-real—including photorealistic textures, skin tones, particle effects, shadows, and lip synching. Photorealistic graphics shrunk down to the size of a screen that is as small as the palm of a player's hand will be muddy and difficult to see; due to this, the screen size and resolution should play a major part in any decision regarding the visual look and feel of the game.

Visual Style

Games cover a wide variety of possible visual styles; in fact, the overall look and feel of the game will set the tone and expectations for players before they even have a chance to read the title screen. Best practices suggest that the overall style should best match the game's genre (e.g., a noir look for a mystery game or a cartoony look for a carnival shooter). However, more often we see successful examples of games with visuals that clash with the gameplay—such as sword and sorcery games with a bright, cartoony palette or murder mysteries that are couched in a sunny suburban backdrop.

Ubisoft   Kairosoft Co., Ltd   Secret Exit

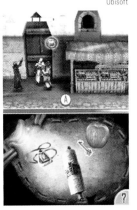  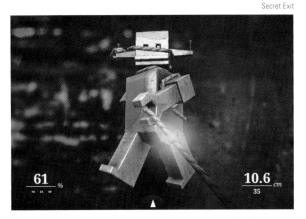

There are almost as many different visual styles as there are game genres. Examples shown here include *Assassin's Creed: Altaïr's Chronicles* (left, for DS), *Game Dev Story* (center, for iPhone), and *Zen Bound 2* (right, for iPad).

::::: *Outwitters*: Creating 2D Art for iOS

One Man Left

For our most recent iOS project, *Outwitters*, the characters and environments I've designed are simply being scaled by a certain percentage between iPhone, iPad, and retina sizes. The final asset generation has been automated with Photoshop scripts. I just make one file and prefix it with what kind of sizes I need spit out (e.g., iPhone, iPad, universal). The character designs in particular were created in vector format in the same way I used to create logos—periodically zooming way out to ensure that the important details would hold up at smaller sizes. Scale had to be determined for each device early on and double-checked for each character before anything was animated. The user interface (UI) between iPhone and iPad are designed separately, out of necessity. On iOS, screen sizes between phones are consistent—so we don't have to worry about accommodating weird, "red-headed step children" sizes. We just have to adjust the menus between phone and tablet.

—*Adam Stewart (Co-Owner, One Man Left Studios)*

Character Design

All games should have a memorable *character*—and we mean this in the broadest sense of the word. There should be a core element that sets a visual tone and style—whether it's a distinct character, an iconic game piece, or a significant recurring background component. The goal is for the player to see, instantly recognize, and identify with this element.

Silhouette

One of the precepts of character design both in traditional art (e.g., animation, fine art, comic books) and in games is the use of a strong *silhouette*. The game's main character or character class needs to be clearly recognizable against the game background, and it needs to stand out against the other characters in the scene. This is one of the reasons background or "filler" characters look somewhat generic in comparison to the hero of the scene. It is also a sure-fire way to help players identify one set of characters over another. Human beings are designed to recognize patterns; it's hard-wired into our brains. If members of the Bad Guy Squad wear hats with horns on them—and members of the Good Guy Squad have funny dome-shaped helmets—then it's a quick and easy task to tell them apart when the rockets are flying. Silhouettes are often based on bold, primary shapes (e.g., squares, triangles, circles), and each shape tends to evoke a certain idea—in part because we have already been trained by all media to recognize a certain silhouette as a powerful "hero" type, or a brick-like, impenetrable "warrior" type.

::::: Silhouette Check

A quick way to see if you have an effective design is to do what is called a "silhouette check." Shade your characters completely black and look to see if you can tell them apart just from the silhouette they show.

Square Enix   Sega

Do you recognize these characters by just looking at their silhouettes?

When you have a strong silhouette to start with, it becomes a simpler thing to reduce that character down to a miniscule size while still maintaining those distinctive features that make them stand out from a distance. This is the reason the "bobblehead" character design is so popular on smaller screen sizes. Reducing the body down to a generalized stick figure, and focusing on the defining characteristics of the face, sets up a clearly recognizable form with which the player will be able to identify in an instant. The same goes for large-scale or exotic weaponry; visually distinctive elements such as the "buster" swords from the *Final Fantasy* franchise become part of that character silhouette and should be taken into account as such.

Color

With the smallest screen sizes, having a distinctive silhouette simply isn't enough. There's barely enough room to determine one eight-pixel tall warrior from another. This is when the internal design of the character comes into play—such as using unified colors to represent a particular group of characters, or coloring the main character in a different palette than the rest of the world (e.g., placing a flaming orange t-shirt on a character when all the backgrounds have been colored in shades of blue). These design precepts can be applied to non-character elements that are important for players to observe and identify—such as vehicles, structures, props, spaceships, giant stone obelisks, or sliding puzzle pieces.

Rovio Ltd.

Nintendo

THQ

The color palette and costuming of game characters can often be as great an identifier as their overall body shapes and silhouettes (Angry Bird, The Incredibles, and Link, shown).

A Dimension's Worth of Difference

The real distinction between 2D and 3D games is the programming that lies beneath—or the game's engine. In console and PC titles, the game engine comprises core bases of code that can be used to build a whole range of different games. In a 3D game, the code handles *polygons*—either created on the fly or imported from an extraneous program such as 3ds Max or Maya—while in a 2D game, it relies on *sprites*. (A sprite is a "cutout" image—whereas a polygon is an actual piece of geometry, defined by the placement of three corner points called *vertices*.) Even if the end result seems to be 2D, it is entirely possible that a 3D code base is being used; this might seem like a waste, but it has been and is still being done. Many times, the use of a 3D engine can allow designers greater freedom and flexibility than they might have with a 2D engine—not only within the confines of a single game, but as a production house as well. The 2.5D "hybrid child" (discussed on the following page) that is beloved by the role-playing game (RPG) genre is actually a function of the visual design rather than a defining characteristic of the underlying programming. In all cases, however, the graphics must be designed to take advantage of the strengths and weaknesses of each type of base code.

2D

Although *2D* might be considered the "older" way of doing things, most games for mobile—particularly the older smart and feature phones—are built in 2D. In many cases, the graphics are entirely drawn and animated by the underlying programming. In the case of mid-grade to higher-end smartphones, the art is created separately by the artist. Flat, two-dimensional animated sprites are moved around on painted backgrounds. ("Flat" does not mean lifeless and stiff; in fact, there are a number of 2D games with spectacular painted or pre-rendered backgrounds and innovative gameplay.) An illusion of 3D depth is created by applying various perspective and parallax tricks, but the code underlying them is geared toward moving 2D animated elements around in the x/y axis only. Any illusion of depth is created in the art itself, rather than being handled by the programming.

Speed is a feature. The advantage of 2D is that games are running at 60fps and faster—something harder to achieve with detailed 3D graphics. Smaller screens require instantly understandable user interfaces (UIs).

—*Chris Ulm (Chief Executive Officer; Appy Entertainment, Inc)*

Bolt Creative

Simple parallaxing and creative visuals in games such as *Pocket God* can give depth to a game without moving to a true 3D environment.

3D

The rule of thumb has been that unless some aspect of *3D* is needed to make the gameplay function, it's better to go with 2D. It's important to carefully consider the cost of a larger game size against the effect it will have on the gameplay of the mobile game. At the moment, 3D is reserved for leading edge smartphones with larger screen sizes. In 3D, there are several different solutions; for example, some games are technically 3D—using polygons to allow the movement of a 2D sprite in all three axes—but they still heavily employ painted 2D backgrounds and sprites. In the case of 3D, the programming has been designed to handle polygons and to work with an x, y and z axis space (rather than just the x and y axes of 2D). The polygons are either created by the programming or with their animations in another program and brought into the game engine, where they function very much like sprites; the programming slides them sideways, up, and down—but the animation (limbs moving, guns firing) is all created by the artist.

> I'm a proponent of 2D until the 3D capabilities of the smartphones get better. I think in a generation or two we'll be able to produce true PSP level games, but until then 2D is simpler and cheaper.
>
> —James Portnow (Chief Executive Officer, Rainmaker Games; Professor, DigiPen Institute of Technology)

Bushi-go, Inc.

Games such as *The Agiliste* rely on 3D geometry to deliver a deeper visual experience.

2.5D

Pseudo 3D or *2.5D* is an old and established way of giving a 3D look and feel to what is essentially a 2D game. Especially popular in "sim" type farming games and "plate-spinning" style puzzlers, 2.5D involves backgrounds that have been painted in perspective and sprites that are *scaled* (sized up and down) by the underlying game programming in order to give the illusion of moving forward and backward in space. Now that smartphones are capable of full 3D, many games incorporate painted 2.5D backgrounds with animated 3D characters—or tiled 2D backgrounds with 3D animated characters—to help push the illusion even farther while still keeping file sizes to a minimum.

Digital Chocolate, Inc.

Pseudo 3D or 2.5D, used in games such as *Mafia Wars: Yakuza*, is an excellent way to add depth to a game environment without pushing a game into true 3D.

::::: Layering Program Graphics & Art

One area that doesn't get explored very often is the layering of program-generated art with painted 2D art and sprites which keeps the game size small while still allowing for larger gameplay areas. A good example of this is Digital Chocolate's *3D Beach Mini Golf*—which uses programmed art for the backgrounds and animation associated with the waves, sky, sand, and green. However, more detailed elements such as golfers and mini golf obstacles were created as 2D sprites and have been layered on top of the programmed background art—which served to significantly reduce the size of the game while still giving a very effective, pseudo 3D look. Sometimes, the effect is reversed—and programmed game art is layered on top of painted 2D art to enable random generation of different elements. For example, in *3D Rollercoaster Rush*, the tracks of the rollercoaster are generated by the underlying programming. There is no "right" way to create many of these games. Layering 2D, 3D, and programmatic elements can be effective ways of building the visuals in a game while still keeping the file sizes as small as possible.

Digital Chocolate, Inc.

Digital Chocolate, Inc.

In *3D Beach Mini Golf* (left), 2D characters and props are layered over programmed art backgrounds—while in *3D Rollercoaster Rush* (right), programmed art is layered over 2D art.

Why 3D?

I'm working on one project right now that is trying to push the limits of 3D rendering. In the case of mobile development, I sometimes think 2D or 2.5D is best—since having a truly 3D experience with the current technology can really impede other areas of the game (CPU power, performance, controls and playability) and create a game with a very large data size. While I appreciate the team's passion and drive to create something amazing, sometimes less is more. You have to draw a line in the sand to re-evaluate whether having 3D is really worth all of the costs and limitations placed on other parts of the game.

—*Nathan Madsen (Composer & Sound Designer, Madsen Studios LLC)*

"It's All About the Gameplay"

I've been in the game industry for so long that mobile art seems more like a throwback than a restriction. I actually like mobile art a lot; instead of sweating over graphic power and amazing shaders, it's all about the gameplay. In a small screen size, you can make things really pretty without having to go crazy on the poly count. Whether 3D or 2D, mobile gaming is about the experience—not full immersion.

—*Alex Bortoluzzi (Chief Executive Officer, Xoobis)*

Pixel Art vs. Vector Graphics

Pixel art is somewhat of a misnomer, since practically all still images are made up of pixels. Early game artists were referred to as "pixel painters" because their work consisted primarily of drawing characters and backgrounds pixel by pixel. As the memory available for graphics expanded, and the tools for drawing and painting digitally became more advanced, pixel painting has given way to more advanced techniques. With the advent of mobile games, however, a new market for an old skillset emerged—and the term "pixel art" stuck. The big problem with what is known as "pixel art" is that it's limited by the information contained in the pixels; "bitmap art" is more fitting. When the art is scaled up, the new space must be filled by a (somewhat sophisticated) guess: The program takes the existing pixels (e.g., a black and white pixel side by side) and averages out the color in a technique known as *anti-aliasing* to create the new pixels. The larger a bitmap image is scaled up, the blurrier it gets. However, this technique works well for reducing graphics down to their smallest possible size; manipulating the image on the pixel level, choosing which pixel to cut, and determining whether to make the pixel 80% black or 60% black will provide the greatest degree of control while minimizing the size of the game.

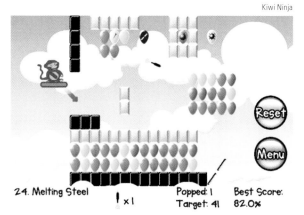

Kiwi Ninja

The smooth, vector-based 2D images in *Bloons* are scaled up and down to fit the screen—and they can be pulled and used in print and web advertising for the game without a loss in quality.

Vector graphics comprise entirely different types of images. In layman's terms, vector graphics are generated by a mathematical function or series of functions. Since the images are created on the fly by the program, based on a set of numbers, they can be scaled up and down with only a bare minimum of loss. Programs such as Flash and Illustrator use vector graphics to great effect for clean, easily scaled graphics for web and print use. Web-based games use vector graphics so heavily in part because the image file size is based on the vector file—not the size of the end graphic. This is a key component in many games developed using Flash for delivery on web and mobile platforms.

As efficient as this all sounds, it is far more common in mobile for vector graphics to be used in the initial creation of the visuals, which are then rendered out into a bitmap or pixel-based format for use in a mobile game. Utilizing the original art as a vector file opens up a wealth of opportunities for the creation of high-end print, web, and broadcast marketing materials.

Use Your Space Wisely

As memory space continues to expand, there is a tendency to let best practices slip and file sizes bloat to fill the space. Artists and programmers should keep in mind that space is precious—and every bit wasted could have been used to add value to the game.

Art for the Small Screen: painting angels on the head of a pin

chapter 5

Palette Tricks

Palettizing is perhaps the oldest trick in the book. Early game developers used it to reduce the file size for an entire level's worth of images, dramatically cutting down the information that needed to be stored within those files. The fewer individual colors available in any given image, the smaller the file size for that image. For example, an image with a 128-color palette is smaller than an image with a 256-color palette—and if the colors can be cut down to 32, 16 or even 8, a large amount of space will be saved.

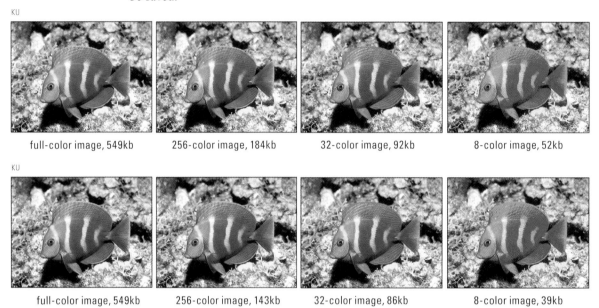

full-color image, 549kb 256-color image, 184kb 32-color image, 92kb 8-color image, 52kb

full-color image, 549kb 256-color image, 143kb 32-color image, 86kb 8-color image, 39kb

Reducing the number of colors used to create an image also reduces the file size (top row). Hand-retouching images to consolidate colors as they are reduced in the palette can also help to reduce file size (bottom row).

The images in the top row above show adjustments to the palette, allowing the program (Photoshop in this case) to handle all of the decision-making during this process. Note the big differences in file size as the palette is reduced to eight colors. Notice how the image gets more "speckled" as it is reduced to fewer and fewer colors? Each of these images reflects a reduction to a smaller palette directly from the original image; for example, the final image reflects a 24-bit color image that has been reduced to eight colors in a single action.

Now for a little hand-retouching: A process known as *walking down* has been applied in the to the images in the bottom row. Starting with a single, 24-bit color image and reducing its number of colors results in a file size reduction but preserves some of the quality as well. Although this is a much more time-consuming method of adjusting images, the final product looks far superior. Adding the step of hand-retouching each image before reducing the palette results in a higher level of quality.

This time, the change in file sizes occurs not only due to storing color data but location data; the file stores the location of each individual pixel and its color—but when those colors are consolidated, making the image more cartoony, the image doesn't have to save the color of all those pixels but the information for the entire swatch of color (which can be far less). This same trick can be applied to characters and other smaller sprites. In the case of animation sequences, an even greater decrease in file size can be achieved by combining all the animation frames into a single file with a single palette; this reduces the number of colors and the overall number of palettes that need to be saved.

Masking

When mobile graphics are set up with an element of transparency, the end result is commonly referred to as *masking*—which involves trimming or blocking out areas of the bitmap that should not be visible—much like using masking tape to cover up parts of the wall you don't want to get paint on. While this may not seem like such a big deal at the outset, this technique is at the core of many visual tricks that can be used to enhance both 2D and 3D games without doing too much damage to the file size.

KU

There are two ways to handle the edges on a masked object; the method used will depend on the mobile device and associated programming. Older smartphones will be restricted to hard-edged, aliased masking. The instance in the accompanying image depicts a hard-edged mask; a stair-step effect results where the square pixel of the character's color backs up against the square pixel of the background color (which will ultimately be invisible). This is called *aliasing*—and the larger the image, the less noticeable the effect. However, for mobile games sizes as small as 8x8 pixels, this effect will be very noticeable and will help to define the end result of the art.

KU

The color used for the background or masked color can be set in a number of ways. Sometimes, the color is set in the code—and it will be necessary to check with the programmers to see what was used; this happens quite a bit on smaller smartphones. When using a custom-built game engine, it's often possible to choose the color. In this case, we recommend a color that is not used in the game—such as RGB 236, 16, 137—a particularly deep shade of pink); this will ensure that the color isn't accidentally used elsewhere, and it will also make it easier to spot in more complex background images.

The pink-colored portions of the above images will be transparent when they are used in the game. Setting a rarely used color offsets the risk that your game will show false transparencies.

To choose a color, access the palette in Photoshop and manually set the first color in the palette to that color. When a file is set to use masking, Photoshop will automatically assign that first color slot to be transparent. When the file is saved, Photoshop will ask if transparency should be used. (Double-check this with the programmers, since sometimes the masking information saved into the file by the graphics editing programs will clash with what the programmers are doing.)

If the file will be saved in .png format (the most common compressed file type currently used in mobile development), there will also be an option of creating an "anti-aliased" edge on the graphic. Since animated sprite sizes are so small, it is not usually recommended to use anti-aliasing on characters—but it helps to smooth out the transition for backgrounds and larger animated images. In this case, the file is being anti-aliased to a transparent background rather than a background color.

Fun with Sprites

A quick way to handle transparency colors in Photoshop is to create a sprite in layers, but be sure to leave the background layer empty. After creating the sprite, delete the background layer under the "Layers" tab to the right. The resulting sprite will be on a background that looks like a soft grey checkerboard. When indexing the file, be sure "transparent" is checked—and it will save with the anti-aliasing intact. Note that this trick will not work when using a masked color; the program will only mask out the specific color assigned and leave any blended colors behind.

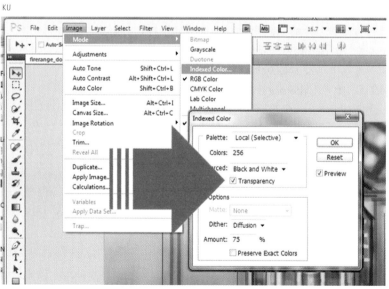

Many programs will automatically use the first position in a 256-color palette as the "transparent" color. Checking the "transparency" box during indexing will ensure that no color ends up in that box, which stays empty.

Scrolling Backgrounds & Parallax Motion

Let's be blunt, shall we? The 176 x 208 resolution still reflects a tiny screen size. Odds are that the entire game won't fit on a single screen. It's big enough for classic puzzle games such as *Tetris*. However, for larger games such as RPGs, more space will be needed—and this means utilizing *scrolling backgrounds*. The classic form of a scrolling background is an image that is long enough so that it won't be very noticeable when it repeats—and where the front and back edges have been matched up so it can tile seamlessly from end to end.

Digital Chocolate, Inc.

This background (from *Ghost Train Ride*—a Halloween-themed version of *Rollercoaster Rush*) has been matched up edge to edge so that it can be looped seamlessly.

Remember those old Hanna-Barbera cartoons where the same door and end table showed up over and over again in the background as one character chased another down a never-ending hallway? This is the same sort of thing. The real key is to make the background seamless enough so that it doesn't distract the player from the game.

It's also possible to have a background that scrolls in all directions—up and down, side to side—but in this case, there is usually a finite edge rather than a looped background. A smartphone screen operates like a little window onto the larger playfield. These large backgrounds are often con-structed of *tiles*—small image squares that can be repeated by the program where needed. The advantage is that the game only needs one copy of each of these tiles, which can then be repeated as often as they are needed to fill the spaces defined by the level designer.

KU

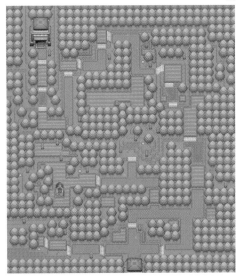

This background is composed of different tiles that can be matched up edge to edge, like puzzle pieces, to create a complete image.

Like a Puzzle

There are a number of free or inexpensively licensed tile editors such as Tile Ed and Mappy that will allow developers to load in 32 x 32 tiles and use them to lay out a complete map. Once the map is designed, the tile location data can be exported in a format the programmers can use to build the map in the game.

The trick that makes these backgrounds come to life is called *parallax motion*, which relies heavily on masking to give the illusion of realistic depth of field to a scene. Screen elements are layered and moved at slightly different speeds in order to add this illusion of depth. Parallax motion has been used in games since the 1980s to achieve additional depth of field. It can work equally well on side-scrolling backgrounds or the larger format tiling backgrounds just discussed.

Different layers scroll past the player at varying speeds in order to give an illusion of depth.

In the background image above, each of the elements shown is a looping, side-scrolling background. As the player moves along the screen, each of these backgrounds scrolls at a different rate; the one in front is usually fastest, while the one furthest back is the slowest. Another option might be to overlay layers on top of a tiled background. The motion will be different, and it is likely that a subtler hand will be needed than with side-scrolling—but this can add a great deal of vertical depth.

Sprites & How to Make Them

Animated characters and objects are usually handled by creating sprites. The actual movement of the object on the screen is done by the programming, but the internal movement (e.g., the back and forth movement of a character's legs, the unfurling of wings, swinging of swords, the folding and unfolding of the puzzle piece) is a part of the animated sequence for files or frames.

Depending on the programming for a game, sprites can be handled in several ways. First, there could be a list of individual frames; each file is named in sequence (e.g. walk001.png, walk002.png, walk_003.png), and the program calls a particular sequence when it needs it.

> Processing power and data throughput are always going to be concerns when developing for mobile platforms. We try to create our art in as efficient a manner as possible, and we heavily manage our data.
>
> —*Gary Gattis (Chief Executive Officer; Spacetime Studios)*

KU

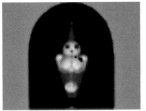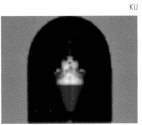

Sprite animation sequences can be saved as separate files with sequential filenames (e.g. Trumpet001.bmp, Trumpet002.bmp, Trumpet03.bmp).

Secondly, a separate filmstrip can be used for each animation. It will be necessary to discuss this with the game's programmers; some code for a specific file width (each frame of the animation is presumed to be a specific size), while others code so that specific colors can be used to indicate the location of the center point of the sprite. The latter is helpful for clever secondary animation tricks where the edges of the frame need to be (which is especially useful when there are animation frames of different sizes).

KU

Sprite animation sequences can be saved as a single strip of images. Note the green-colored, one-pixel wide markers, telling the program where one frame starts and the other ends.

Art for the Small Screen: painting angels on the head of a pin

chapter 5

Thirdly, in a holdover from RPGs on handheld devices, an animation block can be used—where every single animation frame for a specific character is placed. The end result is a large block of animation files that are on the unwieldy side, particularly for mobile titles—but they allow the file size to be reduced by palletizing all the frames at once.

Sprite animation sequences can be saved as a large block of images. Note the same green-colored, one-pixel wide markers; these tell the program where one frame starts and the other ends. Blocks can be unwieldy and hard to use for mobile.

Break It Up

For a very large sprite with only portions of the character animated (e.g., a big boss), it can be beneficial to break the image up into individual animated pieces and reassemble them in-game rather than trying to animate the entire character over a series of overly large sprite images.

Christopher Onstad on Mobile Art Asset Restrictions :::::

Christopher Onstad is a 2D/3D artist and game developer who loves all aspects of production. Currently a freelancer, Christopher has worked as a lead modeler, production artist, graphic artist, illustrator, and web designer. He lives in San Francisco, California with his wife, Kerri, and his son, Warren.

There are numerous restrictions on art assets when developing for mobile platforms—far more than for games developed for consoles or the PC. First and foremost, there's file size. Whether you're using Unity to develop a 3D game for iOS, or Flash/HTML5 for a heavily stylized 2D game, file sizes must be kept to the absolute minimum—as small as possible without lessening the quality of the images produced. In some cases (and in my own experience), even the best-looking designs need to be redesigned occasionally in order to maintain a fast frame rate. No player wants to encounter choppy frames while navigating the world or engaging in a battle with an enemy. The bottom line is playability. A great looking game on the iPhone 4 will only be as successful as its gameplay and "hook." Great art enhances the experience, but it has the potential to hamper it. Artistic designers understand and take technical limitations into consideration while they develop graphics, 3D models, and texture maps so that re-designs are only merely done to adjust aesthetics.

Screen size and resolution directly influence the design direction of any game. Moreover, the more pixels one has to play with, the more one can push the limits of the aesthetics. The iPhone 4, for instance, has more pixels on its display than prior generation iPhones and smartphones—so more details can be seen on textured 3D models and 2D graphics look crisper, sharper, and cleaner. This means that as an artist you can add more details to your assets and only worry about the pure processing capabilities rather than final output of displayed images. With 3D on mobile platforms, there's the advantage of developing full-blown first-person shooters (FPSs) and third-person games that closely mirror those played on the PS2 and Xbox. *Mid-core games*, as they are now being called, are on the rise—and they offer compelling full-blown stories to accompany highly developed art assets in three dimensions. The only technical limitation is on the device itself (processing power), which requires artists and designers to produce a lower *level of detail* (*LOD*) in order to achieve playable frame rates.

The advantage of 2D art is that it takes much less time to revise and animate, since you're only working in two dimensions on any device. What you see is what you get, literally. Every pixel needs to be accounted for—and players are less forgiving of poorly executed 2D graphics than they are with a seam in a 3D textured object.

CO

Christopher P. Onstad (Lead 3D Modeler & Texture Artist, Mega Pickle Entertainment)

3D Art Options

There is 3D and then there's 3D. On the older or less game-oriented phones, 3D simply isn't an option. On the higher-end smartphones, 3D needs to be handled with custom programming and is often restricted to primitive shapes rather than the detailed worlds we are used to thinking of when we hear "3D." On the highest-end units, 2D and 3D game engines are emerging much like those found in game console development—as well as custom application programming interfaces (APIs) for mobile development environments such as Java ME. Working in 3D for mobile requires a different set of constraints, but many of the tricks for 2D discussed in this chapter cross-apply to 3D. Animated 2D sprites can be applied to flat, moving polygons to help provide added visual effects without going through the trouble of creating 3D models.

Firemint

In games such as *Real Racing 2*, 2D masked images and sprites can be combined with 3D to add extra depth and detail.

To the right end of the accompanying screenshot, there are crowds of people watching the player put the pedal to the metal and rip down the track. Rather than individual characters, however, the player sees a flat plane with a masked image of a crowd placed on it. This gives the player the feel of a crowded space without the cost of modeling 20 or 30 people. Remember, just because the game is 3D doesn't mean every little bit of it has to be a 3D mesh.

Mobile Art Guidelines

A good rule of thumb is that a mobile game must look like a higher-end 2D SNES game, at the very least—something that would sell for at least $30 but realistically only costs a buck or two. Design and layout must be at the forefront of aesthetic considerations, and elements must all work on a tiny screen without looking excessively cluttered. Generally, 2D implies "easier to jump into and control," whereas 3D might mean "early PlayStation gaming"—which implies more value if done with a budget. Higher budget 3D often looks quite stellar and can command higher price points, even (and often) at the expense of gameplay depth.

—Ron Alpert (Co-Founder, Headcase Games)

Powers of Two

One of the key restrictions of dealing with a 3D engine (as opposed to custom-coded 3D) is that the graphics need to be developed in *powers of two*. This can result in a little extra waste on the sprites, but it will allow the opportunity for extra space savings on the textures used for the environment. Numbers that are powers of two (2, 4, 8, 16, 32, 64, 128, 256, 512, 1024) are the ideal measurements for most computer memory to process, and mobile units are no different.

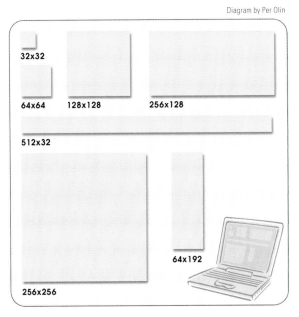

Diagram by Per Olin

"Powers of two" refers to the number of pixels on a side.
Image sizes can be square as well as rectangular.

It is worth noting that the dimensions of the file must be in powers of two, but these can be mixed and matched to use rectangular as well as square files. Stretch or squash the textures to fit so that a texture of a door that might be 128 x 300 could be squashed down to fit onto a 128 x 256 texture, then stretched back out to fit when applied to the in-game 3D object. By its very nature, the stretch and squash distorts the image—so it's better to place a masked sprite into a file with larger dimensions to retain the integrity of the hard-edged mask.

Limited Palette

Be sure to palettize textures before applying them to 3D models. This will help ensure that they are as small as possible before the files are sent to the game engine.

Art for the Small Screen: painting angels on the head of a pin

chapter 5

Batching Files

Let's say that each of 100 animation frames needs to be reduced to the exact same 64-color palette and each needs to have the background color (currently a lurid green) replaced with pepto-pink that has been coded by the programmers. Sounds pretty tedious, doesn't it? Without planning ahead (and let's face it: planning ahead isn't always in the plan!), each individual file will most likely need to be opened, modified, and re-saved. Fortunately, this problem was solved a long time ago by art programs such as Photoshop and DeBabelizer—which have the ability to *batch* files. Batching involves setting up a macro to execute a certain set of instructions and then asking the program to execute that set of instructions on an entire folder full of files. Photoshop makes this easy by allowing a set of actions to be recorded as they are executed. For example:

```
Open File → Select Color → Delete Color → Reduce File to
32 Colors → Save File with a New Name → Close File
```

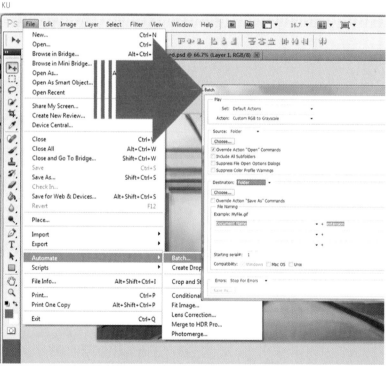

The ability to "batch" files—making the exact same alteration to many images—through a program such as DeBabelizer or Photoshop, can shave hours off a product's development time.

Art generation for mobile devices is almost uniquely universal. First and foremost, mobile game artists must take into account the resolution (pixels per inch) of the target device—which means that a single set of high-resolution art assets can be created, then adjusted for different handheld devices rather than having to create a custom set of assets for each iteration.

Something Old, Something New

Developing art assets for a mobile title is a blend of both old and new techniques. Tricks that worked for developers back when *Pac-Man* was king are still just as valid today and can help go a long way toward keeping file sizes as low as possible. There are new uses for old ideas in game art development being put forth all the time; the openness of mobile games allows a lot of room for innovation—for mixing and matching and trying new ways of building games while still staying within the constraints of file and screen size.

::

Now that we've taken a look at the wants and needs of the artistic development side of the mobile game process, it's time to tackle the programming. Chapter 6 focuses on engineering development tools and techniques associated with different operating systems and mobile devices.

Expanded assignments and projects based on the material in this chapter are available on the Instructor Resources DVD.

:::CHAPTER REVIEW EXERCISES:::

1. Using a smartphone and tablet sketch/wireframe template or idea sheet found at http://www.smashingmagazine.com/2010/03/29/free-printable-sketching-wireframing-and-note-taking-pdf-templates, sketch out ideas for backgrounds, title screens or basic interfaces for an original game idea. How does platform screen size affect your results?

2. Create 3 characters for your game—sketching front, back, and side views. Conduct a "silhouette check" on your characters by shading them in with a black pencil or marker. Can you tell them apart? Are the silhouettes visually interesting? Create a few signature poses for each character—adding accessories when needed and conducting additional silhouette checks on preferred poses. Use some of the color schemes you already developed (Chapter 3 / Exercise 1) on your characters and see if they "fit."

3. Create a scrolling background for your game—utilizing the color schemes you experimented with in Exercise 2. Be sure to make your background seamless enough so that it doesn't distract the player. Now that you've experimented with color schemes for your characters and background, finalize your color palette—applying it not only to your background and characters, but props, structures, and vehicles (when applicable).

4. Play 3 popular mobile games in different genres and observe their visual styles. How do general style (e.g., cartoony, hyperrealistic, iconic, classic/historical), color scheme, and typography vary based on genre? If additional games have been released by the same mobile developers, play those games and determine whether or not each of the developers have successfully maintained "signature" visual styles.

5. Play 3 mobile games that utilize 2D, 2.5D, and 3D. What are some factors that might have affected choice of dimension? Consider platform, genre, use of input devices/controls, gameplay complexity, and visual style.

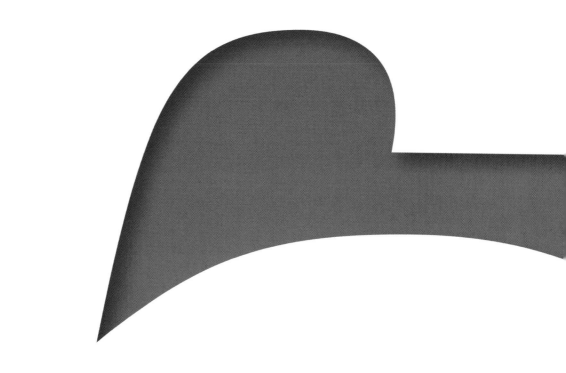

CHAPTER

Programming on the Go

ones and zeros

Key Chapter Questions

- What *languages* are needed for mobile devices?
- Which mobile devices work best for *testing*?
- Is an *emulator* required for mobile programming?
- Where are mobile programming *resources* found?
- Can using a *pre-built game engine* boost development speed?

With so many devices available to the consumer, you might think an epic staff of programmers is required just to cover them all. Programming is one of the key areas in which a decision made early on will greatly affect the rest of the process. If you're still in the early design phase, the choice of programming platform will not only affect where the game is sold, but what can be included within that game. Many of the larger publishers have developed a set process and pipeline for the programming end of their mobile titles—moving from one language to another and focusing on a cleaner flow of assets from one project to the next. This chapter provides a broad introduction to the programming tools and elements associated with the primary operating systems of current mobile and handheld devices. Rather than going into depth on the programming process, we'll give you a "producer-level" overview of different programming environments and the languages that work best with certain mobile devices.

Shoot for the Moon . . . or Just Across the Hall

With the current competition between smartphones in full swing, smaller development studios have an opportunity to focus on a single device. Whether or not this will be sustainable in the long run, the die has been cast—and many new mobile developers are scrambling over one another to get a foot into the ring. Developers who expect to be around in the long run should consider developing for multiple platforms, but this is no longer a stone cold requirement. As the general, mobile-using public continues to learn about app stores as places to purchase games and applications targeted specifically to their devices, the industry is being freed from the restrictions of the carrier deck. It was once necessary to develop for several hundred different smartphone devices—but a small one- or two-person studio can now focus on a single format.

The most influential microprocessor in mobile handsets is the ARM (Advanced RISC Machine). Initially intended as a processor for desktops during the x86 era, it found new life as a low-power microprocessor for mobile phones, handheld game consoles, and music players. According to ARM Holdings, almost all (~98%) smartphones on the market utilize at least one ARM processor—and console-style handhelds such as the Nintendo 3DS and Sony PSVita utilize custom versions of this hardware as well. One of the key factors in the development of the ARM architecture is that ARM Holdings (the company that developed the technology) does not actually produce these chips but provides the design specifications on a license basis; when a licensee provides ARM Holdings with a set of parameters, the company will respond with the specification for a chip that meets those parameters. This practice allows for a great deal of flexibility; different handset manufacturers can also customize their handhelds without spending the massive amounts of time and money required to develop their own custom chips from the ground up. This means that, while these systems all use ARM processors, they can still be very different.

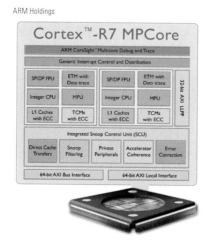

Almost all smartphones have at least one ARM chip.

The Big Four

There are four predominant development platforms associated with mobile and handheld hardware. Android, JavaME, iOS, and Windows Phone are currently the "top dogs"; the majority of mobile handhelds that are capable of playing complete games or applications can run content coded in one of these formats. Let's take a look at the high end of the market first: the smartphones.

- *Android* is Google's entré into the market and is a complete operating system unto itself that can be used to run netbooks and tablets as well as mobile handhelds. Developers that program for Android work with Java, but the operating system itself is based on Linux; this means the development process is quite different from JavaME. In addition, Google has provided a development environment and tools specifically tailored to working with the Android platform.

- *JavaME* (formerly *J2ME*), in its various forms, currently enjoys the broadest penetration across the board when it comes to mobile devices. However, these figures result from the massive number of feature phones on the market, rather than smartphones.

- *iOS* is very hardware specific, unlike its competitors. Only one or two versions of the operating system and hardware are supported by Apple at any given time— which makes development much simpler, since it's not necessary to change the code and bug test on more than a handful of devices. However, focusing solely on iOS puts developers under the thumb of Apple in a way—where their titles are sold only under the umbrella of the iTunes store and are subject to Apple's controls and restrictions.

- *Windows Phone* is perhaps the quiet contender in the race for smartphone dominance. Since programming for Windows Phone is, in essence, very similar to programming for Windows 7, there are many programmers with a very broad range of talents already primed and ready to move into the market rather than having to learn an entirely new set of skills. The big downside is that there is no massive marketing push for any of the Windows phones as seen in Apple or Android units. This means that there's a much smaller (yet devoted) user base—which will limit potential sales figures but possibly give the product line more "stickiness."

Ed Magnin on Developing on Real Hardware :::::

EM

Ed Magnin
(Director of
Development,
Magnin & Associates)

Ed Magnin is the Director of Development for Magnin & Associates, an authorized iPhone/iPad developer. Over a 30-year career, Ed has worked for some of the top game developers in the industry—including MicroProse, Cinemaware, Virgin Games, and Park Place Productions. He has taught undergraduate and graduate level courses on game development, game design, game programming, and the history and business aspects of the game industry. Ed has been credited in dozens of published games for the Apple II, Apple IIGS, Super Nintendo, Game Boy, Game Boy Color, Nintendo DS, iPhone, and iPad.

Real hardware is always better than emulators. The nice thing about iPhone development is that you can develop directly on devices you register with Apple. This also means you have to go get this newest iPhone and iPad as soon as they are released. The emulators Apple supplies are actually very robust, but there are still differences that you can only notice when you have the real hardware as a comparison. Most of the time, we develop on real hardware and even force ourselves to plug in our slowest devices (an old iPod Touch or iPhone 3G) to see how the game plays on them.

Never Rely on the Emulator

"Emulators emulate everything except the device." This was an old saying we used 10 years ago when we pioneered J2ME game development—a caution to all new team members never to rely on the emulator and always code to the device. Emulators have improved dramatically since then—but I believe game developers should still heed the saying and always assess what's on the device screen, not the emulator.

—*Jason Loia (Chief Operating Officer, Digital Chocolate)*

Android

Android represents one of the most highly anticipated changes in the mobile phone market—pushing the idea of a single, high-end, open-source operating system for all mobile devices that is opening up the market to developers of all types and levels of experience. It initially had a rocky start, with complaints about lack of support and QA infrastructure—but developers still flocked to the device, and simple games such as *Snake* appeared just days after the OS was announced.

The Android SDK provides developers with a robust set of tools—including a debugger, several Google-developed libraries, smartphone emulator (see Chapter 2), documentation, samples of code, and a number of tutorials. Most developers (including those who are already experienced with programming in other languages) recommend that you begin with the tutorials that come with the SDK—since these will walk you through the basics of programming, architecture, and tools.

Android applications are written in Java, then compiled along with all the data and resource files into an Android package file with the .apk suffix. This archive allows developers to ensure that everything stays together when distributing and installing the application on mobile devices. Everything packaged in an .apk file is considered a single application, no matter how many smaller individual files it may contain.

Motorola   Motorola

Android (Droid 3, left; Photon 4G, right) is on a broad range of mobile devices from different manufacturers. Formats can be as varied as the now classic "bar" shaped device or the sliding keypad that combines the functionality of the touchscreen with a physical keypad.

In the case of Android, Eclipse is the development framework most directly supported by developer forums—predominantly because it provides the ability to edit, build, and debug from within a single program. Programmers may choose to develop in a number of other integrated development environments (IDEs) such as IntelliJ IDEA or Gnu Emacs.

IDEs & the Acronym Salad

ARM, SDK, IDE … The software industry is very fond of its abbreviations and acronyms. IDE stands for "integrated development environment," which is in essence the core set of tools used by programmers. The IDE focuses on a specific programming language, and it is intended to provide an all-in-one solution that includes a source code editor, compilers, debuggers, etc.—all with similarly built interfaces that allow a programmer to quickly move between them for maximum efficiency.

While Android apps are often written in Java, there is no Java *virtual machine* (*VM*) within the platform. Instead, the code is recompiled into a Dalvik executable (.dex) and is run on a Dalvik virtual machine designed to work with Android with an eye toward optimization for low power devices with memory limitations (such as smartphones).

Diagram by Per Olin

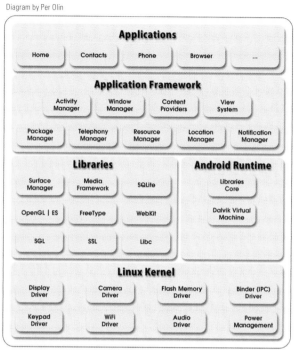

The Android operating system works in a stacked format with available applications shown in blue (representing the visible end result of the programming) and the underlying Linux kernel shown in red. The libraries are all custom developed by Google for use with the operating system and are available to developers as part of the SDK.

Dev Units

On the Android platform, applications will need to work on a number of different smartphones. While the emulator will ensure that the app will work across all devices, be prepared to do some bug fixing once it is released to the public—and factor in some additional time for this. Any Android phone can be used for development—and the application can be installed directly to the phone, either through Eclipse or the command line. Advanced developers might use either a SIM-unlocked *Android Dev Phone* (*ADP*) by applying through the Android Market site or a Nexus S Android phone. In truth, any Android phone could be used as a development phone—but Google makes recommendations for developers based on the best phones for testing. The ADP also features an unlocked *boot loader* (which loads the OS into

E*mulators* can be useful, but development kits are often very affordable; in consideration of issues such as fragmented hardware markets, "real" testing is much more of a necessity.

—Ron Alpert (Co-Founder, Headcase Games)

the device's memory when it is being booted and also starts the OS itself, similar to jailbreaking for the iPhone)—allowing for the development of a complete custom interface and image set for the device if needed.

Android Market

Every app needs a home, and the *Android Market* is the place to be for Android apps. When the Market first opened, it only supported "free" apps—but it has been open to paid applications for several years. The Android Market does not have the lengthy approval process found with Apple; once the app possesses the basic requirements, it is ready to go. However, the comment system is alive and well—and if an app is buggy or has other issues, rest assured someone will say so.

> Memory management is probably the biggest programming restriction, followed by CPU considerations, in order to maintain high frame rates and lag-free performance.
>
> —Caleb Garner
> (Game Producer, Part12 Studios)

::::: Open Source

Many new mobile developers assume all "open source" programs are free and open to anyone, to be used for any purpose—but the reality is often different. In some cases, a "loose" type of open source might exist—where a developer has posted all the code to a project to provide a base from which others can work. Many of these open source projects are woefully incomplete—"open" simply so that more developers are brought in to improve and complete a project at no cost. From a development standpoint, open source situations should be reviewed carefully—since they often lack all but the most basic support and will require a lot of work before becoming viable. When code is released as open, it is usually bound to one of several licenses. Using the code binds the developer to the license as well, so pay close attention to to the license agreement language; for example, don't use open source code that requires developers to release custom libraries and tools if this is not acceptable.

Licenses that are popular and widely used or with strong communities:

- Apache License, 2.0 (Apache-2.0)
- BSD 3-Clause "New" or "Revised" license (BSD-3-Clause)
- BSD 3-Clause "Simplified" or "FreeBSD" license (BSD-2-Clause)
- GNU General Public License (GPL)
- GNU Library or "Lesser" General Public License (LGPL)
- MIT license (MIT)
- Mozilla Public License 1.1 (MPL-1.1)
- Common Development and Distribution License (CDDL-1.0)
- Eclipse Public License (EPL-1.0)

Java ME

Java ME (previously *J2ME*) allows for the greatest penetration when mobile devices are targeted as a class rather than one or two smartphones. However, the information and tools for programming in Java ME are not collected in a single place in a tidy package as with Android or iOS. It will be necessary to spend some time evaluating the smartphones needed and collecting tools and emulators that work for each of them. It is estimated that there are over three billion Java ME enabled phones on the market; this is a very large pool of potential customers to draw from! However, the lion's share consists of feature phones, which means working through a carrier deck.

Much like Android, which is published under the Apache license, Java ME is published under the GNU Public License. This means the source code is open and available to anyone willing to fulfill the requirements laid out by the license. Java ME devices work on mobile units by implementing the *Mobile Information Device Profile* (*MIDP*) specification, which includes *MIDP2*, a basic 2D gaming *API* (*application programming interface*—used extensively on many of the mid to low range smartphones), *GUI* (*graphical user interface*), and a data storage API. Herein lies the trick: Most mobile phones now come with an MIDP already installed and can only run packages (known as *MIDlets*) that have been approved by the carrier.

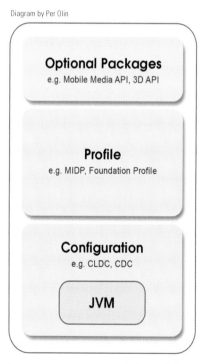

Diagram by Per Olin

Since Java ME relies on an already installed Mobile Information Device Profile (MIDP), the file sizes on Java ME applications are smaller and the structure is simpler. The user-friendly elements are in green above, running on top of the MIDP.

Java ME for BlackBerry

A Java ME end product is usually associated with RIM's line of BlackBerry handhelds. While BlackBerry requires Java ME, there are a number of significant differences between programming an application for a "feature" phone and programming for the BlackBerry—most notably the custom APIs that RIM has developed to use the more powerful capabilities of the hardware. At this time, the BlackBerry does not use a Java VM, but a "Java-like" VM that has been optimized for the BlackBerry hardware. Although Eclipse or other platforms can be used for development, the tools provided by RIM must ultimately be used to ensure that the app is compiled into a BlackBerry-friendly format.

Motorola

Programming for the BlackBerry has its own unique challenges not found in other Java ME devices.

Dev Units

Unlike the iOS and Android markets, which use proprietary operating systems, the market penetration for Java ME is massive—with hundreds of development phones to choose from. The Java ME development phones of choice have been Motorola's RAZR, LG's Chocolate and the BlackBerry Torch—but as new models of feature phones are developed, this will continue to change.

Carrier Deck Distribution

Unlike the iPhone and Android platforms, there is no centralized market for Java ME applications. Instead, primary distribution being handled by the carrier deck associated with each cellular carrier. While there are smaller aggregate sites that collect and distribute mobile applications, finding the right one and installing it on a mobile device may be beyond the skillset of the average cell phone user.

Courtesy of Apple Inc.

iPhone 4

iOS

The most recent entry into the mobile market has been Apple's new line of products that use *iOS*. Whether you love or hate Apple (and the iPhone versus Android rivalry can border on the truly fanatical in some places), the biggest advantage iOS smartphones have is the relative simplicity of testing and distribution. Apple has only two or three iOSs it supports at any given time. Any applications must be distributed through the Apple App Store. While the process of getting into the App Store is somewhat tedious, this is a much simpler process overall from a developer point of view. That said, the iOS market is limited to iPhones, the iPod Touch and iPads, which hold a very small overall market share when compared to the number of "feature" phones already in place worldwide.

Developer Support

Like many of the manufacturers discussed thus far, the Apple developer's program requires a yearly fee ($99) just to get approved. Access to Xcode and a number of tools and support is available to unregistered developers—but only Apple Registered Developers can get applications signed and published through the App Store. There are additional benefits provided to registered developers, such as early access to tools and other special releases (e.g., access to Game Center, announced along with iOS 4 in 2010). It's essential for mobile developers to have early access to these elements if they want their products to be available for release at the same time a new piece of technology becomes available to the general public. Being on the front line of a new software release can heighten exposure for a developer's products and increase the number of downloads significantly.

iOS and Xcode

Since it is derived from the Mac OSX, iOS is oddly enough very much like a UNIX operating system. Mac developers are already familiar with Xcode—a free set of tools and compiler that Apple releases with every computer, which is also the primary programming tool for the iOS. This is does not mean that all programming must be done on a Mac, in Xcode. A number of compilers are available that will allow developers to program in C#, then port to Xcode for the final version. However, like the BlackBerry, the app must be pushed through the manufacturer's (Apple) proprietary tools in order for iOS to use it.

Diagram by Per Olin

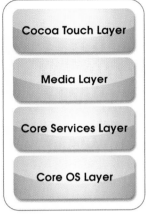

| Cocoa Touch Layer |
| Media Layer |
| Core Services Layer |
| Core OS Layer |

Like Android and Java ME, Apple's platform
is divided into multiple "abstract" layers.

Dev Units

"Unlocked" or open development units cannot be acquired for iOS as they can for
Android devices. However, the Apple developer program does provide the tools
and access needed to test an app on any available iPhone through a process known
as *provisioning*—where a profile is created for a single iPhone or iPad—and the app
can be installed on that unit only through the developer's local version of iTunes.
The catch is that provisioning profiles have limited lifespans, and only 100 of them
are available to each registered developer. This isn't an issue for small studios that
develop only a few games a year, but studios with more products can run out of
available provisions quickly.

Beam Chess: Creating Artificial Intelligence

Quinn Dunki & John Burnett

My best moment so far in mobile development was getting the AI opponent in
Beam Chess to play reasonably well. Chess AI on small hardware is challenging
enough, but the move tree for *Beam Chess* is much, much larger. It was a huge
challenge that took me months to debug and optimize. I just kept at it, coming back
to it in the evenings and weekends while I did other things. I researched chess
algorithms like crazy and discovered that many of the examples and explanations
online are wrong. Once I had it working, getting the code fast enough for the
device was even more difficult—and it required a lot of cheating and creative
corner cutting (commonplace in game AI). You learn a ton from a big challenge
like this, though! I'm so much better at getting code to run fast on an iPhone than
I was before I started.

—*Quinn Dunki (Chief Sarcasm Officer, One Girl, One Laptop Productions)*

Windows Phone

Don't ever count Microsoft out of the race. When the computing giant announced that it was going to enter the game console market, the general consensus was that it would simply produce a half-done Windows box that would hardly be better than

Sprint

a desktop PC of the same era. Over a decade later, Microsoft remains one of the "big three" console manufacturers (alongside Sony and Nintendo)—and the Xbox 360 continues to gather market share. Microsoft systems accounted for almost 25% of all smartphones sold in 2004, but sales have steadily declined (with only 5.8% market share in Q2 2011). So why are we including the *Windows Phone* operating system here? In 2010, Microsoft completely gutted its Windows Mobile operating system and prepared to release Windows Phone. This massive changeup would seem to indicate that Microsoft is taking the mobile and handheld market seriously. Love 'em or hate 'em, when Microsoft begins to take notice, expect to see results.

The Windows Phone operating system is available on both touchscreen smartphones and more traditional keypad style phones. The HTC Arrive (shown) has both touchscreen and keypad.

SDK and .NET

The Windows Phone operating system uses the .NET compact framework (a subset of the .NET framework, which means that many of the tools available for desktop development are also used for mobile). In previous versions of Windows Mobile, developers had more direct access to the .NET Framework. However, in the newest version of Windows Phone, this access has been subsumed—and developers must work at a higher level using Silverlight or XNA to develop their apps. Like the other competitors in the smartphone market, Microsoft provides an SDK free of charge to interested developers. In Microsoft's case, this includes add-ons for Visual Studio, Expression Blend, a Windows Phone emulator, XNA Game Studio (specifically for developing games), and additional samples and documentation.

Expression Blend is a tool that is specifically used to design an app's user interface. It attempts to take the programming out of UI design, allowing the developer to set up an interface on the visual end and then hook the program code up to it after the fact—rather than requiring the programmer to develop the interface from the ground up. In terms of application design, this is a big step forward because allows the designer to work concurrently with the programmer—rather than have a never-ending pipeline of assets going back and forth, which can slow down the development process. There are third-party development systems available as well—including a version of Python called PythonCE than can be used to develop applications on the desktop and then be brought over to the device.

Interestingly, Microsoft has seen fit to allow close communication between its desktop and mobile development. Applications developed for Silverlight or the XNA framework function on Windows Phone-enabled smartphones—with most necessary changes involving adjustments for screen size and resolution, rather than changes to the core programming itself. This means that programmers who work on Windows desktop applications using these frameworks will have an easy opportunity to make the jump to mobile—giving developers a much larger talent pool to draw from and drastically cutting down on the amount of training needed. Like its competitors, Microsoft uses a proprietary bundling tool to convert an app and all of its required components into a single .XAP file. (XAP is the package file that contains all code for the app.)

Diagram by Per Olin

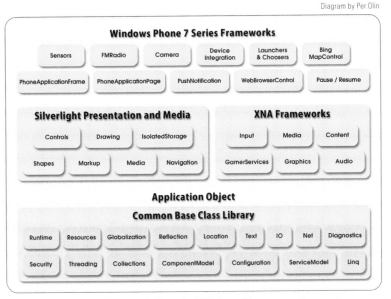

Unlike its competitors, Microsoft views its Windows Phone operating system as part of a larger network—encouraging users and developers to create applications that can smoothly move across and access other Microsoft products, including Xbox LIVE.

Windows Phone Marketplace

Windows does have its own proprietary "app store" known as the *Windows Phone Marketplace* which walks the fine line between the tight control enforced by the Apple App Store and the unconstrained freedom found on the Android Marketplace. Microsoft has openly and publicly announced that it will ban certain types of applications (particularly those with adult or excessively violent content) from its Marketplace. Interestingly enough, apps will need to receive a "rating" from one of three bodies: ESRG (Engineering Software Reliability Group), PEGI (Pan European Game Information) or USK (Self-Monitoring of Entertainment Software). Products that receive a rating below 12 will be admitted to the Marketplace without further review.

Jailbreaking

Whether it's Apple, the government, or even that yoga instructor who thinks that "downward dog" is the best pose ever, the impulse to fight "the Man" is there—and it's what makes us strive to adapt and try new things. Technology fans are no strangers to this impulse; in fact, every device ever brought to market has been hacked, cracked, jailbroken, and otherwise repurposed at the whim of those with the time and intelligence to get through any defenses the manufacturer might have installed. From teaching a Roomba "robot" vacuum cleaner to play soccer, to installing Linux on an Xbox360, new technology begs to be repurposed. Apple's iOS is no different. Before the iPhone hit the market, early adaptors and tinkerers were hard at work finding ways around Apple's control of the system.

Illustration by Ian Vasquez

Benefits

A number of groups have provided instructions and tools for jailbreaking iOS devices; some are better than others, so tread carefully. Jailbreaking can open up a phone for complete customization, allowing users to change the look of the screen display and access applications that Apple would or could not approve for distribution. (This doesn't automatically mean they're "good" apps—but that they were rejected or the developer never submitted them in the first place.) In most cases, if a user makes a mistake during jailbreaking, the phone can be put back into recovery mode and the factory defaults can be reinstalled. Developers with jailbroken iPhones can install and reinstall their apps as needed without using up the allotted number of provisioning profiles provided through the Apple Registered Developer Program.

Jailbreaking vs. Unlocking

Jailbreaking a phone involves modifying it so that it's possible to install unsigned applications and change the icon styles, for example. *Unlocking* goes much deeper, allowing users to make root-level changes that will allow the phone to be used on another carrier. While jailbreaking can be fixed if something goes wrong, make a mistake while unlocking and a user might find that the phone has been *bricked* (rendered useless for any digital purpose, much like an old-fashioned red brick) and can no longer be used at all.

Problems

First out of the gate, jailbreaking will void a phone's warranty. This doesn't really matter to developers that are using smartphones as development devices—and some might even have the technical savvy to fix it whenever an issue arises.

Secondly, and possibly a very important issue for developers, is that jailbreaking reportedly can increase system instability. If an app crashes at random, it may be hard to determine whether or not the fault lies with the system or with the app unless it is installed on a "clean" copy of the OS.

Jailbreaking can make a phone susceptible to virus attacks. The best known of these is the *ikee* worm in Australia, a relatively benign example of hacking that installed a Rick Astley image as the background (in an obvious homage to "Rickrolling"). Now that the genie is out of the bottle, more variations are bound to be released into the wild. Usually, the susceptibility is related to password errors, such as forgetting to change from the default password—but as other exploits are discovered, they will be targeted. Anything that puts a development system at risk for being hacked is something to seriously consider. There's nothing more annoying for a developer than discovering that code has been compromised or stolen. Some people exploit hacks just because they enjoy "peeking through the keyhole"—but for every dozen of these, there are a few that will leave a huge mess behind that will need to be cleaned up. Another thing to consider is that the jailbreaking will get "broken" each time Apple releases an OS update; this means that you will have to jailbreak the phone all over again, possibly with a new set of tools.

All in all, jailbreaking a development phone can make it quicker and easier to test apps without blowing through the Apple Developer 100 install limit. In addition, there is a market for applications for jailbroken phones—so making an app available for phones that have been altered may open up an alternate stream of revenue.

Mobile Ratings

In 1994, the game industry stepped up to the plate and tackled the sticky issue of self-regulation. There had been several ratings agencies in existence previously, and more than a few starts and stops to this process—but by the late '90s, the industry as a whole seemed to reach a level of maturity, which made a voluntary unified rating system possible for consoles and desktop computers. Games for mobile still fall into a grey category where these ratings are only lightly employed. One of the key differences between the sale and marketing of mobile versus box games is the middleman involved. For example, Apple has been very restrictive with regard to content; each game is reviewed and requires approval before it can be sold through the App Store. If a game is determined to contain too much violence or adult content, it will not be allowed through the review process. This "rating by proxy" has been a big source of contention with regard to the unfair removal of many apps. Different carriers have varying approval standards and processes, each tailored to the core audience for that carrier. The types of products approved by T-Mobile, for example, are different in quality and "rating" than those approved by Verizon Wireless. Whereas the game industry at large has been held responsible for regulating game content, it has become the purview of the carriers—those companies maintaining the "walled garden" of mobile content—to control and deliver mobile content.

Shortcuts & Engines

With the recent explosion of mobile applications and the smartphones that run them, there has also evolved a host of "do-it-yourself" systems that, depending on the degree of complexity in an app, can provide a quick turnkey result or an underlying structure—which can save developers from reinventing the wheel.

Mobile programming shortcuts are growing by the minute. There is an increasing number of applications that give mobile developers a leg up. Although none of these is a panacea for actual proper application development, they can serve as useful tools to speed up prototyping and iteration. Even the most "turnkey" solution requires some minor programming for it to become a proper, custom-looking application—rather than just a re-skin of the sample game that was provided with the software.

Cake Mix or Scratch?

Have you ever baked a cake—or helped a friend bake one? There's a decades old-dilemma: Do you go with a box of cake mix, or do you crack open a cookbook and try to make it from scratch? Just like cooking, sometimes programming an app from scratch yields the best result; in other cases, it's best to stand on the shoulders of giants. Be sure to evaluate the project for financial feasibility as well as efficiency of development before having any programmers set fingertips to keyboard.

Benefits of Pre-Built Game Engines

Pre-built game engines are almost always the way to go—especially now that there are so many affordable or free solutions, often with established supportive development communities. A host of restrictions are imposed; for more casual games, it's important to be strict on things such as smaller file sizes.

—*Ron Alpert (Co-Founder, Headcase Games)*

I like to use pre-built game engines because this frees you up from having to start from scratch and spend a lot of time getting ready for when the assets come online. In our case, using Unity, the artists and designers are able to attack the tasks from the get go because it's so user friendly. The fact that you can deploy your game in several different platforms with ease makes it an ideal situation for today's mobile reality.

—*Alex Bortoluzzi (Chief Executive Officer, Xoobis)*

Quinn Dunki on Code & Engines for Mobile Games :::::

Quinn Dunki has been making games for over 25 years (over 15 years as a professional). She was most recently AI Architect at Pandemic Studios on the exciting new open-world title *The Saboteur*. She now pursues consulting, independent development, mixed-media engineering projects, and writing. Her fledgling boutique game company One Girl, One Laptop Productions makes games for Mac, PC, and iOS. In her spare time, Quinn takes pictures, races cars, hacks electronics, and berates her friends with sarcasm.

QD

Quinn Dunki
(Chief Sarcasm Officer, One Girl, One Laptop Productions)

Code needs to be leaner and meaner—but the OS layer is much thicker on phones than on other devices, so you're a bit at its mercy. You need to learn what the hardware is and is *not* good at. You need to learn how to optimize and tailor your code to the platform using various tools. I suppose it's the same as any other console in that sense. I'm not personally a fan of pre-built game engines, because I prefer not to hitch my business wagon to someone else's horse—but I think they could be a good solution for some people. However, I am a fan of well-made middleware. Some problems, such as physics or particle effects, can be solved really well with middleware for minimal risk.

Engines for Mobile

While game engines are everywhere when it comes to console and PC games, they're in mobile development—and they're almost exclusive to smartphones. Unity's product started out as a game engine for desktop systems, but the company quickly recognized there was a rich and untapped market for an engine that allowed for the development of a single product that could be distributed across multiple platforms. GameSalad is geared toward the 2D market, while Unity focuses on 3D. Java ME appears to have gotten the short end of the stick—but since nearly every mobile device that uses it requires a bit of custom tweaking, it seems nearly impossible to develop an engine that will work under those circumstances.

> The Spacetime Engine was written in C++, which allows us tremendous flexibility to port to various platforms as they become more popular.
>
> —*Gary Gattis (Chief Executive Officer, Spacetime Studios)*

GameSalad Inc

Unity Technologies

Engines for mobile games include GameSalad (left) and Unity (right).

In the case of Unity or the mobile version of Unreal 3, game programmers work with *object-oriented programming* (OOP)—not accessing the source code itself, but rather just specifics associated with individual objects and elements. The code for moving an object or character from Point A to Point B has already been written, and the code for making a projectile fly across the screen is already available; the programmer's task is to make sure it completes these operations when asked. This requires a different programming mindset, where nothing needs to be written from scratch; however, programmers must work atop someone else's thought process—and as any programmer can confirm, this is sometimes a very frustrating process.

As might be suspected, OOP is all about "objects." In layman's terms, an object is a packet; think of it as a small box (most often referred to as a "black box") with a series or multiple series of instructions (code) and a bunch of information that is used with those instructions (data). As a user, you are never ever supposed to (or should need to) look inside that box—though, like us, you might probably want to take a peek from time to time!

Once the boxes or "objects" are built, they are inviolate. (With Unity or Unreal 3, they are already built for the user.) They run instructions and spit information back out again, but they cannot be modified. By restricting information in this manner, the original developers of the source code can provide developers with a consistent tool—one that will continue to function and run because the source (underlying code) cannot be changed or broken by a misplaced colon. Since the developer should only be working with the objects, the process is simplified and the tool is protected from missteps.

> We have built all of our core technology ourselves, but we are happy to use third-party pieces (such as physics engines).
>
> —Chris Ulm (Chief Executive Officer, Appy Entertainment, Inc.)

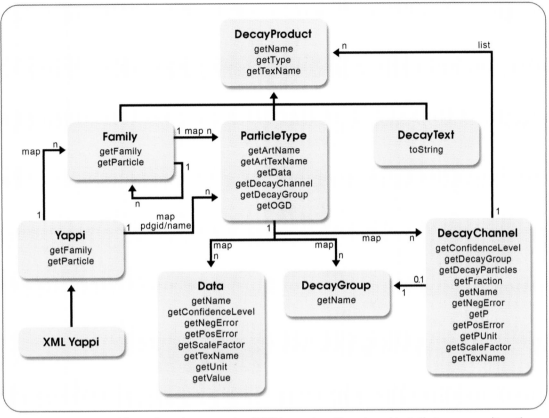

Flowchart showing how object-oriented programming (OOP) is structured based on objects that are grouped together into classes.

Engines for Handheld Devices

When coding for proprietary handhelds, developers work predominantly in C++. Occasionally, it might be necessary to dip into a native language for speed-critical issues, but both Sony and Nintendo systems currently require a solid knowledge of C++. An official devkit designed to work with these systems will include compilers that will convert C++ into code than can be run on the hardware.

Once upon a time, if you were programming for a console style handheld such as the Nintendo GBA or Atari Lynx, you had to develop the product from the ground up. The systems were too closed to really support the licensing of pre-made game engine software. This line of thinking—on the part of both hardware manufacturers and developers—has changed dramatically with the most recent line of devices. In line with this, there is now at least one first-party engine and two third-party engines available for licensing of Sony's line of products (including the PS3, PSP, and PSVita).

Homebrew for Handhelds

Homebrew is an intriguing side element to the handheld console market. Predominantly seen with Nintendo and Sony handhelds, it involves communities dedicated to finding ways to utilize these systems without employing any of the official development hardware or software. The majority of the time, homebrew games and projects are developed on a community and freeware basis rather than being sold for commercial purposes. Once a new handheld is released to the public, the race is on to see who can find a way to access it first. Sometimes this involves circumventing hardware locks or finding ways to take advantage of backdoors left open for bug hunting and development.

DsiBrew

"Homebrew" covers a wide range of topics—from increasing the memory on a proprietary chip to developing custom software.

Who's on First?

The terms "first-party" and "third-party" refer to the relationship between the product developed and its associated platform. For example, an in-house studio for Glu Mobile would be a "first-party" or "in-house" developer. A "third-party" developer would be self-owned—developing games independently (either their own IPs or contract work for larger publishers). The same relationship holds for hardware manufacturers. A "first-party" product is usually developed by a production team working directly for the hardware manufacturer and is marketed and distributed by that manufacturer (e.g., Sony). A "third-party" product is developed by an outside studio and is sold and distributed by an outside source (like the MadCatz controllers made for the Xbox 360).

Sony's first-party engine, PhyreEngine3, has been made available for free to licensed developers who wish to create games for the PSVita. The Phyre engine works on a similar object-oriented system as other engines discussed in this chapter, but it has the added benefit of being not only developed as a first-party product (which often means better access to the handheld and any internal libraries as the engine is being developed) but of being an upgrade to the PhyreEngine 2.X rather than a new product developed from the ground up. This suggests that all of the rookie bugs have been sorted out and the product is well-supported and stable. Other game engines from third-party development houses and previously used with the Sony PSP and PSPGo have also made the jump to the PSVita; these include Trinigy's Vision Game Engine and Vicious Software's Vicious Engine.

Sony Computer Entertainment America

First-party game engines developed by associated hardware manufacturers, such as Sony (PhyreEngine 3, shown) are often built to help showcase the strengths of the hardware product (e.g., the PSVita title, *Gravity Rush*).

Nintendo has also begun opening its development to game engine software. The 3DS handheld is powerful enough to run some of the middle grade versions of the more powerful PC and console engines available, including Epic's Unreal 2 engine. (Although the current version is Unreal 3, Epic has modified this second-generation version of the engine to showcase the 3DS's processing capabilities.) Terminal Reality's Infernal Engine has also been approved for the 3DS.

Entering the Walled Garden

For years, working with the tightly closed handheld console systems required becoming a registered developer and purchasing the software directly from the hardware manufacturers. However, with the massive influx of content available from thousands of independent and small third-party developers focusing on smartphones, console manufacturers have opened up their systems to allow content to cross over into their own walled gardens. There will be some give and take as lessons learned through smartphone game development are translated into older and more structured programming and development practices used in handheld consoles. Regardless of which platform and operating system you choose, be sure to make your decision early in the development process. It will also be necessary to look at the big picture and consider whether or not to take on the broader publication of a game by tackling distribution through a carrier or through a single platform.

Now that we've taken a run through the different areas of specialization that go into making a mobile game, it's time to take a look at assembling and distributing the finished product. There are many quality games out there, so one of your key areas of focus will be how to get your game into the hands of the people who want to play it— and make no mistake, there are people who want to play it! The mobile game market will consume as much content as we developers can possibly deliver. In Chapter 7, we move from the tools and techniques that go into making a game to the production cycle itself—assembling these separate elements together to deliver a finished product.

:::CHAPTER REVIEW EXERCISES:::

1. What are some programming constraints in mobile development? Consider how you plan to overcome or minimize these constraints during the process of programming your own mobile game.

2. Compare and contrast the benefits and disadvantages of operating systems provided by each of the "Big Four" (iOS, Android, Windows Phone, BlackBerry OS). Which operating system makes the most sense for you to choose to develop your own game on first, and why?

3. Play a game that is available on at least two operating systems. (Borrow a friend's smartphone if you have to!) Which game was released first, and which one is a "port" of the other? Compare gameplay characteristics that are directly associated with programming—such as artificial intelligence, pathing, physics, and multiplayer capabilities. Describe any differences in response time, quality, flow, and complexity. Is one of the versions superior to the other in most (if not all) areas?

4. After coding the "Hello, World!" application (Chapter 3 / Exercise 4), begin experimenting with additional tutorials and walkthroughs for Xcode (http://www.icodeblog.com/2009/01/15/iphone-game-programming-tutorial-part-1/) and Eclipse (http://eclipse.dzone.com/articles/beginning-android-game) as you begin to turn your original idea into a mobile game.

5. After experimenting with Unity and/or GameSalad Creator (Chapter 3 / Exercise 5), focus on one program in depth by going through tutorials with your game idea in mind. Unity tutorials are found at http://unity3d.com/support/resources/tutorials/, while GameSalad Creator tutorials are found at http://www.youtube.com/GameSaladCookbook

Part III:
Fruition

Going into Production

"avengers assemble!"

Key Chapter Questions

- What are the pros and cons of being a *third-party studio* vs. *independent developer*?

- What are the key members of a *development team*?

- How can you keep a game from *getting too big to finish*?

- What is the average *time to market* for an indie game?

- How can *going solo* affect design choices?

Every mobile game is different, and the production process is sometimes reinvented to fit the resources and staff on hand. Budding game designers often carry notebooks full of ideas—some questionable, some with potential, and perhaps one that might change the world of games as we know it. Putting an idea into action can get a little scary sometimes, especially for those who are experiencing their "first runs" at being producers. Game production involves managing the hands-on, moment-to-moment development process and working with a team—encouraging, cajoling, and occasionally shouting (but hopefully not too often) to bring a project to fruition. Even an indie developer must understand the needs of the team members. Indie projects are sometimes developed after hours—in the dim time between the day job and before the alarm screams again. Due to this reality, there are special considerations and precautions that should be taken.

Development Phases

The production process for mobile games is different from what is seen in "formal" video game development for console and computer platforms. In traditional game development, there is a "mandate" to make sure the entire product is perfect and complete before it ships—but in mobile games, there is a much greater degree of flexibility. Game elements can be added and expanded upon for months or sometimes even years after a product is released into the market. Gone are the thousand-page design documents with reams of technical detail. Instead, mobile teams use limited documentation that is flexible and changes dynamically on a regular basis. While traditional console games might take years to complete, the entire mobile game production cycle might take place within just a few months.

Pre-Production

Whether the developer is a single-person studio or an in-house team, *pre-production* is the phase in which *what* game will be produced and *how* are both decided. What elements and functions need to be included and at what point can the game be released? The pre-production phase involves setting a "plan of attack." Keep in mind that for mobile, this master plan must stay flexible—so rather than building out an entire production plan (which is often done for a console title), focus instead on individual functionalities and break the project down into small chunks that can be completed and checked off the 'to do' list.

Production

During the *production* phase, the goal is to get the game up and running as quickly as possible in one form or another; this is a key component to solving unseen design issues. In an ideal situation, the goal is to have a working build of the game functions every week or two; this means that the product as a whole is constantly being *prototyped*, rather than having a single distinct phase for the process.

Alpha & Beta

Traditionally, by the *alpha* phase, the game is code complete—playable from start to finish, with all art assets in place. Not *everything* is necessarily final; there may still be a few bits and pieces here and there that need improvement. This is where the team makes a shift from game creation to game refinement. Code is locked, and the majority of time is spent making the game as polished and complete as possible.

This is one of the major divergent points from more traditional game design. With a console-based product (3DS or PSVita) with a longer development cycle, the Alpha and Beta stages are more clearly defined—but with mobile projects, these stages tend to get mashed together. The end goal for mobile is a viable, shippable product that can be polished as needed through updates after it has been released.

Gold

Goooooooooooooooooooooooooooold! If you're working with console style hand-helds, Gold is still the standard: A complete, finished, shiny product is needed for delivery; once it goes out the door, there are only *very* limited opportunities to change it. However, the Gold stage has become indistinct in mobile releases. Getting a product into the app store is paramount—so if it ships with a few issues, there is still an opportunity to push updates and changes that allow for fixes and upgrades.

Post-Production

Wait—there's more? Even after a mobile product is pushed out the door, there are still changes to be made. By reviewing the *metrics* (information collected about player habits and monetization), the design team can see where players have issues with the product, where they might be getting stuck, or how long they play before the put the game down. These elements drive changes to the design that can then be iterated upon and pushed back out as updates (the mobile version of "patches") to an installed user base.

Speed Changes Everything

While this section provides a general overview of the steps taken during the development process in mobile, keep in mind that we're not looking at extensive periods of time. Pre-production might take just a few weeks—and moving from beta to gold can take a week or two at most, depending on how clean the code is and how well the prototyping process went. In an AAA console title, pre-production might take months or even as long as a year depending on the IP and the titles previously developed by the studio.

Agile Development

The production process for games is constantly evolving. Traditional processes derived from manufacturing and product development just can't keep up with the ultra-high-speed pace of mobile development. These methods were reinvented by game developers working with console and PC products. For mobile game development, these processes are still a bit on the slow side and need some modification if they are going to work. The game industry has a long history of reinventing any process that gets in the way of the intended result—and the mobile game industry is no different.

Diagram by Per Olin

Agile Production Cycle

Games for mobile tend to work better when utilizing an *Agile* development process (introduced in Chapter 4)—a type of software development methodology that involves incremental and iterative components, focusing more on response to change and team members rather than tools and plans. Due to the relatively small team sizes, Agile processes such as iteration become much quicker and simpler to manage. Instead of being pushed forward at the same rate, the entire product is instead broken down into smaller pieces. As each game element is taken from the list of "to-do" items and put into production, the prototyping of that individual element is handled—which results in the occurrence of some sort of prototyping process on an ongoing basis.

Valve's Cabal Process

Valve Software uses its own decentralized *Cabal Process*—separating team members into "Cabal Rooms" while working on new projects or bug fixes. Each room contains 10-15 people, hardware, and one whiteboard. In "The Cabal: Valve's Design Process for Creating *Half-Life*" (*Gamasutra*), Senior Developer Ken Birdwell at Valve discusses how this unique form of teamwork turned a "less impressive" version of *Half-Life* into a "groundbreaking success."

Scrum

Scrum is one of the more broadly known of the Agile development processes. In a nutshell, it is a predefined framework designed to allow a single, cross-disciplinary team to be able to work aggressively and iteratively—producing many versions of a product during its development cycle. The product is broken down into "stories," and the development of those stories is further broken down into "sprints"—with team members pushing one element forward to completion, then returning to the backlog of stories to reassess the remaining tasks and choosing the next element to "sprint" on.

Diagram by Per Olin

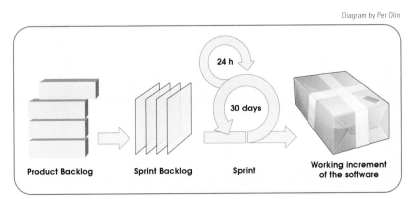

Product Backlog — Sprint Backlog — Sprint — Working increment of the software

Agile development processes such as Scrum aim to keep the product development process flexible and easy to modify in order to keep up with client expectations and a rapidly changing marketplace.

Scrum is a teachable process—and a studio might hire a producer who holds a Scrum Master Certificate or bring in an outside expert to teach an entire production team how to work within a Scrum framework. However, while Scrum works well for large studio teams, it is still a bit unwieldy for the speed at which mobile development operates. Many studios have adapted the Scrum methodology by integrating it with other models to create hybridized production methods that suit their own needs and ideals.

One of the guiding principles of Agile development systems such as Scrum is that working longer hours does not necessarily mean that more work has been produced. Agile processes focus on "effective" hours rather than long hours.

Kanban

Part of *JIT* (*just in time*) production—developed by Japanese businessman, Taiichi Ohno—*Kanban* is a scheduling system that yields larger pieces reflecting several interrelated elements. In most Agile systems, these pieces are pushed to full functionality; the developers then return to the "to-do" list to start on another piece, rather than trying to push production on the entire piece of software forward at the same pace. Kanban begins like Scrum, with the needs and wants of the client determined by assembling a list of "stories"; it also allows features to move from the left of the board (where they are essentially still ideas or stories) to the right (where they are declared completed). However, unlike Scrum, Kanban allows elements to move *back* toward the left if more time is needed, whether during production or another part of the development process; it also makes room for urgent components—elements that can be fast-tracked to rise to the top of the queue and pass through production on a high-priority basis.

alq666 (flikr)

The Kanban system retains much of the flexibility of Agile processes and can be scaled to fit any team size with any set of team positions (or mix of positions, which is often the case in mobile).

Lean Principles

The Agile community has largely embraced Lean development—a set of principles that have been adapted from the Toyota Production System. Lean principles include launching products quickly, empowering the team (no micromanagement), eliminating "waste" (features that don't add value to the player/customer), and delaying decisions (so that they're based on facts rather than assumptions or predictions).

Just like any good production methodology, even the "named" forms of Agile development (there are a great many ways to develop using an Agile process, but not all of them are common enough to be given names or be taught in a formal setting) maintain some flexibility and can be adjusted to better fit the team in question. Keep in mind that Agile is a production philosophy, rather than a hard and fast set of rules.

Gary Gattis on the Mobile Development Process:::::

GG

Gary Gattis
(Chief Executive
Officer,
Spacetime Studios)

Gary Gattis wrote his first game on an Apple II+ in 1984. After graduating with degrees in Sculpture and Computer Science from the University of Texas in 1990, he got his vocational start in gaming when he co-founded Human Code—one of Austin's first multimedia companies. Gary next worked at Digital Anvil as Director of Development. In 2000, he left the game industry for three years to build Fortune 100 enterprise software solutions. In 2003, he joined Sony Online Entertainment to run *Star Wars Galaxies*—and he co-founded Spacetime Studios two years later, in October 2005. Gary served as Chairman of the Board for the Austin branch of the International Game Developer's Association from 2008 to 2009. In April of 2010, Spacetime Studios released *Pocket Legends*, the world's largest mobile MMO. The company continues to expand its content and technology lead in the mobile multiplayer market.

We run a highly iterative development process. At the beginning of the week, we review the game and set our weekly goals. On Wednesday, we do a playthrough to get a sense of where we are. On Friday, the entire team plays and provides feedback. In our games, where literally thousands of people play together all the time, it is impossible to accurately predict what will happen until you release a feature "into the wild." We have a very tight feedback loop with the community, and the technology that allows us to patch our game updates instantly—so we will release something as soon as we think it is good enough. We'll then take feedback from the community and patch it up, usually 1-2 times a day, until it is working flawlessly.

Development Team Roles

Although setting up a development team depends on a number of factors, mobile-specific issues are surprisingly not that relevant early on. Most game design elements are still important, but they're just abbreviated due to device constraints. One of the attractions in developing for a mobile title is that it's unnecessary to have a large team—due to the relative speed of development and simplicity of design. In fact, an entire game can be developed with just a single individual, one laptop, and a dream. However even a single developer must be able to distinguish between different production team roles and how they all fit together in order to lay out a proper plan of attack.

Diagram by Per Olin

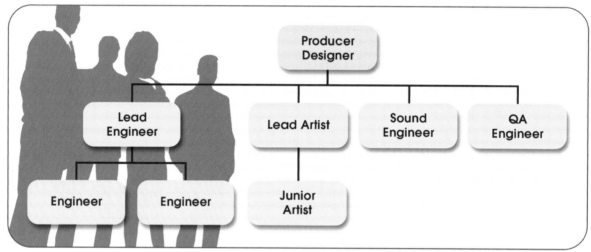

Large Mobile Development Team

Diagram by Per Olin

Small/Indie Development Team

Management

The key *management* position in a development studio is often the *producer*, who is responsible for making things happen and ensuring that everything ships on schedule. In the case of a mobile title, the producer could also be anyone from a team lead (design, art, programming) to the marketing director. For very small and indie studios, the producer often ends up being the person who initially developed the concept (often the designer). This can be a difficult job to juggle— but in the case of a two- or three-person team, it becomes a necessity.

Illustration by Ian Robert Vasquez

Within a larger studio, particularly when sharing resources across multiple projects, the producer position becomes an absolute essential. Even then, it is not always possible to have a wholly dedicated team—particularly in mobile where development times are short, and a single product may need to be pushed out across several thousand devices simultaneously.

Design

In a smaller studio, game *design* is almost always doubled up with another role. The primary role of the game designer, regardless of the studio's size, is to not only create the initial concept of the game but to work with the rest of the team to develop and incorporate any fixes, changes, and new discoveries into the game design as seamlessly as possible.

Illustration by Ian Robert Vasquez

Programming

In full-scale games, *programming* tasks are broken down across multiple disciplines (e.g., graphics, audio, artificial intelligence, engine, tools, network). In mobile, programming teams usually max out at two and more commonly involve just a single programmer. The exception to the rule is when teams program engines for licensing purposes (e.g., GameSalad, Unity).

Illustration by Ian Robert Vasquez

Art

In full-scale game development, *art* involves specializations (e.g., concept, texturing, modeling, animation, character, environment). The industry has rapidly moved away from a few generalists handling all aspects of art production into massive specialization. In contrast, a mobile artist needs to have a "jack of all trades" mentality. In mobile, a single artist often handles concept art and all aspects of the in-game art— from the title screen and backgrounds to cinematics and cut-scenes.

Illustration by Ian Robert Vasquez

Audio

Regrettably, *audio* in mobile games is still in its infancy. With small budgets and tight time constraints, audio is sometimes "kludged" together by a team member. In larger, publisher-backed titles—including stripped-down versions of existing console titles such as *Assassin's Creed*—the audio has already been produced for the larger game and can be re-tasked as needed. The good news is that more audio professionals are getting involved in mobile games—and indie developers are beginning to understand the importance of high-quality music, sound design, and dialogue in their games.

Illustration by Ian Robert Vasquez

:::::: *Super Stickman Golf*: Creating the Soundtrack

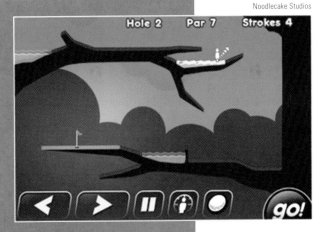

Noodlecake Studios

My most memorable experience so far has been creating the soundtrack for the iOS game *Super Stickman Golf*. Most developers hire me to produce a couple songs and/or sound effects, but Noodlecake Studios commissioned an entire soundtrack of chiptunes from me. This was extremely fun because it allowed me to create a unified collection of songs rather than just a few random ones. I also had a lot of feedback along the way from the developers about what they liked and didn't like. This helped me create music that fit really well with the overall feel of the game.

—Whitaker Blackall (Composer & Sound Designer, Whitaker Blackall Music)

Testing & Quality Assurance

Testing and quality assurance (QA) (whether internal or external) does exist in mobile games. Even single-person micro studios hand the game around to a group of friends and let them bang on it for a while to be sure the worst of the bugs are found. Publisher-backed studios often have access to a more extensive and formalized QA group for testing. Without this luxury, the primary QA tasks need to be handled by the existing team members. Mobile developers can dis-

Illustration by Ian Robert Vasquez

tribute iOS apps wirelessly for "ad hoc" testing purposes—and recipients are easily able to install these pre-releases. TestFlight has further refined this process by letting developers invite testers via email and see who has tested which builds. Android developers can put their Beta builds on the Android Market or send the APK to any number of people who can then side load it onto their systems. When using this method, it's a good idea to build a mechanism within the game so that the testers can easily provide feedback.

Mobile Testing: Internal, External & "in the Wild"

Beta testing is absolutely necessary, but even now it is getting harder to control. Most gamers are less than enthusiastic about helping out an "unknown" pick apart a half-realized app, and these things require a lot of TLC late in the game. I will often take a later-stage app into the bar and have strangers test it out (while I keep mum) to see how it performs "in the wild."

—*Ron Alpert (Co-Founder, Headcase Games)*

We do most testing in-house and with friends and other indie developers. We are thinking about using an external QA team, to free up some time at the end of the projects. I haven't used the open beta on Android yet; it could be a good strategy.

—*Alex Bortoluzzi (Chief Executive Officer, Xoobis)*

We hire our own testers, provision their iPhone devices, and provide them with the latest build so they can test the games for us remotely. Good playtesters provide two functions—the obvious one of finding bugs, but they also help us tweak the gameplay to make sure it is fun and challenging.

—*Ed Magnin (Director of Development, Magnin & Associates)*

Scale & Scope

Mobile games need to be smaller in both *scale* and *scope*. In traditional game development, it is often said that "more is better"—and many developers begin with a larger, grander idea that is trimmed to fit within constraints. In contrast, many mobile developers prefer to "keep it simple"; by initially focusing on mechanics—the nuts and bolts of gameplay—the design process naturally provides constraints than help to keep the game on task.

Feature Creep

Feature creep, sometimes called *scope creep* or "featuritis," has been the death of more great game concepts than anyone is willing to reveal. The producer and game designer need to spend time engaging in *scope control*—reining in scope creep and ensuring that the team focuses on the core elements of the game—with additional features kept on a separate "feature list" in case there is time and budget to add them later. Any new feature or design element must be carefully evaluated with two questions in mind:

- Will including it positively affect the gameplay?
- Will omitting it hurt the game?

If the new feature will negatively affect the game or will not be absolutely essential to it, then it should not be added to the feature list.

Evaluating the Three Lists

One of the simplest ways to keep scope creep under control is to separate the game design elements into three categories, as discussed in Chapter 4: "must have" (features the game cannot function without); "want" (items that require a small amount of extra effort); and "wish" (enhancements that will require a significant amount of effort). Focus on the "must have" elements and polish those first before going back and adding more features to the product.

Time to Market

Mobile games are quick to conceptualize and develop—and they're also fast to hit the market, bloom, and fade away. It's a known fact in software development that 10 people cannot dig a hole 10 times faster than a single person. The more people that are added to any given project, the more it will slow down simply due to supporting the project (e.g., everyone plays well together, all the ducks are in a row, Programmer A delivers code that works well with Programmer B's interface, artists deliver assets that fit with the overall visual style). The more complex the team, the easier it is to break something. Time to market alone in mobile games necessitates smaller, faster, more Agile team structures—even within the confines of large publishing houses.

::::: And the Winner Is . . .

Despite the popularity of indie development on more "next gen" mobile phones such as iPhone and Android platforms, most of the top-selling games on mobile (in the case of *Tetris*, the biggest selling mobile game of all time) are still developed under the wing of and published by large houses that develop more traditional video games. This is partially because large publishers have resources to push titles out over thousands of different smartphones currently available both in the US and in international markets.

Namco Network

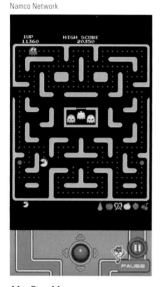

Ms. Pac-Man

▨ *Ms Pac-Man*	Namco Bandai
▨ *Frogger*	Konami
▨ *Diner Dash*	Glu Mobile
▨ *Zuma*	Glu Mobile
▨ *Tetris Mania*	Electronic Arts
▨ *Pac-Man*	Namco Bandai
▨ *Guitar Hero III*	HandsOnMobile
▨ *Are You Smarter than a 5th Grader?*	Capcom
▨ *Bejeweled*	Electronic Arts
▨ *Tetris*	Electronic Arts

In contrast, take a look at 10 of the top games on the iPhone for 2009 listed below (in alphabetical order). In the broader arena of mobile game development—pushing games out to thousands of platforms—the big name publishers have the edge, time, and resources to port games to every available mobile device. However, when focusing on a single smartphone, the indies and smaller studios start to emerge—and solid, innovative gameplay carries the day!

Halfbrick Studios

Fruit Ninja

▨ *Assassin's Creed*	Gameloft
▨ *Civilization: Revolution*	Take-Two Entertainment
▨ *Cooking Mama*	Taito
▨ *Flight Control*	Firemint
▨ *The Oregon Trail*	Gameloft
▨ *Peggle*	PopCap Games
▨ *Sally's Spa*	Games Café, Inc.
▨ *The Sims*	Electronic Arts
▨ *Tiger Woods PGA Tour*	Electronic Arts
▨ *Wheel of Fortune*	Sony Pictures Television

Going Solo

It's 2:00 a.m., and the very last build complies without a hitch. There's no boss to call, and no milestones to meet. It's just you, with your trusty code library and all the coffee you can drink. Sound like a dream job? With the advent of app stores that are specific to a single smartphone, the market for individual and independent developers has broken wide open.

Individual Scope

In theory, there is no limit to what can be done with mobile games as a lone developer. However, to see a return—which should at least cover the costs of coffee and sugar packets consumed during development—it's important for lone developers to pick and choose their battles. Develop quickly and cleanly—and *keep* developing. Producing, developing, and publishing a single game is an achievement that not just anyone can match—and the second game is even more difficult to finish. Single developers or even very small teams who earn incomes doing this often push beyond that single title. First, it's important to decide just why you're doing this. Is it because you love games? Do you have the coolest idea ever and the programming skills to back it up? Are you looking at this as your entré into the larger world of game development? Fame and glory? Money? Bragging rights? The look on your dad's face when you download your game onto his new iPhone?

> It's possible to start an indie mobile company on sweat equity alone—which means if you want creative freedom, this is probably the avenue to take.
>
> —*James Portnow*
> *(Chief Executive Officer, Rainmaker Games; Professor, DigiPen Institute of Technology)*

> The best part of being indie is right there in the label: you're independent. You're free to polish and iterate as often as you like, and you're spared from arbitrary deadlines imposed by outside forces. (Plus, I can go sit in a café any time I want.)
>
> —*Quinn Dunki (Chief Sarcasm Officer, One Girl, One Laptop Productions)*

Semi Secret Software, LLC

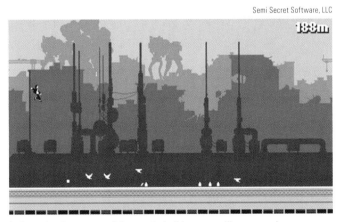

It doesn't take a team of dozens to build a compelling gameplay experience. Semi Secret Software, developer of *Canabalt*—the popular one-button game that emulates parkour (free-running)—consists of a four-person team: programmer, artist, sound designer, and producer.

The exact reasons don't matter, but it's important to know what they are. Your games will need to address these reasons, or the great swampy middle of the development process will bring you to a standstill.

Design Choices

Going solo means working within your own capabilities. If you have a full-time job and are building games as a hobby in your spare time, make sure to "keep it simple" by first creating a game you know you can finish. Keep in mind that a complex game isn't necessarily going to be better. Elements such as gameplay, platform suitability, short entertaining play sessions are the hallmarks of great mobile games. Puzzle and physics games are often perfect starting choices, since there are so many great examples available that can be created using a very simple set of rules.

Anthropophagy LLC

1:20

Physics or puzzle games such as *Stay* can deliver a compelling game experience with a basic, straightforward set of rules.

> **B**eing independent allows Appy Entertainment to take chances and create original games that would not be attempted at larger, more bureaucratic companies.
>
> —*Paul O'Connor (Brand Director, Appy Entertainment)*

> **B**eing an indie developer means building the experience that you are passionate about, owning and controlling your IP and brand, and communicating directly with your customers.
>
> —*Chris Ulm (Chief Executive Officer, Appy Entertainment)*

The Joys of Indie vs. Third-Party Development

Being an indie gives you two things: freedom, and the stress that comes with it. Money is always a concern, but the satisfaction of creating something unique that resonates with a wide range of people is really addictive. The teams are smaller, and people benefit from being 'jacks-of-all-trades' instead of 'super specialists.'

—Alex Bortoluzzi (Chief Executive Officer, Xoobis)

With mobile, smaller indie developers have a greater opportunity to compete against larger third-party studios. We've seen small (even solo) teams come up with top-10 hits that have made them a great deal of money without the overhead of a large studio. I wouldn't say that the playing field is level, due to the marketing power of a larger company—but it's certainly flatter than in traditional console and PC markets.

—Mark Chuberka (Director of Business Development, GameSalad)

Third-party development has a bit more stability, but it has to answer to someone else's needs. Indie developers have all the freedom and time in the world—but no guarantees.

—Jennifer Estaris (Experience/Game Designer, Total Immersion)

We are enjoying being an indie developer right now, since we are free to create our own IPs—adding value to the studio. The structure of our team is similar to traditional game development (production, design, art, and tech), but we have also added some marketing, analysis, and web-oriented skills to the mix.

—Gary Gattis (Chief Executive Officer, Spacetime Studios)

Indie developers have the advantage of moving more quickly on an idea or concept. This makes them more nimble and likely to innovate. The downside is that the garage shop developer can rarely scale or repeat a hit. It takes a certain amount of process and overhead to operationalize large-scale game development.

—Jason Loia (Chief Operating Officer, Digital Chocolate)

We used to ask publishers for a project or pitch our own projects to them. They would fund us, but eventually insist on their changes—some of which we did despite our own better judgment, only to receive a negative review on those changes. Now we have the freedom to develop the games we want. There are no arbitrary deadlines. Whenever we are convinced we are done, we prepare the game for submission to the App Store. Usually, it's on sale about eight days later.

—Ed Magnin (Director of Development, Magnin & Associates)

RA

Ron Alpert
(Co-Founder,
Headcase Games)

Ron Alpert is a 14-year veteran of the game industry who's seen it all! Charting a history at well-established production studios such as Neversoft and Obsidian to the scrappy and dirty D.I.Y. style of independent development, Ron continues to make waves in and around the game scene. He's having as much of a blast as ever, and his goal is to keep reinventing the definition of gaming while always minding the humble beginnings of the medium.

Third-party developers have many rules in place and can seldom afford to be risky without facing extreme consequences—yet they often have filled-out supportive staff, great marketing/publishing connections, and (relatively) easier access to money to see a project through to proper completion. Independents have no one to lean on and require dedication throughout from an often tiny staff—with skeleton resources that usually rely on a bit of luck to get some necessary components in place. However, project-to-project is nowhere near as risky; there is the ability to put out a lot of great software in a tiny amount of time; and now more than ever, it's easier to develop a brand new creator-owned IP and own it. This is something that many/most third-party devs just cannot do any more, even though it's always their ultimate dream.

MF

Matt Forbeck
(Writer & Game
Designer,
Full Moon Enterprises)

Matt Forbeck has been creating award-winning games and fiction since 1989. He has designed collectible card games, role-playing games, miniatures games, board games, and toys—and he has written novels, short fiction, comic books, motion comics, non-fiction, essays, and computer game scripts/stories for companies such as Adams Media, Angry Robot, ArenaNet, Atari, Boom! Studios, Del Rey, Games Workshop, IDW, Image Comics, Mattel, Playmates Toys, Simon & Schuster, Tor.com, Ubisoft, Wired.com, Wizards of the Coast, and WizKids. Matt has written 15 published novels to date, including the award-nominated *Guild Wars: Ghosts of Ascalon*.

Mobile game teams are often much smaller and nimbler than those for console or PC games. Due to this, the budgets are lower, and the games require less risk. This makes being an indie developer much more tempting if you can muster up the right team for the job. It also means developing a direct relationship with your players on an ongoing basis, though—and not every development team is ready for this.

Platforms

The Android, iPhone, Windows Phone, and BlackBerry hardware platforms are best suited for individual or small-team developers. This is due primarily to the relative ease of publication and distribution on these platforms. With handheld devices such as the PSVita and 3DS, the environment is much more hostile to individual or small-team developers—in part due to the licensing and development kit costs involved.

iPhone

Developing for the iPhone requires registering as an iPhone developer. This allows access to iPhone developer forums, software needed to develop titles, sample code, instructional materials—almost everything needed outside of the original game concept itself. One of the greatest benefits of developing for the iPhone is the limited number of devices that the developer needs to address.

Android

Android is the new kid on the block. The operating system was developed by Google and is available on devices from a number of different manufacturers. And therein lies the rub: While the Android is an extremely open system, and the Android Market approval process is swift and straightforward, the game must be run on several different devices—each with slightly different configurations.

Windows Phone

Developing for Windows Phone is similar to developing for the Android operating system. There are many different Windows Phone devices on the market—but due to the relatively closed nature of the Windows Phone OS, there may be less variation among them.

BlackBerry

With a limited set of devices available on the market, the BlackBerry has something in common with the iPhone. Much like Apple, the differences in these devices are largely generational rather than related to hardware customization for specific carriers—so it's possible to develop and test on just one or two devices rather than a dozen or more.

Publishing

For each development platform, there is an individual publishing process required to make the game or application available for all to see. Until the broader adoption of platform-specific stores such as the Android Market and Apple App Store, distribution for mobile titles was primarily handled through a carrier-specific mobile store referred to as a carrier deck (discussed in Chapter 6)—and a rotating list of titles was promoted and distributed by a mobile carrier through its own purchasing option. Verizon's "Get It Now" is one of the widest known examples.

Verizon Wireless

Most wireless carriers have their own mobile stores, often referred to as "carrier decks," that allow users to purchase games and applications directly from the carrier and charge their purchases to their regular wireless bills. This Samsung Glyde shows Verizon's Media Store.

Since many carriers require developers to support a large number of their devices, often all with different operating systems and requirements, this process becomes prohibitive for individual or small-team developers. In an attempt to push applications designed specifically for their own devices, several manufacturers launched their own, smartphone-specific stores (e.g., BlackBerry's App World—which could be found through the associated web site, but not directly through the phone). The manufacturers didn't have as much ability to push applications developed for their devices; consumers still needed to either go through the carrier's deck, the web or other sources to find and download the programs they wanted. The direct link from the phone to the manufacturer wasn't there.

::::: Application Marketplaces

In an effort to drive more sales and to entice developers to build applications exclusive to specific devices, many hardware manufacturers have created marketplaces where customers are able to purchase apps. When these marketplaces were initially launched, consumers didn't embrace them; the process of purchasing applications online and downloading them to their smartphones trouble-free was intimidating, and they preferred to rely on the "safer" option of purchasing through the carrier deck. The application marketplaces of today are in high demand, while the carrier deck model continues to shrink in popularity.

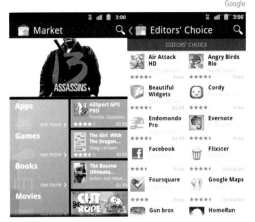

Google

Current application marketplaces such as the Android Market are in wide use today.

Independent mobile developers are faced with the question of just where to publish. There have been a number of smaller web sites that will allow sales of games and applications designed for a single device, but these sites also have no quality control; in some cases, site operators don't even check to be sure an application downloads and plays on the advertised smartphones. These content aggregation sites also contain games by larger publishers that have slipped off the carrier decks because they either weren't generating enough revenue to be worth the associated fees or had outlived their life cycles.

For a game to have a chance, it needs to be available through OS-specific app stores: Apple App Store (Apple), App World (BlackBerry), Android Marketplace (Android), and Windows Phone Marketplace (Microsoft). Each of these outlets has a separate publication process, and all submitted games will undergo a review in some form or another. Registered developers for any of these operating systems have access to the associated app store publication requirements and processes—and they should read and understand the most current set of restrictions. For example, Apple is continually refining and modifying its restrictions for publication based on consumer feedback and Apple App Store abuses. Developers interested in pushing the acceptable boundaries of the iPhone and iPad run the risk of getting an app pulled if these rules shift to the more conservative.

Publishing is a Privilege

Apple has become well known for restricting the types of apps available in its App Store—in particular, restrictions placed on games and products that feature adult content. Less known include restrictions placed on games that involve using a third-party tool for development. In each case, Apple has gone through and swept games from its App Store with a broad brush—requiring developers to contact Apple directly and ask for another review of their titles.

Studio Development

Starting a development studio comes with its own set of problems, not the least of which is funding. It is a common misconception among new developers that having a contract in hand with a publisher is enough to get up and running—but most of the time, putting together a formal development studio requires upfront capital in the form of cash funding or *sweat equity* (working for free for the first game or two until capital increases enough to allow for a more formal salary arrangement).

Needless to say, starting a studio with a fat wad of cash is a lot easier than bootstrapping (discussed in the Financing section). Although there are many enthusiastic new developers who are willing to take financial risks, one of the biggest sticking points across the board is the need to eat; this means getting or keeping a day job, freelance work or other opportunities that will interfere with game development time and may result in the loss of team members at some point during production. Many studios launch with the promise of an equity share in the games expected to be released, but this also means that developers aren't paid until months after products ship.

One advantage of mobile games is the speed of development. The time commitment to develop a game is usually less than six months and can often drop into weeks depending on the simplicity of the title. This means it's possible to develop a game using the good graces and spare time of the other team members, but it *doesn't* mean that a whole catalogue of games should be developed the same way!

Marroni Electronic Entertainment   BurstStudio

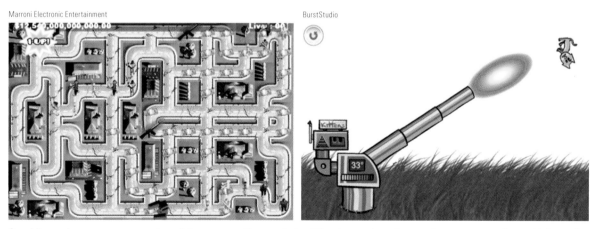

One-hit wonders are as common in mobile games as they are in traditional console and computer games—and even high-quality games aren't always enough to ensure long-term sustainability (Marroni's *iBailout!!* [left] and BurstStudio's *Kitten Cannon* [right], shown).

Office Space vs. Virtual Team Building

There are advantages and disadvantages to leasing office space and working out of a home office with a distributed (or "virtual") team. On one hand, having a virtual team means you don't have to pay the overhead; all team members function as independent contractors, maintaining their own equipment and holding responsibility for their own piece of the project. Meetings can be held on a weekly or even daily basis via various types of multi-party or multi-location conference software and systems (e.g., Skype, WebEx, Google+ Hangouts). A virtual setup requires more discipline and greater personal responsibility on the part of the team members—who must be relied upon to do the work with only limited oversight. If something goes wrong and they stop returning phone calls or vanish from the virtual space, how will you handle this? Drive to their house and camp out on the front lawn? When building a virtual team, it's necessary to have controls in place—including checking art and code assets in and out each day from a common location (whether online through version-control software such as Assembla or Google Docs, or on a private company server). If a team member suffers a personal tragedy (or if the programmer goes to Burning Man and comes back having eschewed all technology), the damage to the project will be minimal. If there's a centralized office space where everyone physically puts in their time—even if it's the basement of your grandmother's house—the discipline is imposed from the outside. All the resources and materials are in one place—and when someone fails to show up for work, everyone else will notice.

Subletting

The cost of maintaining a formal office space can be a problem, especially for a developer starting out—but it's often possible to sublet some offices from a larger corporation interested in maintaining a "lived-in" look at a particular space. It sometimes requires a bit of ingenuity and a willingness to ask around—but some corporations are required to lease an entire floor, even if they don't need all of the offices right away. The manager may be willing to sublet one or two of those offices on a short-term basis. Always be sure to keep up a professional appearance in any lease situation; the lessor will not be happy with the arrangement if the team leaves empty soda cans in the hallways and takes sink showers in the restroom in the morning.

Office Space: The Home Run

My most memorable experience working with a development studio involved building a flexible lease that mirrored the developer's business. We used a leveraged negotiation to force a landlord to fund the entire game studio build-out including servers, furniture, cabling, data connections, extra HVAC, and power required for three dev kits per employee. It was a home run!

—*Greg Lovett (Senior Director, Cushman & Wakefield)*

Keep in mind that there is a difference between an *independent contractor* and an *employee*. Be sure you know the rules, even if you and two of your best buddies have all agreed verbally to work "on spec" for the time being. For example, California workers are classified as employees when they're required to work in the company's office space (even if it's in a private home) at set hours each day on company equipment. Although everyone might be "best friends" when the studio starts up, this might change as time goes on—and one employment-related lawsuit can break a struggling startup.

Profit Share vs. Salary

Diagram by Per Olin

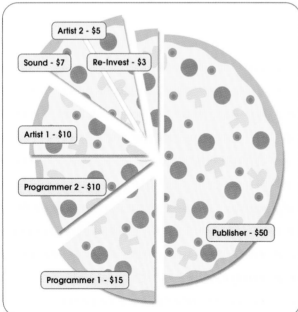

Artist 2 - $5
Sound - $7   Re-Invest - $3
Artist 1 - $10
Programmer 2 - $10
Publisher - $50
Programmer 1 - $15

The pie can get very small if you're using it to pre-pay for your project. For every $100 your game makes, only $3 might be re-invested into the company to fund new projects.

There are two key issues to consider when bringing on developers to work for *profit share*, rather than cash or a salary.

1. *The return is likely to be very small.* Becoming a sustainable mobile game developer isn't so much about having one hit title but developing a long string of moderately successful or even low producing titles that continue to trickle in cash over a long period of time. This means that the *return on investment* (*ROI*) for any individual team member may be fairly low—especially if there are several different people each working on just one game each. While the return over time may cover development costs, the length of time it takes to see a return can simply be just too long for your team members to stick around.

2. *If all the revenue is divided up among the team members, it's not going back into the company.* Sustainability means continuing to pay employees for a while even if there is no new work coming in. This type of sustainability means that a developer can publish original games when it isn't working with a publisher on a third-party title. There's an "ebb and flow" associated with publishing contracts; no matter who you know or how many friends you might have in the industry, the timing might just be off—and your company must have the working capital to survive the shortfall. If you've promised it all away, then it will be necessary to come up with a plan to survive or close your doors. The world of game development is littered with the corpses of studios whose founders came together to develop a game for a publisher but were unable to land a second title quickly enough to keep the momentum going.

Financing

Financing is the great sticky wicket of forming any company. In games in particular, actual saleable *assets* (tangible and intangible items an investor might guarantee against in case of failure) are extremely limited: A handful of computers that will be obsolete in a year, any devkits that have been purchased, and lots of great ideas. (Don't be fooled: There are countless great ideas out there—and having one or even 100 in the company's portfolio doesn't mean it has any value!)

Illustration by Ian Robert Vasquez

Investors

Intellectual property only becomes valuable after it's been developed—so unless a prototype has already been created, a company must have something more to offer that's worth the investment. Every so often, this company or that company is reported to have secured $10 million or upwards of $30 million in venture capital financing. Most of the time, these companies are already established—with products and processes in place, a management team with years of successful shipped games at well-known companies, or some sort of track record that gives investors confidence.

An *angel investor* is the first choice for companies that are just starting out; "angels" are usually individuals who invest $50,000, $100,000 or even $500,000 (usually under $1 million) in a small company for a big fat return in a few years. The best way to meet an angel investor is through an introduction—preferably by someone that has already done business with them. There are also investment summits and conferences that provide opportunities to network with small investors. Angels actively looking for investments are often willing to talk directly with visionary entrepreneurs who are willing to shake things up.

Be Prepared

The fundraising process can happen at lightning speed. Investors who are actively looking might request a full business plan and supporting financials right away. Before making "first contact," be sure to do the research and be prepared with a 1-2 page executive summary at the very least. It's also important to prepare a 30-second verbal "elevator pitch" focusing on the company's vision and business strategy.

Out-of-Pocket

The majority of small, formal studios get started with *out-of-pocket* funding. Perhaps either you've saved up the funding to begin production on a game, you've been a part of a previous startup that was bought out, or you have a wealthy uncle who passed away and left you his prize collection of Victorian-era spittoons; for one reason or another, the cash is in hand to get the process started. This might look at first like total freedom—but your investment could run dry very quickly. It's important to consider the time it will take to secure contracts to continue doing business. Staff lightly at the outset; mobile games in particular take far fewer people to build, so start out with a single programmer and move up from there as the contracts get lined up.

Bootstrapping

Bootstrapping is most common in single developer situations; it's difficult to get four or five passionate people together who are financially secure enough to work on an unfunded project. However, if investors and out-of-pocket funding are not options, consider bootstrapping one or two very small projects as a single developer until enough cash can be saved to grow the company through self-funding. At that point, other financing options might be on the table—if they're still needed!

After assembling a team and growing a game development studio, it will be time to make a decision. Will you sustain a "lifestyle" business (one intended to support the founders/employees for as long as possible)—or will you make a play for bigger money by selling to a larger firm? In mobile development, both of these are equally viable options—but if you have pulled in an outside investor, then the bigger play is where you want to be looking.

The Fast & the Flexible

When it comes to production, mobile games move faster and require a lot more flexibility during the development process than more traditional console or PC games. The same key roles and elements are there, but they're handled in significantly different ways. Especially important is the overall flexibility of the mobile production process. Due to the way mobile games continue to evolve based on player feedback and metrics gathering processes, a single game may go through the production process multiple times over the course of its life.

What happens after the game is complete? Chapter 8 moves beyond the actual development process and into the ever-evolving world of publication and distribution. We'll take a look at what happens after launch, how to tackle the thorny issue of discoverability, and how metrics will provide the feedback needed to improve your game.

Expanded assignments and projects based on the material in this chapter are available on the Instructor Resources DVD.

:::CHAPTER REVIEW EXERCISES:::

1. Choose one Agile production method such as Scrum, Lean or Kanban, and map out a production plan for your original game idea. Which method did you choose, and why? (For Kanban, try to "go analog" and create a Kanban board using a whiteboard and a variety of colored Post-it notes. Take an initial picture of your board for this exercise—and continue to document as you progress through production.)

2. Conduct a "feature creep prevention test" on your game idea. Make a list of features and design elements you'd like to include. Go down the list and ask the following questions regarding each element: (a) Will including this positively affect the gameplay? and (b) Will omitting it hurt the game? If you determine that a feature affects the game negatively, immediately strike it from your list. After evaluating each of the remaining features with the above questions in mind, further streamline your list by eliminating extraneous elements until you are left with the essentials.

3. Conduct "ad hoc" testing on a mobile game of your choice on any mobile platform. As you play the game, hunt for bugs by paying attention to errors in the following categories: graphics, audio, gameplay/logic, physics, AI—even multiplayer/network errors, when applicable. Be sure to play the game for at least one hour. Create a test report that describes and categorizes each of these bugs.

4. The first step in forming your own development studio is to determine your own roles and responsibilities before bringing in other team members. What are your own strengths?

   - *Producer:* Do you have a talent for managing people, projects, schedules, and budget—and are you good at working with spreadsheets and task-driven project management tools?
   - *Designer:* Do you come up with compelling story/gameplay ideas—and are you comfortable with game design tools such as GameSalad Creator or level editors such as UnrealEd?
   - *Artist:* Do you have a background in art (concept, texture, modeling or animation)—and are you familiar with art tools such as 3ds Max/Maya and Photoshop?
   - *Programmer:* Are you familiar with programming languages such as C++ or Java—and have you experimented with Xcode or Eclipse?

   Once you've identified your strengths, it's time to consider whether you're going to take in a partner, hire independent contractors, or recruit an entire team. Which path would you take, and why?

5. Create your own 30-second "elevator pitch" for a funding source (e.g., publisher, angel investor, venture capitalist, wealthy relative). Imagine having to convince that funding source during a short elevator ride that your game or company idea is the greatest ever—or at least worthy of being funded. (No fantasies allowed about getting stuck in that elevator!) Focus on the creative vision and brand strategy behind your game or company.

CHAPTER

8

Publishing & Marketing

life after development

Key Chapter Questions

- How does a mobile game get *published*?

- Are there key *distribution* locations for different mobile devices?

- What are some *marketing* techniques for indie mobile games?

- What can a developer expect from a *publisher*?

- What are some effective *revenue models* for mobile games?

Once a game hits the beta phase, it's time for the development team members to lift their heads from their keyboards and take a look at the world around them. This little baby is about to get kicked out into the public eye—and for good or evil, it will need to stand on its own two feet. How does it get noticed? How does it get into the hands of bloggers, reviewers, and journalists—and how can it be marketed effectively so that it will be discovered among the thousands and thousands of other applications that are out there, swimming in the ether taking up space in the minds of the consumers?

Publishing

Every publication route will have its specific quirks, whether it's a byzantine app approval process or a long and drawn out set of requirements to become a "publisher." Although developers who have secured publishing deals don't need to focus on getting a game or app onto the various marketplaces and outlets (this is the publisher's role), they will be expected to provide support—including screenshots, bug fixes, and gameplay tweaks.

App Store Requirements

Since current smartphone devices are all associated with "walled garden" style app stores, there has been a rush to cut out more traditional publishers. Manufacturers of individual smartphones have gone to some trouble to ensure that independent developers have the tools to publish their games and apps without the need for third-party intervention. Here are just a few examples of app stores and their requirements:

- *Apple* (http://developer.apple.com/programs/iphone/): Fee of $99/year to be included in the developer program. Apple provides extensive documentation and examples of application programming and development. Complete SDK provided as well as support for XCode, Cocoa, and C#. All applications and/or games must undergo Apple's review process before they are allowed to be published through the Apple App Store. This process currently takes 1-2 weeks for a new app with 3-5 days for an updated app.

- *Android* (http://market.android.com/publish/signup): Fee of $25 to sign up as a developer; no additional fee required for publication. Android provides documentation and community-based support, example projects, a complete SDK, and an emulator. Applications and/or games are automatically submitted to the store— currently requiring no outside approval.

- *BlackBerry* (http://na.blackberry.com/eng/developers/appworld/): Submission fee of $200—refundable if the application is not approved. RIM provides documentation, limited support, and access to the plugins needed for Eclipse and other common development programs. Applications require review and approval by BlackBerry both regarding content and technical functionality.

Bug Hunting

Manufacturers that review an app before publication will check for content and general functionality, but they don't engage in game testing; be prepared to take care of this yourself, or face the wrath of the customer base!

Illustration by Ian Robert Vasquez

A developer must take each app store's requirements into
consideration before choosing a lead platform.

Mobile developers need to weigh the requirements and available manufacturer support
associated with each app store before making a final decision on a primary publishing route.
Fees, review processes, and available documentation differ based on operating system.

Deliverables

A mobile game is always delivered as a package file
of some sort—whether it's .ipa (iOS), .apk (Android),
or .xap (Windows Phone). In every case, the manufacturer will provide the software needed to export
the game into a tiny bundle that can be downloaded
to the players' smartphones—along with a handful of
marketing materials with very specific requirements.
Icons for the app (usually in multiple sizes and resolutions), screenshots, and sometimes an animated
.gif showing gameplay can be tricky to build—especially if they need to be compressed down to the
kilobyte range—so be sure to allow time to prepare
them properly. The icons are used by the manufac-

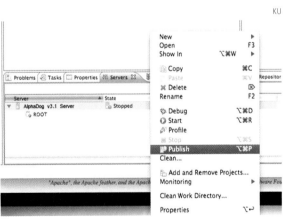

Make sure you have all your deliverables in order before hitting
the "publish" button. Software is kicked back for missing
requirements (e.g., screenshots, icons)—not to mention having
bugs or other more serious issues (Eclipse, shown).

turer to market the game on their web site and other sources; if the game makes a poor
showing there, this can dramatically affect your sales. Be careful to read through the
submission requirements and include *everything* the review board requests. With long
review times, it can be frustrating to see a game get kicked back because the associated
icon was too large or only four screenshots were included instead of five.

Marketing

Marketing strategies come in all shapes and sizes—from word-of-mouth to traditional promotion, advertising, sales, and public relations reserved for most AAA titles. With released mobile games numbering in the hundreds of thousands, it's not easy for a title to get noticed. The market is littered with the dead and dying corpses of great mobile games—including those that introduced some new innovative control scheme, story concept or gameplay feature. In a market that is already saturated yet still hungry for fresh new content, it's essential to stand out from the crowd. Let's take a look at a few guidelines that should provide a foundation for a strong marketing strategy.

Billions & Billions of Apps

One of the advantages to a rating system seen in various app stores is that a game will move up in the rankings if players like it. However, until a game hits that Top 25 or Featured game status, it's still going to be invisible to everyone except those searching for something specific. This means that targeting a game and its advertising to a specific audience is the best way to garner interest. Once a game gets into the Top 25, it will pick up the "curious"—those players who are looking for something new and fresh, but who may not necessarily be searching in the game's genre or category.

Illustration by Ian Robert Vasquez

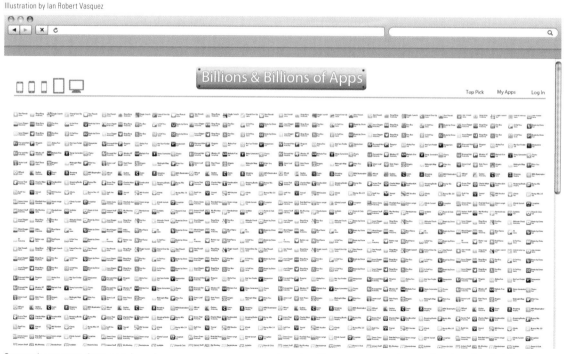

Smartphone manufacturers have become ever more aggressive when it comes to pursuing applications for their hardware. Where a phone might have once shipped with just a dozen generalist applications, now hundreds are put into the pipeline so that they're available when the hardware goes to market.

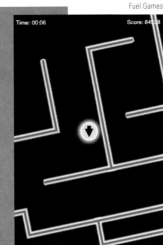

Spinner Prologue: Landing in the Top 25

Fuel Games

Having my game *Spinner Prologue* available the day the App Store launched in July 2008 was a memorable experience. Since we didn't think the game was quite worth paying for, we made it free and were one of 11 free games available that day. As a result, we were in the Top 25 of all apps for the first couple months, which resulted in a huge number of downloads in that time. We didn't realize what we had, and we didn't capitalize on it very well—but it was great being right there at the start of a new platform.

—Brian Robbins (Founder, Riptide Games, Inc.)

Rise of the Indies

The big publishers were spitting out a lot of contractors in 2011. It was our pleasure to help those small studios get back on their feet and become successful as indies. We knew that if we worked hard, we could make a difference—and it was gratifying to see that this was indeed the case.

—Sue Bohle (President, The Bohle Company)

Goals

Whether it's a certain dollar figure, number of downloads, brand building, or positioning, it's essential to have a strong, straightforward, and attainable marketing goal that can be explained in a short phrase or brief sentence. Let's assume the goal is to make $1,000. Make sure to first price the game accordingly. Assuming a price point of 99 cents, the actual profit to the developer would be 66 cents—since the Apple App Store and Android Market both take 30% off the top. In order to make just $1,000, it will be necessary to sell 1,515 copies of the game.

Our publisher deals with all the PR and promotion for the titles, but we are active on forums and social networks to spread the word about the games. It's never enough to just rely on your publisher; you need to keep pushing.

—Alex Bortoluzzi
(Chief Executive Officer, Xoobis)

::::: Conversion Rates

In the world of games and apps, the *conversion rate* is the number of people expected to purchase the full copy of a game after playing through the "Free Trial" or "Lite" version. Is this number 1 out of 100, 1 out of 1,000, or . . . ? In the mobile industry, this number can vary widely depending on the device and point of sale. For example, the conversion rate across certain devices (including the Android, iPhone and iPod) tends to be 1.5% on average—but for a device such as the iPad, the rate is higher (around 2%). The term is also applied to the conversion of clicks on mobile advertisements to actual sales. Monetization of mobile and casual games through advertising has grown almost exponentially over the past few years—and more companies that provide analytics are coming to the fore. These analytics reveal the demographics of a game's purchasers and players—and they show the most effective points of sale. (For example, is the link on the developer's web site pushing sales farther and faster than the Facebook ad?)

Illustration by Ian Robert Vasquez

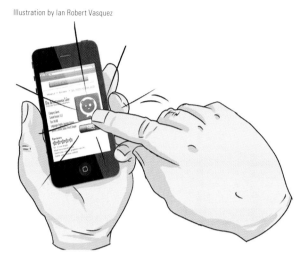

Time Frame

The success of Valve, id, Epic, and Blizzard notwithstanding, the "it's done when it's done" mindset is death to almost any project. Make sure to have a *time frame* in mind. Choose an exact date for your goal and then break it into smaller pieces (months, years, etc.) Using our goal of $1,000 net sales, the timeline breakdown might look something like the data depicted in the accompanying diagram. Once you have a clear breakdown of where you are going, even if some of it is based on educated guesswork, it is a much simpler task to get from Point A to Point B. As you receive information on your application, such as revenue and number of downloads, you will be able to feed this information into the chart—tailoring it to something that will give you a better idea of how your game is doing. As you grow in experience—building and publishing more apps, getting a feel for the marketplace and how it flows—you will be better able to predict the accuracy of these numbers.

Diagram by Per Olin

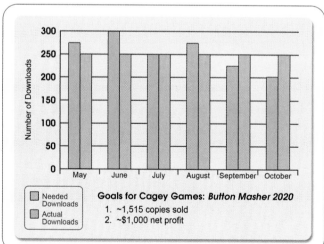

In order to make a net profit of ~$1,000 by October 31, 2014, Cagey Games must sell ~1,515 copies of *Button Masher 2020* within a six-month time frame. An average of 252 downloads is needed per month, but actual downloads will fluctuate from month to month.

Distribution

The walled garden app stores that are aligned with smartphone devices are the cleanest and most obvious mobile distribution avenues—but there are other options as well. Although Apple has the App Store, AT&T sells mobile applications for the iPhone through its own app store (a modern version of the carrier deck). In addition, many smartphones have aggregate sites that collect content for a particular brand or operating system. For example, there are a number of download sites that sell applications not allowed on the Apple App Store for a variety of reasons (including content issues or the existence of competing functionalities that Apple doesn't want enabled yet); these apps could run on phones that have been jailbroken (discussed in Chapter 6), which is perfectly legal but voids the warranty. Here's an example of how distribution channels might be defined for a hypothetical mobile game:

> KriketSmaashen *will be sold primarily through the Android Market. Sales links on the* KriketSmaashen *web site will direct the purchaser to the* KriketSmaashen *point of sale on the Android Market's web interface. Additional opportunities may be found at AndroidsRUs.com and HandyAndy.com, which should be investigated with regard to fit and price point.*

Examine the portals available, then check the Top 10 bestsellers a few times; sometimes these are updated weekly or even daily. This will give you an idea of where the market stands for your game—and the types of games that are preferred by the audience. (For example, a shooter shouldn't be published on a portal that sells mostly romance RPGs!)

Refine the Product

Make sure the game is ready for market, and be prepared to tweak it even after it is released if necessary. Be sure the visual polish is all in and the gameplay is fully functional. Read the comments and keep an eye on what the reviewers are saying to detect any problems or issues that might have been missed.

Bushi-go, Inc.

Bushi-go, Inc.

 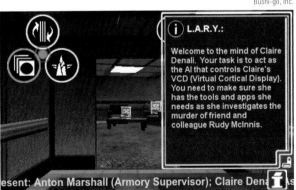

Most games are playable well before the final layer of polish has been put into place. Some games may even undergo a complete transformation—changing their look, feel, and visual style by the time they're finished (*The Agiliste*: raw at left, polished at right).

Shout Out Loud!

The next logical step is to determine how to let everyone know about the game—which could involve driving traffic to the developer's web site for more information, getting them to download the game through an app store, or landing reviews and feature stories in media outlets. The marketing strategy during this stage will depend highly on the type of player being targeted. Keep in mind that players have different, somewhat clearly defined habits. For example, people who play social games (such as those found on Facebook) may have different behavior patterns than those who play console titles—and players obsessed with matching tiles may have different attitudes than those who like to shoot alien zombies. Part of the developer's job is to identify a game's market segment and how it should be targeted. There are three common ways to break up the market:

Diagram by Per Olin

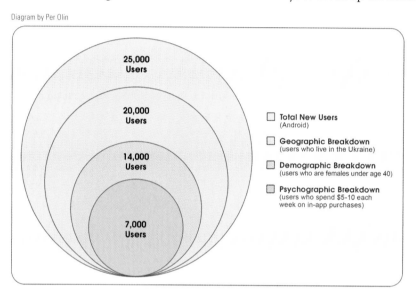

25,000 Users

20,000 Users

14,000 Users

7,000 Users

☐ **Total New Users**
(Android)

☐ **Geographic Breakdown**
(users who live in the Ukraine)

☐ **Demographic Breakdown**
(users who are females under age 40)

☐ **Psychographic Breakdown**
(users who spend $5-10 each week on in-app purchases)

1. *Geographics:* Where are the players located? Players in Japan are targeted differently than players in Sweden, for example. The international markets can be tricky, since not all games appeal to all cultures—and even with translation services, social faux pas are not uncommon.

2. *Demographics:* Discrete elements such as age, occupation, smartphone usage, gender, income, and even political and religious affiliation group players together—often with large areas of crossover between them.

3. *Psychographics:* Attitudes, values, lifestyles, and behavior patterns are known as psychographic elements. There are often areas of crossover between psychographic and demographic breakdowns—so unless a developer prefers to target a very specific niche market (e.g., women over 65 working in the nursing profession who own iPhones), this may be a somewhat limited area to target. This group is defined by elements such as play habits, awareness of products and brands, customer loyalty, preferred genre, level of comfort or access to technology and bandwidth.

After considering the game's target market and ways in which it can be segmented, it's time to create a marketing message. Think carefully about what needs to be said about the game, and be sure to address the target market directly—rather than trying to reach everyone that posts on a player forum or comments on a game industry blog. Here's an example of a brief marketing message for a hypothetical mobile game:

Integrated campaigns involving community contests, promotions, PR, and advertising seem to work most effectively in the mobile space. It takes effort from all parties to coordinate, but the result is more than worth it.

—Sue Bohle (President, The Bohle Company)

KriketSmaashen is targeted toward casual players who hate nothing more than a lack of updates to their social network sites. Casual gamers of this type tend to play games with relatively straightforward "click and harvest" gameplay with heavy social applications, allowing them to invite and include their friends in the gameplay process. The income for these players ranges from $25k to $45k a year, and they will often spend $10-20 a month on upgrades or premium in-game products. Our players spend a significant amount of time online and often own small cats. KriketSmaashen will use a number of different outlets including AdWords and iAds that will target visitors to cricket-oriented games. In addition, banner ads will be placed on major review sites and webcomics relating to and about the smashing of crickets.

After polishing the game's marketing message, focus on ways to reach the target market—such as advertising using in-app placement using a mobile advertising service such as Tapjoy or W3i and sending the game out to magazines and bloggers for reviews. (Be sure to only contact reviewers who are well-versed in the game's genre.) Developers often promote their own games through affiliate sites, contests, newsletters, banner advertising, and press releases—but many also hire professional PR specialists or firms.

We work our press list, direct email list, Twitter, blog, and Facebook channels to communicate that our games are available at launch. All of our original games have been featured by Apple.

—Paul O'Connor
(Brand Director, Appy Entertainment, Inc.)

The key is to get into the Top 25; if you can't do that, you're sunk. If you're a small indie company that has no money for marketing, try to get reviews from every site possible—and submit your game to every competition you can think of.

—James Portnow
(Chief Executive Officer, Rainmaker Games;
Professor, DigiPen Institute of Technology)

::::: The Media Gold Mine

Game reviewers and journalists *want* to see your game. You might feel like a supplicant—closing your eyes, holding up your most treasured possession, and praying that the person on the other end (the one with the sharpened quill and rapier wit) will be merciful and quick. However, as a source of feedback, a game reviewer can be a gold mine. Reviewers and journalists have their fingers on the pulse of everything that's out there within their preferred genres. They will notice if an homage to all things *Blade Runner* comes through to the player—and they will point out (sometimes even before the players do) any issues that the development team might have missed due to being too close to the game.

Pocket Gamer

Slide to Play

The Internet is full of people who review games; some get paid, some just review stuff they love, and some do seem to have the goal of making game developers cry. Research games that are already in the marketplace by reading the reviews to determine what works and what doesn't. This might even help you come up with some new innovations that will make your game stand out (*Pocket Gamer*, left; *Slide to Play*, right).

::::: *Zombie Wonderland*: Making It All Worthwhile

Xoobis

I was exhausted after being awake 31 hours straight at the launch of our game, and then I started reading the early reviews. They were positive, but one user said that *Zombie Wonderland* was the best game he ever played on his mobile, and I just broke down in tears. After five months of grueling work at our home office—with 18-hour days, no weekends or holidays—it was amazing to see that we did our job right and people were enjoying it a lot.

—Alex Bortoluzzi (Chief Executive Officer, Xoobis)

Watch What Happens

Be sure to keep an eye on sales and occasionally change things up to see how it affects your product. Selling your game through the App Store for $2.99? Try dropping the price for a week to see how it affects the number of purchases. Your advertising should provide you with some metrics showing how well it's working (e.g., click rate). Do you see an increase in sales if you offer a free demo, or do they stay static? This is where many indie games get abandoned, shoved out with a single price point, then left to fend for themselves.

Diagram by Per Olin

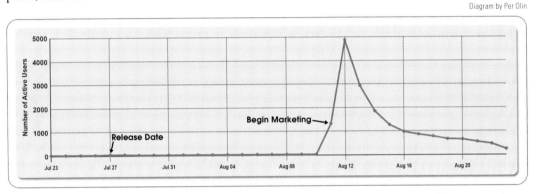

Marketing, even on limited budget, can make a huge difference in sales and downloads of a mobile game product.

Keep the Players Happy

Stay in touch with players after the release of the game through any number of social outlets such as Facebook, Twitter, or game-related blog/review sites like *Gaming Angels*. These social networking tools are invaluable resources when it comes to keeping the fan base interested in your game and keeping track of consumer satisfaction. How do you plan to keep in touch with your customer base and handle issues with your app after it's released? Will you provide customer support yourself, or will you outsource it to a third party?

DCom Solutions   Assembla, LLC

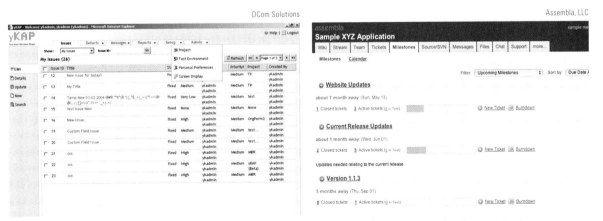

Bug tracking software such as DCom Solution's yKAP (left) and Assembla (right) is available to developers who choose to handle testing and quality assurance internally rather than hiring an outside service.

:::: *Pocket Legends*:
The Little Android in All of Us

Spacetime Studios

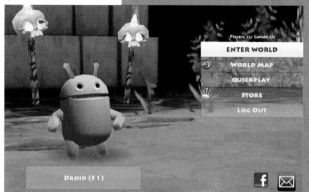

One of my favorite mobile experiences occurred during the Android launch for *Pocket Legends*, the first 3D MMO on mobile platforms. After a very successful launch on the iPhone, we wanted to make sure Android fans would fully embrace the game. Since Android is unlike iOS in many subtle and not-so-subtle ways, the PR firm and the client (Spacetime Studios) decided to first take advantage of a short open beta to generate buzz, then capitalize on the platform's cute mascot (an idea I had during a particularly fun conference call). On iOS, open betas are more difficult to run due to Apple's stringent submission guidelines. Nothing with the word "beta" will ever get approved. Android is the opposite: It embraces beta products like few other mobile operating systems. (Google, the mother ship behind Android, famously left Gmail in beta for more than five years.) Our one-week open beta was followed by an official "launch," and that's when we started offering one Android costume per web site to be given away over comments/Twitter/Facebook contests at each site's discretion. Since *Pocket Legends* is an MMO, the costume could be loaded as a "skin"—a perfect representation of Android in-game if there ever was one. The giveaways generated a massive amount of buzz within the community, with threads overflowing with entries and players literally "on the hunt" for the rare Android costume. Even editors were asking for costumes—via email, Twitter, Facebook, and every conceivable social media avenue. The Android costume is exceedingly rare to this day, with proud "owners" taking them for a spin now and then. *Pocket Legends* on Android was (and is) a huge success, with revenue numbers eclipsing that of the iOS version.

—*Luis Levy (Co-Founder, Novy Unlimited; Director, Novy PR)*

Lifespan

Let's face it: Games don't live forever. You are likely to see your biggest push in sales during the first couple of months unless the title gets mentioned by Conan O'Brien or shows up in an image on the side of a bus as part of the manufacturer's overall marketing push. If you've planned ahead, then updates, additional levels, characters, power-ups, and fancy ringtones will all keep a game fresh in the minds of the players. In fact, the idea that games can (and are) constantly updated for content rather than bugs has become pervasive in mobile games—so when the App Store indicates that there's a free update to your game, the additional downloads will show up in the publisher's metrics and have the power to push the game back into the Top 25 or Top 10 position once again. When updating content, be sure to keep to a reasonable, regular schedule. Many developers have promised regular updates to their games but quickly lost their fan base after being unable to keep up. Don't forget: Your fans will be a vocal group; if you miss your updates or never deliver them as promised, the complaints will appear in game reviews—which will be read by your game's prospective buyers.

We believe that reaching out to game reviewers and engaging the community are key to sustained growth. Advertising can also be effective, but they're costly and won't necessarily result in a high level of adoptions/installations.

—*Caleb Garner (Game Producer, Part12 Studios)*

Diagram by Per Olin

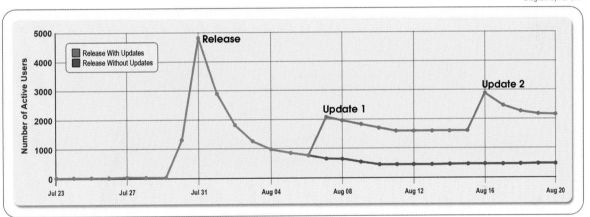

Small updates that add value to the game, such as new character skins or levels, can be effective methods of expanding the experience and extending the game's life.

Mobile Marketing Challenges

Marketing is probably one of the most difficult areas of mobile development, if not *the* most difficult. In a short time, the field has become quite crowded—and we cannot count on the media (or community) to be very supportive anymore. And why should they? They're jaded after the steady oversaturation of quality titles on the market! The developer must either seek out and hire a proper PR person or learn to deal with it alone (which is good for the longer term, since it can be extremely expensive and the connections will only serve you well—later). In spite of what many think, money must be spent—and a lot of painstaking research and trial-and-error must be conducted. Unusual steps (such as viral marketing) should be taken in order to get any kind of headline attention.

—*Ron Alpert (Co-Founder, Headcase Games)*

JN

Luis Levy
(Co-Founder,
Novy Unlimited;
Director, Novy PR)

Luis Levy is the co-founder of Novy Unlimited and the director of Novy PR—a public relations firm specializing in high-
technology, mobile, and indie developers with clients such
as Appy Entertainment, Liquid Entertainment, and Xoobis.
At Novy, Luis manages strategy, planning, media placement,
speaking opportunities, and trade show bookings. Prior to
Novy, Luis was an account executive at The Bohle Company
– where he represented game and high-technology clients
such as Spacetime Studios, The Voxel Agents, Muzzy Lane,
TimeGate Studios, and Dr. Fun Fun. Luis has also worked in
advertising, sales, film and television editing, and as a game
tester at Activision and Treyarch. He co-authored *Play the Game: The Parent's Guide
to Video Games* and *Game QA & Testing* with Jeannie Novak. Luis was born in São
Paulo, Brazil and attended Fundação Armando Álvares Penteado (FAAP), where he
received a B.A. in Film & Television.

The most effective marketing and PR techniques I've seen start with a nar-
row focus on a studio's biggest asset: its fans. The community that forms
around successful game developers and their creations is often one of those
immaterial factors that can drastically change the way a game is perceived—
and how it sells. Community equals commitment. Community can express
itself as friendship and often does so through loyalty. A great way to engage
your audience is to give them preferential treatment. Let them play the game
early, taking part in a closed beta. Let them contribute ideas—and feedback—at an early stage. Reward them with exclusive content and impossible-
to-find in-game items. When sending them newsletters, come bearing gifts.
Developers who listen to their fans get healthy sales and goodwill in return.
On the PR side of things, it's essential to speak their language. Leave buzz-
words and jargon for closed door chats with industry insiders. Your players
want you to describe the game in their words. They need to know you're one
of them. They need to see themselves in you; this applies to press releases,
web sites and social media outlets. Being honest with your audience means
telling the truth—no matter what. It means apologizing if you make a mistake and celebrating a win with the entire player population. If developers
follow these basic tenets, the effort and money spent marketing their games
will pay off in spades.

Sweetening

A few companies have been caught buying five-star reviews or having staff members post positive reviews of the same app over and over again (sometimes by the hundreds) to be sure it gets pushed up the ladder toward the Top 25. This is known as *sweetening*; it's bad form, and you don't need to do it. The last publisher caught doing this egregiously (reportedly giving multiple five-star reviews to a hangman-style app that crashed repeatedly) had all of their apps pulled. Most of the marketplaces reserve the right to yank an app they don't like. It could be because of the questionable content or because the exact same app was published with 10 different names in inappropriate categories (such as a swimsuit model picture show being published in the "children and family" category). If you abuse this, the long-term repercussions could include banishment from app stores altogether. Asking your nephew to download your app and give it a good review isn't a problem—but paying people $1 per star *is*, and it should be avoided at all costs.

::::: *iArrPirate & Pocket Legends*:
Mobile Marketing Lessons Learned

Riptide Games, Inc.

Our title *iArrPirate* was timed and themed to coincide with Talk Like a Pirate Day (TLAPD). We launched a few weeks prior, spent a significant amount on a Free App A Day promotion, and tried to generate as much interest as possible going into TLAPD. Unfortunately, we discovered that pirates are simply not very popular on their own, and most of our advertising expense was completely wasted. In contrast, we've had the best success with typical grass roots marketing—reaching out to our contacts in the mobile gaming press, and encouraging others to share and spread.

—*Brian Robbins (Founder, Riptide Games, Inc.)*

Spacetime Studios

I think the most interesting thing was the day we accidentally banned thousands of players. We very aggressively moderate our games, since a lot of kids play. All mobile devices have a unique ID, which means we can ban a specific device from ever playing our games again. Unfortunately, one manufacturer (who shall remain anonymous) let a batch of phones go that all shared the same unique ID. We banned what we thought was one phone from our system for being naughty, and suddenly thousands of people were unable to play. We reversed that particular ban pretty quickly. :)

—*Gary Gattis (Chief Executive Officer, Spacetime Studios)*

The Publisher's Role

A publisher usually has a marketing plan in place. It may not be big—but there will at least be a standard, basic plan applied across the board to all new products. Ask to see it, or at least get a description of what they are planning to do. Whatever it is, you're not going to think it's enough; that just par for the course. To you, it deserves the Ritz—but to the publisher, it might just deserve a nice, clean Motel Six! Publishers always have to hedge their bets—backing multiple horses and hoping for a "win" while also trying to cash in on the runners- up to help defray the risk. Consider that your game might be one of 20 or so in the publisher's pipeline. The question then becomes how to add to what the publisher already has planned. What can you, the third-party developer, do to push the publisher's reach even farther? If you are work-ing with a publisher, don't clash with what the publisher has already lined up. Don't start your own little developer-based fire sale to drum up more downloads when the publisher has planned something similar just a few weeks in the future.

> Appy Entertainment publishes its own original games. We spend a lot of time reaching out to our customers, the enthusiast press and working with other developers to launch our titles.
>
> —Chris Ulm (Chief Executive Officer, Appy Entertainment, Inc.)

Illustration by Ian Robert Vasquez

Be sure to run special promotions and interviews by your publisher and their marketing team before you pull the trigger.

> We publish our own games through the App Store. We also work with associates; provide them with art, technical and programming support; and share the App Store revenue on a sliding scale.
>
> —Ed Magnin (Director of Development, Magnin & Associates)

> We've published our own stuff directly to Apple's App Store, and we've also done contract work for partners. Both have generated some success; it just depends on the right project and the right partnership.
>
> —Quinn Dunki (Chief Sarcasm Officer; One Girl, One Laptop Productions)

Working With (or Bypassing) a Publisher

With Apple, you simply submit the app to the App Store for review and distribution; with Android, you just upload the .apk—and it's for sale instantly (leaving quality control up to you). In both capacities, a developer must be diligent on follow-through—both with addressing and fixing issues in a timely manner, and communicating this to the user base. A publisher will doubtlessly ease this process for a small independent—but to be true to their name, they must figure out the nuts and bolts of such a process with minimal hand-holding . . . or they won't last very long.

—Ron Alpert (Co-Founder, Headcase Games)

We are being published by Chillingo, which is great with indie developers. From feedback and constructive criticism, they really push the game out to the masses. Communication and transparency always help in dealings with a publisher. If the publisher knows what's going on, they can prepare for whatever is coming their way (good or bad) and plan around it. If you keep your cards too close, you can get into a tight spot and possibly sour the relationship.

—Alex Bortoluzzi (Chief Executive Officer, Xoobis)

The beauty of the emerging mobile market is that we can become our own publisher and don't have to rely on the traditional pub-dev relationships. The partners we are seeking now are hardware manufacturers and telcos, so in essence we can bypass the old model of game distribution.

—Gary Gattis (Chief Executive Officer, Spacetime Studios)

We chose to work with Electronic Arts to distribute our game. Their reach and cross promotion has been fantastic. Since we funded the game ourselves, we had none of the usual publisher/developer "tensions" over costs vs. timing vs. quality. So overall, we've worked with a lot of smart and dedicated people; this has made the relationship a joy for us—and hopefully for them!

—Jason Kay (Chief Business Monkey, Monkey Gods LLC)

Crunching the Numbers

It's a heady moment when a developer first reviews its game's analytics and sees how many copies have been downloaded since first appearing in the app store. Most of the stores will provide at least a daily accounting of a game's performance—allowing you to track sales, make price adjustments, and change up the advertising strategy quickly enough to address trends. Different app stores may have distinct payout timelines (weekly, monthly, quarterly) and payout methods; for example, BlackBerry requires a PayPal account, while the Android Market requires a Google account. Developers who release products across several platforms may quickly reach a point where optimizing and keeping tabs on the applications becomes a full-time job.

Revenue Models: Paid, Freemium & Free-to-Play

I'll go out on a limb and say that free-to-play is by and large the best opportunity we have as tiny independents to get our work seen, but it must be cleverly monetized with experimental gimmicks that won't annoy the player. The game must be more than enjoyable at its base without being cluttered with distracting advertising, and DLC/IAP must feel worthwhile and valuable.

—*Ron Alpert (Co-Founder, Headcase Games)*

Free is irresistible, but usually comes with caveats. I'd rather pay for something that I can have my gaming session uninterrupted. DLC is great. If I can get my game for a lower price, so when I get involved I could add to it or make it mine, that's the sweet spot I'm trying to achieve.

—*Alex Bortoluzzi (Chief Executive Officer, Xoobis)*

The freemium model is a particularly effective business model in the mobile market. If done right, it allows the developer to get as many users to try a game without having to sell them on initially spending money to give it a try. Of course, the model only works if the game successfully entices the user to pay for in-game purchases. From an indie developer standpoint, the least desirable strategy of the freemium model is, sadly, also the most effective: This is when in-game purchases are tied to time limitations—and the user can either wait to play or "pay" to *not* wait to play. Hopefully, this strategy, though profitable, will change over time to something more desirable involving a change in game features or mechanics enticing the players to pay for things they "want" (more levels or the ability to keep an already played character for good) instead of things they "need", and simply use up, in order to "play" the game.

—*Kimberly Carrasco (Developer/Owner, Tiny Tech Studios)*

Revenue Models (continued)

It's freemium all the way! With freemium you can in theory monetize one user multiple times. In paid, you have only one chance to monetize them—and success then depends on the cost and virality of your user acquisition.

—Sana N. Choudary (Chief Executive Officer, YetiZen)

Every app is different. Not every model works well for every game. However, in general we believe in the power of 'free.' It's just a safer bet that free games will be installed more, even if that free download doesn't turn into a direct sale. The developer receives a bit of exposure that could help later projects take hold and turn into a sale at that point. The more eyes, the bigger the potential prize.

—Caleb Garner (Game Producer, Part12 Studios)

Without question, the dominant model for solo mobile gaming has been freemium— where users can try a demo and then decide to purchase the whole game. This is giving way to more social games on mobile, where the superior model will be free-to-play, virtual goods-based monetization.

—Jason Loia (Chief Operating Officer, Digital Chocolate)

The name of the game is DLC!!! I don't care if it is free or paid, the ability to expand my gaming experience as a player is key. Also, a great way to bring players into your game is to offer a free or lite version and a full version, which the player will hopefully purchase if your game is good and fun enough.

—Nathan Madsen (Composer/Sound Designer, Madsen Studios LLC)

We have tried almost all of mobile revenue models, and our experience has shown that strong existing brands and incoming IP can work great for a paid system. For smaller developers launching new titles, having free, ad-based, and/or DLC-supported games is a much more viable option; it largely eliminates the barrier to entry for players and allows the content to drive engagement and adoption without having to pre-sell players on making purchases.

—Brian Robbins (Founder, Riptide Games, Inc.)

Mark Chuberka on the Free-to-Play Model :::::

MC

Mark Chuberka
(Director of Business
Development,
GameSalad)

Mark Chuberka is a 20-year veteran of the game industry, working on the sales and business development side of the business. He has worked for several of the industry leaders, including Electronic Arts, Activision, and Sony Online. He currently works at GameSalad, which produces GameSalad Creator—a visual drag-and-drop game creation tool for mobile and web development.

Paid mobile games is a dying game. Discovering games that sell for $0.99 is incredibly difficult, so making back development costs is unlikely. The free-to-play model in its various forms is growing and is likely to be dominant in the near future. In-game purchases for additional content are great for driving revenue while keeping customers interested and engaged. It's important to keep a perspective on in-game purchases, though; don't make it essential to progress, or you just have a lite version. Give them a reason to pay: faster leveling, cooler items, new looks … and keep it fresh, with regular additions and upgrades.

Patches & Bug Hunting

Developers always handle bug reports from players. For games developed only for a single device such as the iPhone, the probability of users having difficulty after download is fairly small—especially if the developer has already conducted a serious round of beta testing toward the end of the production process. However, games developed for multiple operating systems such as Android and iOS will invariably yield a larger amount of bug reports from players.

There are a number of ways to handle customer issues. Indie developers should set up specific email accounts just to handle incoming complaints and concerns. There are also a number of online companies such as Gamecloud, Ltd. that can provide this service—either on a per game, per call or monthly contract basis. Customer complaints are inevitable. Some players will love the game, some will hate it—and most of them will be more than happy to post a comment or send an email to your customer support line to say so.

In the case of many carrier decks, any new version of a game will automatically be downloaded to the purchaser's phone after logging into the game. Sometimes a dialogue box will appear asking players if they *want* the upgrade—but most often, such upgrades happen without the players' awareness.

With smartphones, the player is usually made aware that an update is available—but player intervention is required to download the update. This is due in part to limitations on download size. When a game or app is updated, a completely new copy of the game is downloaded rather than just a patch. Even if the game was under the 10MB download cap when it was purchased, upgrades and free updates will quickly push it up to a size that requires a Wi-Fi connection—either a download to the user's PC first or directly to the phone in question.

Getting Paid

It's no secret that smartphone stores charge developers 30% off the top for the privilege of publishing a game; in fact, it has become standard with other "e-platforms" (e.g., Kindle, Sony e-Reader). One thing to take into account is whether or not to provide refunds. If some players hate the game, do you give them their money back? The Apple App Store gives a full refund to the purchaser and deducts the funds from the developer's account, whether the developer wants to offer refunds or not. Other app stores may have different return policies. One of the attractive things about the $.99 price point (that no one ever talks about) is that most of the time, people who paid $.99 for the app aren't going to ask for it back; instead, they'll write it off and move onto something new and niftier. For the indie developer, this is a less risky figure than $5.99—which is large enough that a purchaser might consider it to be indispensable.

Kontagent

Mobile user analytics platforms such as Kontagent's kSuite provide a comprehensive set of tracking tools allowing developers to keep track of how many copies an app has sold and check sales against marketing pushes.

The Wild West

Perhaps you've heard about those mysterious "black market" web sites such as Cydia that sell "unapproved" apps—including iPhone apps that didn't pass inspection because the main character is scantily clad or others that allow *tethering* (sharing the smartphone's Internet connection with other devices such as laptops). Much of the time, these apps might actually be innocuous—but due to the Wild West nature of the point of sale, you will often see one of two things: Either the comments on a given app will be policed and moderated by those running the site (particularly if they're concerned with maintaining the site's reputation), or there will be a free-for-all with alternating ads for adult or illegal warez sites and political rants.

Illustration by Ian Robert Vasquez

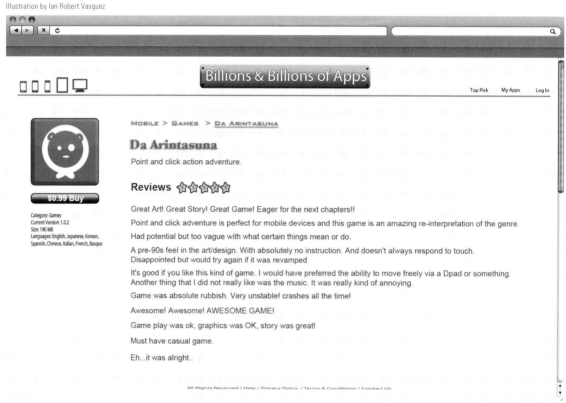

Comments are enabled everywhere, from app stores and review sites to "black market" destinations. Although some of these "brutally honest" comments can be painful, they often provide insight into genuine problems that can be fixed in the next update.

These sites—the ones that allow you to purchase software for jailbroken phones from any manufacturer—are not illegal, and a large percentage of the software they peddle isn't illegal either. This is where you go for more useful apps that are rejected because they conflict with the manufacturer's master plan, it can be a gold mine. Many people are willing to pay a premium price to be able to multitask, tether their phones to their laptops, view spreadsheets or Flash-based web sites and games from their smartphones. An app or a game that might have been driven down to the $.99 price point on the more formal app store might find an audience willing to pay that extra $5.00 just for the privilege. These sites serve as alternatives to the app stores' walled gardens, but they mean significantly more work for the developer. Companies such as Tapjoy that handle cross-app marketing don't handle independent sites, for example. The discoverability issue becomes much more difficult. In addition, the licensed app stores may pull a product if the developer is found to be cross-selling on an independent site. While these sites may be an option, they do take a lot more time and effort.

Life After Production

Completing production on a game or application and getting it ready for market is only the first part of the process. Once the game has been launched on the app store, there is still a whole ocean of marketing and management needed to keep the game on the top of the pile and producing revenue. Many indie developers feel that, once the game goes out the door, that's it—but on the contrary, they've only really just hit the halfway mark if they expect the game to be a success.

:::

Now that we've covered the entire game development, marketing, and distribution process, it's time to shift to a more reflective mode. In the final chapter, we'll take a look at what's next—including "pie in the sky" (and more plausible) technologies, and where the mobile industry seems to be heading in the near future.

Expanded assignments and projects based on the material in this chapter are available on the Instructor Resources DVD.

:::CHAPTER REVIEW EXERCISES:::

1. What is your "bottom line" goal as a mobile developer? Is it a dollar amount, number of downloads, brand building, positioning, or another discrete goal? After coming up with a goal, give it a "reality check." How many units do you have to sell in order to reach your goal? How extensive of a marketing campaign must you launch in order to sell that many units? Once you're satisfied that your goal can become a reality, describe it in a brief sentence.

2. Choose a primary revenue model for your game. Will you focus on paid, advertising-based, free-to-play, subscription, "freemium," DLC—or a combination? Discuss your rationale for your choice(s) based on your game's features, player market, and associated distribution channels.

3. Define and segment the player market for your original game idea. Consider geographics, demographics, and psychographics as you go through the process of identifying the characteristics of your market. Now create a one-paragraph marketing message for your original game idea. In the message, describe your market in detail—using the example in the chapter for reference.

4. Familiarize yourself with several mobile game review sites such as 148Apps, TouchArcade, and Pocket Gamer. Identify at least three journalists that you feel would be a good match for your game idea. Who did you choose, and why? Now draft a hypothetical pitch to generate coverage for your game—addressing one of the journalists you chose. The pitch should be 3-4 paragraphs long, clear, concise, and to the point. Be sure the focus of your pitch directly relates to the journalist's beat and provide links to assets (such as screenshots, trailers, and other views on Flickr and YouTube)—and end with a "call to action" (ask if the journalist is interested in an interview, promo code, in-game currency, etc.).

5. Take a look at analytics presentations and samples from companies such as Flurry (http://blog.flurry.com, http://www.flurry.com/product/analytics/index.html) or Kontagent (http://www.slideshare.net/kontagent/top-7-social-metrics-gdc-europe-2011), and familiarize yourself with how usage statistics can change over a period of time. Pay special attention to spikes in downloads and theorize why they are there. Examine this trend in comparison to other similar products over time. Note differences in the applications and consider how they might be affecting download trends.

CHAPTER

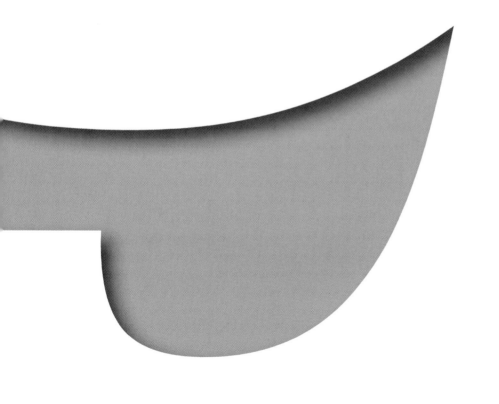

What's Next?

a view of the mobile future

Key Chapter Questions

- Will mobile games be driven more by *innovation* or *technology* in the next 10 years?

- How will built-in *hardware features* and *peripheral accessories* affect the way mobile games are played?

- What is the fate of technologies such as *augmented reality* and *3D* in the mobile space?

- How will the *Apple vs. Google* battle be settled?

- How will innovations such as *cloud computing* and *implanted technology* help shape the mobile future?

There is no question in the business or consumer mind that the world of mobile development has exploded over the last few years—and it seems to be moving forward at a rate that is only controlled by the amount of content than can be pushed out to the consumer. The mobile industry is still in its infancy, particularly when it comes to games and applications. There are many new opportunities on the horizon—some that will come to fruition in the next few years, and others that will take greater installed base and perhaps a few false starts before hitting their stride.

Mobile: No Longer the Little Kid on the Playground

What was once viewed as a niche industry sidelined by major publishers and producers of game content has become a major force in global game development. In countries without a pre-existing infrastructure for communications such as

> "**M**obile game" does not mean phone or tablet. It means, 'Oh, I wore this shirt today, which has connectivity with this bus stop, which alters the world via my sunglasses, and I control the game with my hands . . . or voice . . . or . . . thoughts.'
>
> —*Jennifer Estaris (Experience/ Game Designer, Total Immersion)*

fiber optics, the penetration of mobile phones and the potential installed base for consumers and players have outstripped anything the inventors of the devices might have imagined. Add to this the meteoric rise of the smartphone and the ever increasing depth and breadth of wireless connections, and you are looking at a market that will expand as quickly as new and innovative content can be delivered to its door. There are innovations just appearing on the market—some new to everyone, some adapted from other areas of the computing industry—that will help to push mobile even further forward.

People have become used to having information at their fingertips, and this is not going to change anytime soon. In fact, what is considered information overload right now is ultimately going to be the norm—with people who grow and adapt to the technology; those who learn to sort the good from the garbage will be able to make the best use of what's out there right now.

Illustration by Ian Robert Vasquez

Is this our mobile future?

Video Phone

With the advent of the video chat feature, the new generation of smartphones has provided users with an easily available opportunity. *Video phone* calls never really hit their stride until a few years ago on PC and desktop computers—when Skype fueled the use of webcams, and social sites such as *Chatroulette* gave them a use outside web conferencing.

Courtesy of Apple Inc.

With 3G capabilities now available on all carriers, video chat has appeared on smartphones (FaceTime on iPhone 4, shown).

The Mobile-Social Revolution

The next billion gamers will be playing social games on mobile devices. A whole new generation of Facebook and IM-savvy gamers are being groomed to stay connected with friends, and social games have already proven to be that glue. Mobile will be the rocket booster that lets them play with their friends 24x7.

—*Jason Loia (Chief Operating Officer, Digital Chocolate)*

Platforms get faster and have better sound and graphics, more game input methods (speech recognition), and more multiplayer games. The push toward social gaming and playing games over Facebook or through Apple's Game Center are creating new challenges and opportunities for us.

—*Ed Magnin (Director of Development, Magnin & Associates)*

The future of mobile game development will likely be in the interaction and competition within your immediate and extended social network. Communicating and connecting with one another through games on mobile devices is a natural step beyond simple chat.

—*Drew Tolman (Producer, Beach Plum Media)*

foursquare

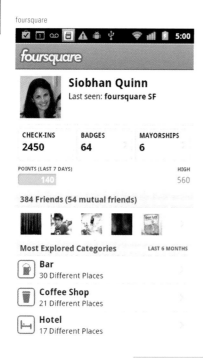

Location-Based Games

Location-based games began to hit their stride in mid-2010. Although there were a number of previous attempts to use location-based games to support entertainment venues such as theme parks and movie theaters, having to support so many different potential mobile devices was a problem—and they didn't show the expected returns. Apps such as *foursquare* have taken location-based games in a different direction; rather than delivering custom content based on players' locations and events, *foursquare* makes a game out of location check-ins (easily mapped through a smartphone's built-in GPS)—using traditional game features such as points and leaderboards.

Location-based apps such as *foursquare* focus exclusively on real-world check-ins, but developers are pushing toward game environments interposed on real-world locations.

"Passive" & Location-Based Gaming

We feel strongly that "passive gaming" is going to be huge; to some degree, it's happening already—but not to the level it could be. People are busy, and face time is precious. Providing games that allow a player to check in on and interact with others casually can be a lot of fun. Location-based encounters offer some exciting possiblities.

—*Caleb Garner (Game Producer, Part12 Studios)*

:::::Google the World

Wikitude

With companies such as Google attempting to map every square inch of the known world, it is becoming easier to build games that take advantage of those locations either under the guise of games or other apps that allow users to achieve a better understanding of their surroundings. This extends into augmented reality (discussed later in this chapter)—where users can see business names, building details, historical facts, directions or otherwise access information by simply pointing their phones or handheld devices at the building in question.

Wikitude allows players to collect information on real-world places—incorporating it into live gameplay.

Battery Life

A consistent complaint among smartphone users, *battery life* will continue to be a sticking point for the next couple of years. However, this hurdle has been jumped many times before in mobile devices—with portable computing, scientific and medical equipment, and any other device that requires a battery source. The technology for power delivery and the refinement of the electronics that use that power must "catch up" as devices get more sophisticated and consumers are trained to expect a certain set of basic amenities. No one would have batted an eye at the thought of having to charge a mobile device nightly 10 years ago—but when the iPhone was first released with a battery life of approximately one day with average usage, one of the loudest complaints concerned limited battery life. Improved battery life is significant for mobile games in particular; of all the applications available on smartphones today, games and videos use the most power—going so far as to cut the battery life in half!

Diagram by Per Olin

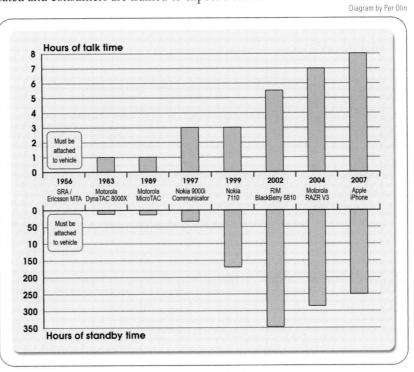

Increase in Battery Efficiency of Mobile Phones Over Time

Limited Battery Life & Casual Play

Much like the console arena, everything will continue to get more powerful—which will allow developers to create more immersive games. I do believe that, at least to a point, mobile gaming will always be a bit more casual than console gaming. This is because the phone has a limited battery life and is often a "go to" device during short breaks—whereas consoles are placed in environments (such as living rooms with couches) that promote much longer gaming periods. I'm very excited to be a part of mobile gaming and can't wait to see where it goes next!

—*Nathan Madsen (Composer & Sound Designer, Madsen Studios LLC)*

::::: Tech Trickle-Down

Let's consider the nature of technology: When the first model of the iPhone was released to the public in 2007, it was sold for around $500 ($600 for the 8GB model); by 2011, the much improved iPhone 4 was sold for $200 ($300 for the 32GB version). Compare this to flat screen televisions: When first available, the prices were well into the thousands—but four or five years later, they found their way down to the hundreds. While smartphones are certainly at the high end of the market right now, technology will continue to trickle down and the market will expand—with various smartphones replacing feature phones and being replaced by yet another form of technology at the top of the food chain.

Diagram by Per Olin

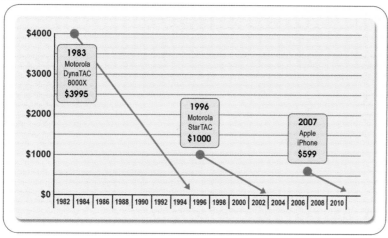

Mobile Phone Price Drops Over Time

Democratizing Development

As development tools become more user-friendly, people who can't program but have talent in art and design (or really great ideas) will be able to create their games and bring them to market. There's a lot of untapped potential in the world, and some great games are coming from the most unlikely of sources.

—*Mark Chuberka (Director of Business Development, GameSalad)*

In the not too distant future, development tools will advance to the point where a programmer isn't necessary. A simple storyteller will be able to walk through a wizard-driven process that will reduce or eliminate technical concerns and enable authors to put their complete focus on characters and what happens to them inside the story. It will democratize the process of game design in the same way that automatic HD cameras and YouTube democratized video production and distribution. Simultaneously, the easy function of development software will enable players to re-design the story as they experience it.

—*Catherine Clinch (Adjunct Professor,
Department of Mediated Instruction & Distance Learning, California State Dominguez Hills)*

"The Future Will be Decided by Creativity . . . Not Technology"

Platforms come and go, but creativity is needed to instill life in successful new IP. A studio doesn't make a name for itself by taking project after project, licensed properties, and advergames. New IP *defines* studios like nothing else. Looking at the evolution of mobile platforms, I see Android and iOS coexisting with a third platform in the background—similar to what we have with game consoles. Devices will become smaller, but screens will grow; the only way to make this physically possible will be through heads-up displays [HUDs] and other "discrete" display technologies (think *Minority Report*). Touch and voice control will be pervasive—but even if we have what amounts to Microsoft's Kinect everywhere, I bet we'll still have a need for functional game pads and D-pads. Mobile games will be next-gen in every way: true surround sound, high-definition graphics (or the next step, high-vision)—and always-on, 4G Internet connections that work anywhere in the globe. Consoles as they exist today might disappear in favor of smartphones that "dock" wirelessly with home entertainment systems, which the iPad can partially accomplish already with an HDMI cable. It will be harder and harder not to be a gamer—similar to not watching movies or TV in the late 1950s. The only challenge to this upcoming "golden age" is the rock bottom pricing of most games and a legion of developers dumping low-quality games on the unsuspecting masses. Unless we find a way to balance the conflicting interests of studios and publishers looking to make quick money and customers lost in a sea of cheap games, the mobile game industry might go the way of Atari in 1984. And no one, absolutely no one, wants to live through that again.

—Luis Levy (Co-Founder, Novy Unlimited ; Director, Novy PR)

Mobile is the fastest growing sector of game development. New devices appear almost weekly, whereas the larger console platorms get a new version every four or five years. The budget-minded consumer will continue to use this platform for gaming.

—Ben Long (Composer, Sound Designer, Audio Director & Author, Noise Buffet)

JS

Jeff Scott
(Editor, 148Apps)

Jeff Scott is the founder of the 148Apps network of sites covering mobile applications and the business surrounding the development of apps. An innovator in the mobile apps space, 148Apps was launched in 2008 and was one of the first sites to publish statistics and metrics on the app marketplaces it covers. Based in San Francisco, Jeff's background is in web and mobile application development—having worked for a variety of startups before launching his own web publishing company.

In the future, the only difference between mobile and more traditional console games will be the size of the screen. Mobile games are growing up quickly. In the not so distant future, you will be able to start a game on your mobile device, continue playing that game on your TV when you get home, and then resume playing it on your computer when you are at that screen. You'll be able to play your favorite games when, where, and how you choose. This is the real future of mobile games; developers should be looking in that direction and facilitating it whenever possible.

CU

Chris Ulm
(Chief Executive
Officer, Appy
Entertainment, Inc.)

A 20-year veteran of both the publishing and video game industries, Chris Ulm is CEO and co-founder of Appy Entertainment—an iPhone-centric game publisher dedicated to providing blasts of fun for busy people on the go. Appy's games have been downloaded more than 10 million times, have all achieved Top 20 status in their category, and have all been featured by Apple. Titles include *Tune Runner*, *Zombie Pizza*, "Best App Ever" winner *Trucks & Skulls*, the popular brawler *FaceFighter*, and the confectionary puzzler *Candy Rush*. Prior to Appy, Chris co-founded console game developer High Moon Studios and was co-creator of its original video game property, *Darkwatch*. As Chief Development Officer, Chris was a key player in building High Moon into an AAA developer—and he was integral to the acquisition of High Moon by Vivendi Games in 2006 and in its later transition to Activision-Blizzard.

We firmly believe that there will be a time in the next 10 years when a single game is downloaded by a billion players. Between "post-PC" devices such as tablets and smartphones, the vast majority of human beings on Earth will be able to download our games by the end of the decade. This is an unparalleled opportunity for talented game makers, though it will be fraught with rapid disruptions and chaos as the market grows exponentially. Our mission at Appy is to entertain the world through our games, and there has never been a better time for that.

As CEO, Mary-Margaret Walker leads the new business endeavors for Mary-Margaret Network. She brings to the role 14 years of experience in career and hiring services and 6 years of experience in video game development. Prior to creating Mary-Margaret Network in 1996, she was Manager of Studio Services for The 3DO Company—managing the milestones and development process of all projects in production and the hiring of over 200 employees. Previously, Mary-Margaret was at Origin Systems where she created the company's Human Resources department and contributed to titles in development as Design Manager. She is a regular speaker at international trade shows and has authored numerous articles. A founding member of the IGDA, Mary-Margaret holds a Bachelor of Arts degree from Texas Christian University and an M.B.A. from Sacred Heart University.

Mary-Margaret Walker (Chief Executive Officer, Mary-Margaret Network)

I have watched the game industry grow since I started at Origin in 1992. I love watching the cycles in the industry and the new developments in technology. It's been exciting to see the recent growth in mobile game development—including the resurgence of small teams and budgets accomplishing widely enjoyed and successful games. It's also fantastic to see whole new types of companies growing in this space as they continue to hire and expand development while also acquiring smaller companies. Mobile game development is truly international with many companies maintaining studios in multiple cities in the US and strategic areas throughout the world. This realm of game development is leading the industry in mainstream gaming. It appeals to every type of player and has created fresh types of games that weren't possible before such as location-based gaming. Mobile gaming will continue to morph and grow in terms of game companies, support services, deeper layers of positions in all disciplines—and, of course, revenue.

> Gameplay has become a constant form of entertainment—filling all those little moments when you have to wait in line or wait for someone to finish what they need to do. Mobile gaming fills that gap.
>
> —*Sue Bohle (President, The Bohle Company)*

Way Out There

Within the next 10 years, we are going to see another run at the oft chased all-in-one solution. As consumers move toward devices with less personal freedom in favor of the "out of the box" solution, there will be a brief trend toward consolidation—quickly followed by additional market fragmentation as players move back to devices that specialize. For everyone who's been waiting for the Gibson and Kurzweil tech-heavy futures to arrive, we've got news for you: We're already there. Granted we missed out on drilling holes in the skull and the massive dystopia, but the technology is already available to make many similar things a reality; it's just a question of adoption rather than "Can we do it?" Once the visions of the future have been translated into the consumerism of the now, where do we go from there?

Augmented Reality

Augmented reality will take a big leap in the next five years as the eminently trainable younger generation of mobile phone users moves up into areas of higher disposable income. As always, there will be a "training period" of two to three years before the technology really becomes embedded, and it will require wholehearted adoption and support by Apple or Google in order to achieve proper integration rather than just remaining a cool "tech toy."

Hunter Research and Technology, LLC

Presselite

Based on a centuries-old astronomical instrument, *Theodolite* (left) serves as a compass, GPS, map, zoom camera, rangefinder, and two-axis inclinometer. The *Firefighter 360* (right) fire-fighting game uses a unique augmented reality engine.

The Return of the Daisy Chain

There was a time when users had to link three, four or five devices together and utilize a single serial port on their desktops—forming what was known as a *daisy chain*. This functionality will be reinvented as consumers demand the ability to link their wireless mobile devices together. Rather than having multiple devices with cellular capability, consumers will just need one—a type of mobile router that allows them to connect multiple devices to it wirelessly, much like the connection between a Bluetooth headset and a mobile phone. Instead of moving to a single, all-in-one device, we will see user-enabled customization as people buy or rent single wireless cellular routers, then purchase the pieces they want (e.g., text-based messaging handhelds, web browsers, video devices).

Digital Living Network Alliance

The Digital Living Network Alliance (DLNA) was established by Sony in 2003 with the goal of using standards-based technology to make it easier for consumers to use, share, and enjoy digital photos, music, and videos. As of 2011, over 9,000 devices have obtained "DLNA Certified" status, indicated by a logo on their packaging and confirming their interoperability with other devices.

The Fate of 3D

As *3D* makes the jump to mobile phones, it might fail terribly. One of the requirements for success in mobile seems to involve serving an actual function that adds value to the experience. Games and apps take advantage of these technological advances once they are already in place, but they do not necessarily engender their adoption. Larger color screens added value because they solved issues relating to readability and information flow; they enabled people with camera phones to see the pictures they had taken, and they allowed for the touch-style input devices to come into play in more recent years. As of now, 3D has not fulfilled its promise on traditional console systems—due in part to the need for 3D glasses or headsets; although devices such as the HTC EVO 3D smartphone and the Nintendo 3DS handheld both use *autostereoscopy*, which does away with the need for these accessories, there hasn't exactly been a run at the market for the these systems. It will take much research and development to come up with a 3D gaming experience that truly satisfies, with the potential to move mainstream.

HTC Corporation

Only time will tell if the 3D so popular in movies can successfully make the jump to games. Devices such as the HTC EVO 3D smartphone (shown) and the Nintendo 3DS handheld hope to lead the way in 3D mobile gaming.

Cloud Computing

Mobile technology will simply replace workstation technology where consumers are concerned. As the laptop continues to gradually replace the workstation in the home and office, mobile computing devices will completely replace laptops—and those large workspaces taken over by wires and cables will eventually vanish completely. This will, incidentally, give *cloud computing* an opportunity to really shine. Savvy users and businesses still demand a hard backup of all their data, but storage and documentation kept on large server farms like those maintained by Google will be where the vast majority of data is handled. Most devices will become a variation on the old "dumb terminal," where the mobile unit is only used to access the cloud space. Once this is adopted, mobile units the thickness of a sheet of construction paper will come to the fore. With the need for local powerful processors eliminated, device manufacturers will be free to focus on connectivity and input technology rather than on processor speed, licenses, and heat.

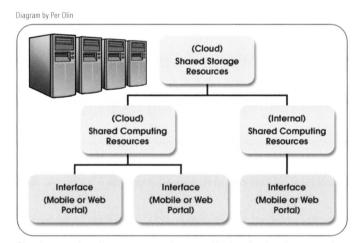

Diagram by Per Olin

Cloud computing allows games to be stored in the cloud and accessed through a player's mobile device.

Cross-Platform Access through the Cloud

I think we will see more cross-platform access—and I don't mean separate games: I mean playing a game on your PC, then continuing to play that same game on your iPad or smartphone, and then back to your PC. As more games are stored and played in the cloud, players will have multiple ways to access their games—similar to the way Facebook or Twitter is used now.

—*Chris Parsons (Product Manager, Muzzy Lane Software)*

Open Sim?

What do cellular companies really do? Like AOL before them, they provide a point of access to a broader network. Some companies such as Verizon Wireless own the network to which they provide access. Other smaller networks might have negotiated the right to provide access, but they don't own the infrastructure themselves. At some point, the balance between subsidizing the purchase of mobile devices and providing access is going to tip—and when it does, the networks will no longer be in a position to restrict access to one model of phone or another, and users will be able to purchase phones and use them on any desired point of access. It will be a sad day for mobile if this happens. The fight for customers is what keeps everything fresh, priced just within reach of the average consumer, and moving forward at the speed of thought.

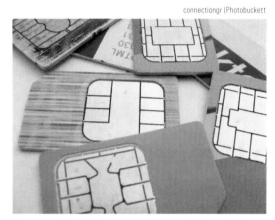

connectiongr (Photobuckett

The sim card gives a mobile device access to one cellular carrier's network versus another. If mobile carriers lose their incentive to subsidize phones, we may see fewer reasons to build "custom" units that suit a particular carrier.

Apple vs. Google

Everybody expects there to be a knock-down, drag-out fight to the finish between iOS- and Android-based smartphones. The problem is that this is simply not going to happen in any appreciable sense. Apple and Google are fighting in two completely different arenas and are never going to directly come to blows unless Google steps up to the plate and "owns" Android systems in the same way that Apple owns the iPhone. Right now, Apple has a single operating system associated with a few devices that are controlled from inception to distribution and beyond. Google's Android is much more of a workhorse and is targeting, for the most part, the broad penetration that is currently covered by Java ME feature phones. This means that as the technology trickles down, Google is going to be in the position to have its OS on every single one of the handsets that goes out into the feature phone market; Google will, in essence, be the successor to Java ME rather than trying to be the master of the smartphone. Google has its foot in the ring on the high end as well, but it is playing the long game. Within the next 5-10 years, we'll see Android as the dominant player where it really counts: in the feature phone market.

Apple, on the other hand, will dominate the independent market for applications. It's reasonably quick to develop for iOS, you don't have to build different versions of a game to satisfy carrier requirements, and there are significantly fewer issues when developing for only one or two operating systems. Some indies may not like it, but Apple is still the best bet for getting their titles produced and out into industry. Despite the occasionally Draconian rules and regulations that Apple has in place, most developers will work within those parameters—in part because having an app in the Apple App Store puts you in a place with some semblance of control. Moral pulchritude notwithstanding, most users will first want to have a product that will work with a minimum of fuss or nasty surprises. In the comparative Wild West of the Android store, there is a much greater percentage of unknowns—which may give a consumer pause before hitting the "buy" button.

Illustration by Ian Robert Vasquez

It might look like an epic "Apple vs. Google" battle—but these two members of the "Big Four" will most likely not engage in a deathmatch, since they're fighting in two completely different arenas.

Apple is all about control—while Android looks like the wave of the future because it's open . . . and free. Indie developers might initially gravitate toward the Android, since it might be easier to get one game into the market on a single device. However, once there, you are—for all intents and purposes—dead in the water. There is no real marketing plan, no opportunity for your game to appear on a television spot (or to have its icon up in the local store or on the side of a bus)—no matter how it may revolutionize the industry. You are truly indie with all the hassle, word-of-mouth requirement, blood sweat and tears that go along with it. This is precisely why the Apple App Store is going to remain the 800-pound gorilla in the room for the next five years. Apple might be a tight-fisted control freak, but the company's interest is in making sure that enough of its library of apps pays out to keep developers coming back—and it offers support and tools to help make that happen.

Under Your Skin

Some far flung futurists point to mobile as being the beginning of *implanted technology*. Already, there are plans and speculative designs for items such as flexible keypads under the skin that are driven by blood supply rather than a battery—and medical inroads are already being paved for devices that are able to draw an image directly onto the visual cortex. The evolution of mobile devices will help push this technology further along—and while it may never enjoy the kind of mainstream consumer use envisioned by William Gibson or Neal Stephenson, most of the tools and tricks you see will have been brought over from the mobile world even if you don't immediately recognize the roots.

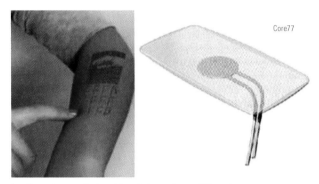

Core77

Implants beneath the skin might make mobile units an even more literal part of our lives.

Goggles

Augmented reality *goggles* and other "personal view screen" devices will finally get their tech sorted out to the point where they will achieve the same plug-and-play ubiquitousness enjoyed by mobile hands-free headsets. Right now, these devices are most often used to privately watch movies on long plane flights or play video games without disturbing your roommates. However, with augmented reality services preparing to kick into full swing, these devices will be pulled into the same loop—allowing an overlay of Google Maps onto the world around you or visual access to information without having to look up and back at your mobile handheld as you type in a URL. Some current generation smartphones are built to allow the use of goggles for private movie watching, but it remains to be seen if they can make the jump to game and app usage.

Vuzix

The accessory market for mobile handhelds has already surpassed the $2 billion mark for the current generation of smartphones. Add-ons such as Bluetooth headsets, and eventually VR goggles (Wrap 310 with iPhone, shown), will be made available for many different handsets over the lifetime of the product.

Looking into the Crystal Ball . . .

We are in the infancy of all of this right now. Some people say "the get-rich days have come and gone"—but to be honest, we're still a long way from the real beginning. It's so exciting to be active during this crazy period; the *most* exciting part is to be able to do what I know how to do, on my own terms, and be in control of it all—with what is historically the first time that mass distribution of such software is as simple as a button press. Mobile is going to revolutionize everything, and it's moving quickly already.

—*Ron Alpert (Co-Founder, Headcase Games)*

I think mobile development is the *future* of game development. The audience is gigantic, and the devices keep getting more powerful—especially tablets: Once wireless streaming HDMI becomes standard, there's no reason they won't replace the living room console.

—*Quinn Dunki (Chief Sarcasm Officer, One Girl, One Laptop Productions)*

The next billion gamers will be playing social games on mobile devices. A whole new generation of Facebook and IM-savvy gamers are being groomed to stay connected with friends, and social games have already proven to be that glue. Mobile will be the rocket booster that lets them play with their friends 24x7.

—*Jason Loia (Chief Operating Officer, Digital Chocolate)*

The future of mobile game development is bright. Venture capitalists are investing like mad right now, and start-ups are beginning to see the fruits of their labor with huge returns. Soon, however, we'll see over-saturation of the marketplace and investors slowing or stopping their investments altogether. At that time, companies will stop actively recruiting for new talent and instead focus more on restructuring and growing their already proven IPs. As mobile devices become more powerful, we'll also see more mid-core games being produced. Eventually, you'll be able to play a game as graphically impressive and complex as *Halo: Reach* on a handheld. At this point, the industry will revolutionize yet again as the pinnacle achievement is reached. Games created in 2D will remain popular and financially successful until there are so many developers and games to choose from that oversaturation will all but end their reign. If larger developers and publishers such as EA acquire these smaller studios, then there will still be breathing room for others to emerge and compete with new and original games of their own.

—*Christopher P. Onstad (Lead 3D Modeler/Texture Artist, Mega Pickle Entertainment)*

Looking into the Crystal Ball (continued)

The budgets for mobile apps and games pale in comparison to other platform, so you'll hear far less celebrities doing voices for them—which, in my opinion, is a very good thing. Celebs—who needs 'em anyway?

—*Lani Minella (Master Creator, AudioGodz Inc)*

Everyone has a smartphone and buys all of our games all the time. We are very rich, and I own a small fleet of helicopters. I hold annual races where other helicopter pilots from around the world can challenge my helicopters, but mine always win. The races aren't rigged or anything; my helicopters are just that fast.

—*Adam Stewart (Co-Owner, One Man Left Studios)*

In mobile games, the development of new technologies drives innovation in graphics and gameplay. Useful (and ubiquitous) applications may push manufacturers toward including specific hardware in the next generation of handheld devices; for example, *foursquare* greatly contributed to the adoption of GPS antennas in smartphones. Over the next few years, we will witness the continued forward march of the smartphone into the lives of consumers leading directly into what many describe as the "post-PC" world.

The Societal Evolution Barrier

Perhaps one of the biggest barriers to mobile computing, and oddly enough one of the easiest to overcome, will be societal evolution. Today, you can carry enough computing power in your backpack to make art and code for an entire AAA console title—but it's the compartmentalization that gets you. It's the integration with society that is now at issue: how people evolve to work with these new technologies, how they structure their lives, and how their employers allow them to work within the scope of these changes. As much as we might try to embrace them, these changes can take a generation to take hold and become viable. Much like how the introduction of factories put workers on a time clock—and the wholesale adoption of the automobile allowed people to live in the suburbs and commute to their businesses—the integration of mobile computing has the potential to change the way our society functions. All that's needed at this point is time.

: :

Mobile development offers unique opportunities and challenges. Mobile isn't "easy." It requires out-of-the-box thinking and a fearlessness that hasn't been seen in game development for a very long time. Milestones are short, file sizes are minuscule, and art requirements could make a minimalist weep—but if you're up to the task, if you enjoy working fast and smart, then mobile is the place to be for the foreseeable future.

Expanded assignments and projects based on the material in this chapter are available on the Instructor Resources DVD.

249

:::CHAPTER REVIEW EXERCISES:::

1. Do you feel that social and mobile games are beginning to intersect? After playing a social game on a mobile device and a PC, discuss the benefits and disadvantages of playing social games on mobile devices.

2. What is the appeal of location-based and augmented reality games? After exploring a smartphone app that focuses on providing a "hybrid" between the digital realm and the real world (e.g., *foursquare*, *Wikitude*, *Layar*), discuss how these apps could be turned into actual games.

3. What are the pros and cons of 3D mobile gameplay? Play a stereoscopic 3D game on the Nintendo 3DS or 3D-enabled smartphone such as the HTC EVO 3D. What do you like (and dislike) about the gameplay? Do you feel 3D has a future in mobile gaming? Why, or why not?

4. What are your views on the Apple vs. Google "race"? Provide a rationale for your answer. Choose another company that's involved in the mobile arena in any way (e.g., developer, publisher, hardware manufacturer, software provider). Discuss your thoughts on the trajectory this company might take in the next 5-10 years depending on market conditions.

5. What is your vision of the "mobile future"? Compare your predictions with those in this chapter and discuss whether you agree or disagree with them.

Resources

There's a wealth of information on game development and related topics discussed in this book. Here is just a sample list of books, news sites, organizations, and events you should definitely explore!

Communities, Directories, Libraries & Tutorials

Android Game Programming Tutorial (DZone) eclipse.dzone.com/articles/beginning-android-game

APM Music www.apmmusic.com

Apple Developer Connection developer.apple.com

ArtBarf.com www.artbarf.com

Betawatcher.com www.betawatcher.com

Beyond3D www.beyond3d.com

Bitmob.com www.bitmob.com

CG Society www.cgtalk.com

CG Textures www.cgtextures.com

Design Instruct www.designinstruct.com

Destructoid www.destructoid.com

DevMaster.net www.devmaster.net

DevShed Forum forums.devshed.com/game-development-141

Gamasutra www.gamasutra.com

Game Audio Forum www.gameaudioforum.com

Game Audio Pro Tech Group groups.yahoo.com/group/gameaudiopro

GameDev.net www.gamedev.net

Game Development Search Engine www.gdse.com

GameDevMap www.gamedevmap.com

GameFAQs www.gamefaqs.com

Game Music.com www.gamemusic.com

Game Music Revolution (GMR) www.gmronline.com

GameSalad Creator Tutorials www.youtube.com/GameSaladCookbook

Games Tester www.gamestester.com

Gaming (Reddit) www.reddit.com/r/gaming

GarageGames www.garagegames.com

Giant Bomb www.giantbomb.com

Guide to Sound Effects www.epicsound.com/sfx/

iDevGames Forum www.idevgames.com/forum

Indiegamer Forum forums.indiegamer.com

IndustryGamers www.industrygamers.com

International Dialects of English Archive (IDEA) web.ku.edu/idea/

iOS Developer Program developer.apple.com

iPhone Game Programming Tutorial (iCode[blog]) www.icodeblog.com/2009/01/15/iphone-game-programming-tutorial-part-1/

Machinima.com www.machinima.com

Mayang's Free Texture Library www.mayang.com/textures

mobiForge www.mobiforge.com

MobyGames www.mobygames.com

NeoGAF www.neogaf.com

Nokia User Experience Library www.developer.nokia.com/Resources/Library/Design_and_UX

Northern Sounds www.northernsounds.com

Overclocked Remix www.overclocked.org

Professional Sound Designers Forum psd.freeforums.org

PS3 www.ps3.net

Sketching, wireframing & note-taking PDF templates
www.smashingmagazine.com/2010/03/29/
free-printable-sketching-wireframing-and-note-
taking-pdf-templates/

Sound Design Forum   groups.yahoo.com/group/
sound_design

3D Buzz   www.3dbuzz.com

3D Total   www.3dtotal.com

Tongue Twisters   www.geocities.com/Athens/8136/
tonguetwisters.html

TrueGaming (Reddit)   www.reddit.com/r/

Unity Tutorials
www.unity3d.com/support/resources/tutorials/

VGMix   www.vgmix.com

Video Game Music Database (VGMdb)
www.vgmdb.net

Voicebank.net   www.voicebank.net

Voiceover Demos   www.compostproductions.com/
demos.html

Wii-Play   www.wii-play.com

Xbox.com   www.xbox.com

Xbox 360 Homebrew   www.xbox360homebrew.com

XNA Creators Club   creators.xna.com

Career Resources

BlueSkyResumes www.blueskyresumes.com

Craigslist www.craigslist.org

Creative Heads   www.creativeheads.net

Dice www.dice.com

Digital Artist Management
www.digitalartistmanagement.com

EntertainmentCareers.net
www.entertainmentcareers.net

Entertainment Technology Source   www.etsource.com

Game Career Guide   www.gamecareerguide.com

GameJobs   www.gamejobs.com

Game Recruiter   www.gamerecruiter.com

Games-Match   www.games-match.com

Hot Jobs   www.hotjobs.com

International Search Partners   www.ispards.com

LinkedIn   www.linkedin.com

Mary-Margaret Network   www.mary-margaret.com

Microsoft/Monster Career Center   office.microsoft.com/
en-us/help/FX103504051033.aspx

Monster   www.monster.com

Premier Search   www.premier-search.net

Prime Candidate, Inc.   www.primecandidateinc.com

Resumé Samples   www.freeresumesamples.org

Sample Resume   www.bestsampleresume.com

2015   www.2015.com

Colleges & Universities

Academy of Art University
www.academyart.edu

American Intercontinental University
www.aiuniv.edu

Arizona State University   www.asu.edu

Art Institute of Pittsburgh Online
www.aionline.edu

The Art Institutes   www.artinstitutes.edu

Austin Community College
www.austincc.edu

Becker College   www.becker.edu

Bunker Hill Community College
www.bhcc.mass.edu

California College of the Arts
www.cca.edu

Carnegie Mellon University/Entertainment
Technology Center   www.cmu.edu

Champlain College   www.champlain.edu

Cornell University   gdiac.cis.cornell.edu

Dartmouth College   www.dartmouth.edu

DePaul University   www.depaul.edu

DeVry University   www.devry.edu

DigiPen Institute of Technology
www.digipen.edu

Ex'pression College for Digital Arts
www.expression.edu

Full Sail Real World Education
www.fullsail.edu

Georgia Institute of Technology
dm.lcc.gatech.edu

Guildhall at SMU   guildhall.smu.edu

Indiana University - MIME Program
www.mime.indiana.edu

International Academy of Design &
Technology   www.iadtschools.com

Iowa State University   www.iastate.edu

ITT Technical Institute   www.itt-tech.edu

Lehigh Carbon Community College
(LCCC)   www.lccc.edu

Los Angeles Film School   www.lafilm.edu

Massachusetts Institute of Technology
(MIT)   media.mit.edu

Mercyhurst College   www.mercyhurst.edu

New England Institute of Art
www.artinstitutes.edu/boston

Northeastern University
www.northeastern.edu

Rasmussen College   www.rasmussen.edu

Rensselaer Polytechnic Institute
www.rpi.edu

Ringling College of Art & Design
www.ringling.edu

Rochester Institute of Technology
www.rit.edu

SAE Institute   www.sae.edu

Santa Monica College Academy of
Entertainment & Technology
academy.smc.edu

Savannah College of Art & Design
www.scad.edu

Tomball College   www.tomballcollege.
com

University of California, Los Angeles
(UCLA) Extension
www.uclaextension.edu

University of California, San Diego
(UCSD) - Experimental Game Lab
http://www.experimentalgamelab.net/

University of California, San Diego
(UCSD) - Mobile Systems Design Lab
esdat.ucsd.edu/index.shtml

University of Central Florida - Florida
Interactive Entertainment Academy
fiea.ucf.edu

University of North Florida   www.unf.edu

University of Ontario Institute of
Technology   www.uoit.ca

University of Southern California (USC)
Information Technology Program
itp.usc.edu

University of Southern California (USC) School of Cinematic Arts interactive.usc.edu

University of Washington Bothell Center for Serious Play   www.uwb.edu/csp

Vancouver Film School   www.vfs.com

Westwood College   www.westwood.edu

Worcester Polytechnic Institute   www.wpi.edu

Development & Post-Production Tools

Adobe: Audition/Flash/Dreamweaver/ Illustrator/Photoshop   www.adobe.com

Assembla   www.assembla.com

Autodesk: 3ds Max/Maya/Mudbox/ MotionBuilder/Softimage   usa.autodesk.com

Bethesda Softworks: Elder Scrolls Construction Kit   www.bethsoft.com

Crystal Space: Graphics engine   www.crystalspace3d.org

Crytek: CryENGINE   www.crytek.com

Dassault Systemes: 3DVIA   www.3dvia.com

DigiDesign: Pro-Tools   www.digidesign.com

Emergent Game Technologies: Gamebryo   www.emergent.net

Epic Games/Unreal Technology: Unreal Engine   www.unrealtechnology.com

Flurry (analytics)   www.flurry.com

Game Maker   www.yoyogames.com

GameSalad Creator   www.gamesalad.com

Gamestudio: www.3dgamestudio.com

Genesis 3D   www.genesis3d.com

Havok   www.havok.com

id Software: id Tech   www.idsoftware.com

Irrlicht Engine   irrlicht.sourceforge.net

Kontagent (analytics)   www.kontagent.com

Monolith Productions: Lith Jupiter Engine   www.lith.com

Nvidia: PhysX   www.nvidia.com

Panda3D: 3D game engine   panda3d.org

Pixologic: Zbrush   www.pixilogic.com

RAD Game Tools   www.radtools.com

RealmForge: Game engine   sourceforge.net/projects/realmforge

Relic Entertainment: Essence engine   www.relic.com

Sony Creative Software: Sound Forge   www.sonycreativesoftware.com

Steinberg: Cubase Studio/ WaveLab   www.steinberg.com

Torque 2D Game Builder/3D Game Engine Advanced   www.garagegames.com

Unity   www.unity3d.com

uScript   www.detoxstudios.com

Valve Software: Source Engine   www.valvesoftware.com

Xcode   developer.apple.com/xcode

Organizations

Academy of Interactive Arts & Sciences
(AIAS)   www.interactive.org

Academy of Machinima Arts & Sciences
www.machinima.org

Association of Computing Machinery
(ACM)   www.acm.org

Audio Engineering Society (AES)
www.aes.org

Business Software Alliance (BSA)
www.bsa.org

Digital Games Research Association
(DiGRA)   www.digra.org

Entertainment Software Association (ESA)
www.theesa.com

Entertainment Software Ratings Board
(ESRB)   www.esrb.org

Game Audio Network Guild (GANG)
www.audiogang.org

Game Audio Technical Committee   www.
aes.org/technical/ag

Interactive Audio Special Interest Group
(IASIG)   www.iasig.org

International Computer Games Association
(ICGA)   www.cs.unimaas.nl/icga

International Game Developers Association
(IGDA)   www.igda.org

News, Reviews & Research

AppAddict.net   www.appaddict.net

The APPera   www.theappera.com

Appolicious   www.appolicious.com

Ars Technica   www.arstechnica.com

Blues News   www.bluesnews.com

CNET   www.cnet.com

Computer & Video Games
www.computerandvideogames.com

Computer Games Magazine
www.cgonline.com

Curse.com   www.curse.com

Develop Magazine   www.developmag.com

Digital Playroom   www.dplay.com

DIYgamer   www.diygamer.com

Edge Online   www.edge-online.com

Electronic Gaming Monthly (EGMi)
www.egmnow.com

The Escapist   www.escapistmagazine.com

Eurogamer   www.eurogamer.net

FingerGaming   www.fingergaming.com

Game Developer Magazine
www.gdmag.com

Gamers Hell   www.gamershell.com

Game Industry News
www.gameindustry.com

GameInformer.com
www.gameinformer.com

Game-Machines.com
www.game-machines.com

GamePolitics   www.gamepolitics.com

GamePro   www.gamepro.com

GameRankings   www.gamerankings.com

Game Revolution
www.gamerevolution.com

Games.com (blog)   blog.games.com

GamesBeat (VentureBeat)
www.venturebeat.com/category/games

GameSetWatch   www.gamesetwatch.com

GamesIndustry.biz
www.gamesindustry.biz

GameSlice Weekly   www.gameslice.com

GameSpot   www.gamespot.com

GameSpy   www.gamespy.com

Games Radar (PC Gamer)
www.gamesradar.com/pc

GameTrailers   www.gametrailers.com

Gamezebo   www.gamezebo.com

GamingAngels   www.gamingangels.com

GayGamer   www.gaygamer.net

Girl Gamer   www.girlgamer.com

IndieGames.com   www.indiegames.com

Internet Gaming Network (IGN)
    www.ign.com

Jay is Games   www.jayisgames.com

Joystiq   www.joystiq.com

Kotaku   www.kotaku.com

The Loop   www.theloopinsight.com

Mac|Life   www.maclife.com

Macworld.com   www.macworld.com

MCV   www.mcvuk.com

Metacritic   www.metacritic.com

MMOGChart.com   www.mmogchart.com

MMORPG.com   www.mmorpg.com

MPOGD.com   www.mpogd.com

MTV Multiplayer
    multiplayerblog.mtv.com

Music4Games.net   www.music4games.net

Nine Over Ten   www.nineoverten.com

148Apps   www.148apps.com

1UP   www.1up.com

PC Gamer   www.pcgamer.com

Penny Arcade   www.penny-arcade.com

Planet Unreal   planetunreal.gamespy.com

Pocket Gamer   www.pocketgamer.co.uk

PolyCount   www.polycount.com

Recording History: The History of
    Recording Technology
    www.recording-history.org

Ripten   www.ripten.com

Showfax   www.showfax.com

Slashdot   games.slashdot.org

Slide to Play   www.slidetoplay.com

Star Tech Journal
    www.startechjournal.com

Ten Ton Hammer
    www.tentonhammer.com

TouchArcade   www.toucharcade.com

TouchGen   www.touchgen.net

UnderGroundOnline (UGO)
    www.ugo.com

Unreal Technology
    www.unrealtechnology.com

Unreal Wiki   wiki.beyondunreal.com

Xbox Developer Programs
    www.xbox.com/ en-US/dev/
    contentproviders.htm

Wired Game | Life   blog.wired.com/games

WorkingGames   www.workingames.co.uk

Events

Month	Title	Location	Site
January	Consumer Electronics Show (CES)	Las Vegas, NV	www.cesweb.org
February	DICE Summit (AIAS)	Las Vegas, NV	www.dicesummit.org
March	Game Developers Conference (GDC)	San Francisco, CA	www.gdconf.com
	Penny Arcade Expo East (PAX East)	Boston, MA	east.paxsite.com
April	Engage! Expo	San Francisco, CA	www.engagedigital.com
	LA Games Conference	Los Angeles, CA	www.lagamesconference.com
May	LOGIN Conference	Bellevue, WA	www.loginconference.com
	Games For Health	Boston, MA	www.gamesforhealth.org/index.php/conferences/
June	Electronic Entertainment Expo (E3)	Los Angeles, CA	www.e3expo.com
	Games For Change Festival	New York, NY	www.gamesforchange.org/festival/
	Game Education Summit (GES)	varies	www.gameeducationsummit.com
	Origins Game Fair	Columbus, OH	www.originsgamefair.com
July	Comic-Con	San Diego, CA	www.comic-con.com
	Casual Connect	Seattle, WA	seattle.casualconnect.org
August	SIGGRAPH	varies	www.siggraph.org
	GDC Europe	varies	www.gdceurope.com
	BlizzCon	Anaheim, CA	www.blizzcon.com
	Gen Con	Indianapolis, IN	www.gencon.com
September	Dragon*Con	Atlanta, GA	www.dragoncon.org
	NY Games Conference	New York, NY	www.nygamesconference.com
	Tokyo Game Show (TGS)	Tokyo, Japan	tgs.cesa.or.jp/english
October	MIPCOM	Cannes, France	www.mipworld.com/mipcom
	Brasil Game Show	Rio de Janeiro, Brazil	www.brasilgameshow.com.br/
	GDC Online	Austin, TX	www.gdconline.com
	IndieCade	Los Angeles, CA	www.indiecade.com
	SIEGE (Southern Interactive Entertainment & Game Expo)	Atlanta, GA	www.siegecon.net
	FailCon	San Francisco, CA	www.failcon.com
	IGDA Leadership Forum	Los Angeles, CA	www.igda.org/leadership
	Project Bar-B-Q	Lake Buchanan, TX	www.projectbarbq.com
November	Social Gaming Summit	London, UK	www.mediabistro.com/socialgamingsummit
	GDC China	Shanghai, China	www.gdcchina.com
December	Dubai World Game Expo	Dubai, UAE	www.gameexpo.ae

Game-Related Companies

Activision Blizzard
www.activisionblizzard.com

Alelo www.alelo.com

Amaze Entertainment www.amazeent.com

Apogee Software / 3D Realms
www.apogeeosoftware.com

Appboy www.appboy.com

Appy Entertainment
www.appyentertainment.com

ArenaNet www.arena.net

Atari www.atari.com

Atlus USA www.atlus.com

AudioGodz www.audiogodz.com

Bethesda Softworks www.bethsoft.com

Big Fish Games www.bigfishgames.com

Big Huge Games www.bighugegames.com

Binary Finery www.binaryfinery.com

BioWare www.bioware.com

Bluepoint Games
www.bluepointgames.com

Boost Mobile www.boostmobile.com

Breakaway Games
www.breakawaygames.com

Bungie Software www.bungie.net

Bushi-go www.bushi-go.com

Cafe.com www.cafe.com

Capcom Entertainment www.capcom.com

Carbine Studios www.carbinestudios.com

CDV Software www.cdvusa.com

Chronic Logic www.chroniclogic.com

Codemasters www.codemasters.com

Concrete Software, Inc.
www.concretesoftware.com

Course Games www.coursegames.com

Crave Entertainment www.cravegames.com

Cryptic Allusion Games cagames.com

Cryptic Studios crypticstudios.com

Crystal Dynamics www.crystald.com

Cyan Worlds, Inc. cyanworlds.com

Digital Chocolate
www.digitalchocolate.com

Disney Interactive Studios disney.go.com/
disneyinteractivestudios/

Double Helix Games
www.doublehelixgames.com

DreamWorks
www.dreamworkanimation.com

EA Mobile www.eamobile.com/Web/

Eidos Interactive www.eidosinteractive.com

Electronic Arts www.ea.com

Enemy Technology
www.enemytechnology.com

Enspire Learning
www.enspirelearning.com

Epic Games www.epicgames.com

Firaxis Games www.firaxis.com

5 Elements Entertainment
www.5elementsentertainment.com

Foundation 9 www.foundation9.com

Freescale Semiconductor
www.freescale.com

Frogster America
www.frogster-america.com

Funcom www.funcom.com

Gameloft www.gameloft.com

GameSalad www.gamesalad.com

GarageGames www.garagegames.com

Gas Powered Games www.gaspowered.com

Gideon Games www.gideongames.com

Glu Mobile
www.glu.com/noram/Pages/home.aspx

Gravity Interactive
www.gravity.co.kr/eng/index.asp

Hanako Games www.hanakogames.com

Hands-On Mobile www.handson.com

Harmonix www.harmonixmusic.com

Headcase Games www.headcasegames.com

Hidden Path Entertainment
www.hiddenpath.com

Icarus Studios www.icarusstudios.com

id Software www.idsoftware.com

Insomniac Games
www.insomniacgames.com

Interplay Productions www.interplay.com

I-play www.iplay.playp.biz

iWin www.iwin.com

Koei Corporation North America
www.koei.com

Konami www.konami.com/mobile

Large Animal Games
www.largeanimal.com

Last Day of Work www.ldw.com

LucasArts Entertainment
www.lucasarts.com

Mad Monkey Militia
www.madmonkeymilitia.com

Madsen Studios www.madsenstudios.com

Magnin & Associates www.edmagnin.com

Majesco Entertainment
www.majescoentertainment.com

Max Gaming Technologies
www.maxgaming.net

Microsoft Corporation www.microsoft.com

Mine Shaft Entertainment, Inc.
www.mineshaft.org

Mobile Deluxe mobiledeluxe.com

Monkey Gods www.monkeygods.com

Monolith Productions www.lith.com

MSN Games
zone.msn.com/en/root/default.htm

Muzzy Lane Software www.muzzylane.com

Namco Bandai Games
www.namcobandaigames.com

Namco Mobile www.namcomobile.com

Naughty Dog www.naughtydog.com

NCsoft www.ncsoft.net/global/

NetDevil www.netdevil.com

Neversoft Entertainment
www.neversoft.com

Nexus Entertainment www.nexusent.com

Nintendo of America www.nintendo.com

Noise Buffet www.noisebuffet.com

Oasys Mobile www.oasysmobileinc.com

Obsidian Entertainment
www.obsidianent.com

One Girl, One Laptop Productions
www.quinndunki.com

One Man Left Studios
www.onemanleft.com

On Your Mark Music Productions
www.onyourmarkmusic.com

Paramount Pictures Interactive & Mobile
Entertainment www.paramount.com

Part12 Studios www.part12studios.com

Petroglyph Games
www.petroglyphgames.com

Pixar www.pixar.com

Playdom www.playdom.com

PlayFirst www.playfirst.com

Playfish www.playfish.com

PopCap Games www.popcap.com

Rainbow Studios www.rainbowstudios.com

Raven Software www.ravensoft.com

Red Storm Entertainment
www.redstorm.com

Reflexive Entertainment
www.reflexive-inc.com

Retro Studios www.retrostudios.com

Riptide Games www.riptidegames.com

Rockstar San Diego rockstarsandiego.com

Sega of America www.sega.com

SkyZone Entertainment
www.skyzonemobile.com

Smith & Tinker, Inc.
www.smithandtinker.com

Sneaky Games www.sneakygames.com

Snowblind Studios
www.snowblindstudios.com

Socialize, Inc. www.getsocialize.com

Sony Computer Entertainment America
www.us.playstation.com

Sony Online Entertainment
www.soe.com/en/soe.vm

Sony Pictures Animation
www.sonypictures.com

Sound For Games Interactive
sfginteractive.blogspot.com

SouthPeak Interactive www.
southpeakgames.com

Spacetime Studios
www.spacetimestudios.com

Square-Enix USA
www.square-enix.com/na/

SRRN Games   www.srrngames.com

Stardock www.stardock.com

Star Mountain Studios
www.starmountainstudios.com

Sucker Punch Productions
www.suckerpunch.com

Surreal Software www.surreal.com

SyFy Games   www.syfygames.com

Take-Two Interactive
www.take2games.com

Tecmo www.tecmogames.com

THQ www.thq.com

3DVIA/Dassault Systemes
www.3dvia.com

Three Rings   www.threerings.net

TikGames www.tikgames.com

TimeGate Studios
www.timegatestudios.com

Tin Man Games Pty. Ltd.
www.tinmangames.com.au

Tiny Tech Studios
www.tinytechstudios.com

Total Immersion   www.t-immersion.com

Uber Entertainment www.uberent.com

TubettiWorld Games
www.tubettiworld.com

2K Games www.2kboston.com

21-6 Productions www.21-6.com

2015 www.2015.com

Twisted Pixel Games
www.twistedpixelgames.com

Twittering Machine   www.twittering.com

Uber Entertainment www.uberent.com

Ubisoft www.ubi.soft

Unity www.unity3d.com

Valve www.valvesoftware.com

Vicarious Visions www.vvisions.com

Vigil Games   www.vigilgames.com

Walt Disney Animation Studios
www.disneyanimation.com

Whitaker Blackall Music
www.whitakerblackall.com

WildTangent www.wildtangent.com

WorldWinner www.worldwinner.com

Xoobis www.xoobis.com

Yahoo! Games games.yahoo.com

YetiZen www.yetizen.com

YoYo Games www.yoyogames.com

ZeniMax Online Studios
www.zenimaxonline.com

Zynga www.zynga.com

Books & Articles

Adams, E. (2003). *Break into the game industry.* McGraw-Hill Osborne Media.

Adams, E. & Rollings, A. (2006). *Fundamentals of game design.* Prentice Hall.

Ahearn, L. & Crooks II, C.E. (2002). *Awesome game creation: No programming required. (2nd ed).* Charles River Media.

Ahlquist, J.B., Jr. & Novak, J. (2007). *Game development essentials: Game artificial intelligence.* Cengage Delmar.

Aldrich, C. (2003). *Simulations and the future of learning.* Pfeiffer.

Aldrich, C. (2005). *Learning by doing.* Jossey-Bass.

Allison, S.E. et al. (March 2006). "The development of the self in the era of the Internet & role-playing fantasy games. *The American Journal of Psychiatry.*

Allmer, M. (February 27, 2009). "The 13 basic principles of gameplay design." *Gamasutra* (www.gamasutra.com/view/feature/3949/the_13_basic_principles_of_.php).

Atkin, M. & Abercrombie, J. (2005). "Using a goal/action architecture to integrate modularity and long-term memory into AI behaviors." *Game Developers Conference.*

Axelrod, R. (1985). *The evolution of cooperation.* Basic Books.

Bartle, R.A. (1996). "Hearts, clubs, diamonds, spades: Players who suit MUDs." *MUSE   Multi-User Entertainment Ltd* (www.mud.co.uk/richard/hcds.htm).

Bates, B. (2002). *Game design: The art & business of creating games.* Premier Press.

Beck, J.C. & Wade, M. (2004). *Got game: How the gamer generation is reshaping business forever.* Harvard Business School Press.

Beshera, T. (2008). *Acing the interview: How to ask and answer the questions that will get you the job.* AMACOM.

Bethke, E. (2003). *Game development and production.* Wordware.

Birdwell, K. (1999). "The cabal: Valve's design process for creating *Half-Life.*" *Gamasutra* (http://www.gamasutra.com/view/feature/3408/the_cabal_valves_design_process_.php)

Birn, J. (2006). *Digital lighting and rendering (2nd ed.).* New Riders Press.

Boer, J. (2002). *Game audio programming.* Charles River Media.

Brandon, A. (2004). *Audio for games: Planning, process, and production.* New Riders.

Brin, D. (1998). *The transparent society.* Addison-Wesley.

Broderick, D. (2001). *The spike: How our lives are being transformed by rapidly advancing technologies.* Forge.

Brooks, D. (2001). *Bobos in paradise: The new upper class and how they got there.* Simon & Schuster.

Busby, A., Parrish, Z. & Van Eenwyk, J. (2004). *Mastering Unreal technology: The art of level design.* Sams.

Byrne, E. (2004). *Game level design.* Charles River Media.

Campbell, J. (1972). *The hero with a thousand faces.* Princeton University Press.

Campbell, J. & Moyers, B. (1991). *The power of myth.* Anchor.

Castells, M. (2001). *The Internet galaxy: Reflections on the Internet, business, and society.* Oxford University Press.

Castillo, T. & Novak, J. (2008). *Game development essentials: Game level design.* Cengage Delmar.

Castronova, E. (2005). *Synthetic worlds: The business and culture of online games.* University of Chicago Press.

Chase, R.B., Aquilano, N.J. & Jacobs, R. (2001). *Operations management for competitive advantage (9th ed).* McGraw-Hill/Irwin

Cheeseman, H.R. (2004). *Business law (5th ed).* Pearson Education, Inc.

Chiarella, T. (1998). *Writing dialogue.* Story Press.

Childs, G.W. (2006). *Creating music and sound for games.* Course Technology PTR.

Christen, P. (November 2006). "Serious expectations" *Game Developer Magazine.*

Clayton, A.C. (2003). *Introduction to level design for PC games.* Charles River Media.

Co, P. (2006). *Level design for games: Creating compelling game experiences.* New Riders Games.

Cooper, A., & Reimann, R. (2003). *About face 2.0: The essentials of interaction design.* Wiley.

Cornman, L.B. et al. (December 1998). A fuzzy logic method for improved moment estimation from Doppler spectra. *Journal of Atmospheric & Oceanic Technology.*

Cox, E. & Goetz, M. (March 1991). Fuzzy logic clarified. *Computerworld.*

Crawford, C. (2003). *Chris Crawford on game design.* New Riders.

Crowley, M. (2004). "'A' is for average." *Reader's Digest.*

Csikszentmihalyi, M. (1991). *Flow: The psychology of optimal experience.* Perennial.

Dawson, M. (2006). *Beginning C++ through game programming.* Course Technology.

Decker, M. (2000). "Bug Reports That Make Sense." *StickyMinds.com* (www.stickyminds.com/sitewide.asp?Function=edetail&ObjectType=ART&ObjectId=2079).

DeMaria, R. & Wilson, J.L. (2003). *High score!: The illustrated history of electronic games.* McGraw-Hill.

Demers, O. (2001). *Digital texturing and painting.* New Riders Press.

Dickens, C. (April 1, 2004). "Automated Testing Basics." *Software Test Engineering @ Microsoft* (blogs.msdn.com/chappell/articles/106056.aspx).

Dickheiser, M. (2006). *C++ for Game Programmers.* Charles River Media.

Digital Media Wire. *Project Millennials Sourcebook (2nd Ed.).* (2008). Pass Along / Digital Media Wire.

Donovan, T. (2010). *Replay: The history of video games.* Yellow Ant.

Duffy, J. (April 2009). "8th Annual Game Developer Salary Survey." *Game Developer Magazine.*

Duffy, J. (August 2007). "The Bean Counters." *Game Developer Magazine.*

Dunniway, T. & Novak, J. (2008). *Game development essentials: Gameplay mechanics.* Cengage Delmar.

Eberly, D. H. (2004). *3D game engine architecture: Engineering real-time applications with wild magic.* Morgan Kaufmann.

Egri, L. (1946). *The art of dramatic writing: Its basis in the creative interpretation of human motives.* Simon and Schuster.

Eischen, C. W. and Eischen, L. A. (2009). *Résumés, cover letters, networking, and interviewing.* South-Western College Pub.

Eisenman, S. (2006). *Building design portfolios: Innovative concepts for presenting your work.* Rockport Publishers.

Erikson, E.H. (1994). *Identity and the life cycle.* W.W. Norton & Company.

Erikson, E.H. (1995). *Childhood and society.* Vintage.

Escober, C. & Galindo, J. (2004). Fuzzy control in agriculture: Simulation software. *Industrial Simulation Conference 2004.*

Evans, A. (2001). *This virtual life: Escapism and simulation in our media world.* Fusion Press.

Fay, T. (2003). *DirectX 9 audio exposed: Interactive audio development,* Wordware Publishing.

Feare, T. (July 2000). "Simulation: Tactical tool for system builders." *Modern Materials Handling.*

Friedl, M. (2002). *Online game interactivity theory.* Charles River Media.

Fristrom, J. (July 14, 2003). "Production Testing & Bug Tracking." *Gamasutra* (www.gamasutra.com/view/feature/2829/production_testing_and_bug_tracking.php).

Fruin, N. & Harringan, P. (Eds.) (2004). *First person: New media as story, performance and game.* MIT Press.

Fullerton, T., Swain, C. & Hoffman, S. (2004). *Game design workshop: Designing, prototyping & playtesting games.* CMP Books.

Galitz, W.O. (2002). *The essential guide to user interface design: An introduction to GUI design principles and techniques.* (2nd ed.). Wiley.

Gamma, E., Helm, R., Johnson, R. & Vlissides, J. (1995). *Design patterns: Elements of reusable object-oriented software.* Addison-Wesley.

Gardner, J. (1991). *The art of fiction: Notes on craft for young writers.* Vintage Books.

Gee, J.P. (2003). *What video games have to teach us about learning and literacy.* Palgrave Macmillan.

Gershenfeld, A., Loparco, M. & Barajas, C. (2003). *Game plan: The insiders guide to breaking in and succeeding in the computer and video game business.* Griffin Trade Paperback.

Giarratano, J.C. & Riley, G.D. (1998). *Expert systems: Principles & programming (4th ed).* Course Technology.

Gibson, D., Aldrich, C. & Prensky, M. (Eds.) (2006). *Games and simulations in online learning.* IGI Global.

Gladwell, M. (2000). *The tipping point: How little things can make a big difference.* New York, NY: Little Brown & Company.

Gladwell, M. (2007). *Blink: The power of thinking without thinking.* Back Bay Books.

Gleick, J. (1987). *Chaos: Making a new science.* Viking.

Gleick, J. (1999). *Faster: The acceleration of just about everything.* Vintage Books.

Gleick, J. (2003). *What just happened: A chronicle from the information frontier.* Vintage.

Godin, S. (2003). *Purple cow: Transform your business by being remarkable.* Portfolio.

Godin, S. (2005). *The big moo: Stop trying to be perfect and start being remarkable.* Portfolio.

Goldratt, E.M. & Cox, J. (2004). *The goal: A process of ongoing improvement (3rd ed).* North River Press.

Gorden, R. L. (1998). *Basic interviewing skills.* Waveland Press.

Gordon, T. (2000). *P.E.T.: Parent effectiveness training.* Three Rivers Press.

Guilfoyle, E. (2007). *Half Life 2 mods for dummies.* For Dummies.

Guilfoyle, E. (2006). *Quake 4 mods for dummies.* For Dummies.

Habgood, J. & Overmars, M. (2006). *The game maker's apprentice: Game development for beginners.* Apress.

Hall, R. & Novak, J. (2008). *Game development essentials: Online game development.* Cengage Delmar.

Hamilton, E. (1940). *Mythology: Timeless tales of gods and heroes.* Mentor.

Hart, S.N. (1996-2000). "A Brief History of Home Video Games." *geekcomix* (www.geekcomix.com/vgh/main.shtml).

Heim, M. (1993). *The metaphysics of virtual reality.* Oxford University Press.

Hight, J. & Novak, J. (2007). *Game development essentials: Game project management.* Cengage Delmar.

Hofferber, K. & Isaacs, K. (2006). *The career change résumé.* McGraw-Hill.

Hornyak, T.N. (2006). *Loving the machine: The art and science of Japanese robots.* Kodansha International.

Hsu, F. (2004). *Behind Deep Blue: Building the computer that defeated the world chess champion.* Princeton University Press.

Hunt, C.W. (October 1998). "Uncertainty factor drives new approach to building simulations." *Signal.*

Jensen, E. (2006). *Enriching the brain: How to maximize every learner's potential.* John Wiley & Sons.

Isla, D. (2005). "Handling complexity in the *Halo 2* AI." Game Developers Conference.

Johnson, S. (1997). *Interface culture: How new technology transforms the way we create & communicate.* Basic Books.

Johnson, S. (2006). *Everything bad is good for you.* Riverhead.

Jung, C.G. (1969). *Man and his symbols.* Dell Publishing.

Kennedy, J. L. (2007), *Résumés for dummies.* For Dummies.

Kent, S.L. (2001). *The ultimate history of video games.* Prima.

King, S. (2000). *On writing.* Scribner.

Knoke, W. (1997). *Bold new world: The essential road map to the twenty-first century.* Kodansha International.

Koster, R. (2005). *Theory of fun for game design.* Paraglyph Press.

Krawczyk, M. & Novak, J. (2006). *Game development essentials: Game story & character development.* Cengage Delmar.

Kurzweil, R. (2000). *The age of spiritual machines: When computers exceed human intelligence.* Penguin.

Laramee, F.D. (Ed.) (2002). *Game design perspectives.* Charles River Media.

Laramee, F.D. (Ed.) (2005). *Secrets of the game business. (3rd ed).* Charles River Media.

Levy, L. & Novak, J. (2009). *Game development essentials: Game QA & testing.* Cengage Delmar.

Levy, P. (2001). *Cyberculture.* University of Minnesota Press.

Lewis, M. (2001). *Next: The future just happened.* W.W.Norton & Company.

Mackay, C. (1841). *Extraordinary popular delusions & the madness of crowds.* Three Rivers Press.

Marks, A. (2008). *The complete guide to game audio.* Elsevier/Focal Press.

Marks, A. & Novak, J. (2008). *Game development essentials: Game audio development.* Cengage Delmar.

Maurina III, E. F. (2006). *The game programmer's guide to Torque: Under the hood of the Torque game engine.* AK Peters Ltd.

McConnell, S. (1996). *Rapid development.* Microsoft Press.

McCorduck, P. (2004). *Machines who think: A personal inquiry into the history and prospects of artificial intelligence (2nd ed).* AK Peters.

McKenna, T. (December 2003). "This means war." *Journal of Electronic Defense.*

Meigs, T. (2003). *Ultimate game design: Building game worlds.* McGraw-Hill Osborne Media.

Mencher, M. (2002). *Get in the game: Careers in the game industry.* New Riders.

Meyers, S. (2005). *Effective C++: 55 specific ways to improve your programs and designs (3rd ed).* Addison-Wesley.

Michael, D. (2003). *The indie game development survival guide.* Charles River Media.

Montfort, N. (2003). *Twisty little passages: An approach to interactive fiction.* MIT Press.

Montfort, N. & Bogost, I. (2009). *Racing the beam: The Atari video game computer system.* The MIT Press.

Moore, M. & Novak, J. (2009). *Game development essentials: Game industry career guide.* Cengage Delmar Learning.

Moore, M. E. & Sward, J. (2006). *Introduction to the game industry.* Prentice Hall.

Moravec, H. (2000). *Robot.* Oxford University Press.

Morris, D. (September/October 2004). Virtual weather. *Weatherwise.*

Morris, D. & Hartas, L. (2003). *Game art: The graphic art of computer games.* Watson-Guptill Publications.

Muehl, W. & Novak, J. (2007). *Game development essentials: Game simulation development.* Cengage Delmar.

Mulligan, J. & Patrovsky, B. (2003). *Developing online games: An insider's guide.* New Riders.

Mummolo, J. (July 2006). "Helping children play." *Newsweek.*

Murray, J. (2001). *Hamlet on the holodeck: The future of narrative in cyberspace.* MIT Press.

Negroponte, N. (1996). *Being digital.* Vintage Books.

Newheiser, M. (June 28, 2010). "Adventure game puzzles: Unlocking the secrets of puzzle design." *Adventure Classic Gaming* (www.adventureclassicgaming.com/index.php/site/features/423/)

Nielsen, J. (1999). *Designing web usability: The practice of simplicity.* New Riders.

Nomadyun. (February 23, 2006). "Game Testing Methodology." *CN IT Blog* (www.cnitblog.com/nomadyun/archive/2006/02/23/6869.html).

Novak, J. (2011). *Game development essentials: An introduction (3rd ed).* Cengage Delmar.

Novak, J. & Levy, L. (2007). *Play the game: The parent's guide to video games.* Cengage Course Technology PTR.

Novak, J. (2003). "MMOGs as online distance learning applications." University of Southern California.

O'Donnell, M. & Marks, A. (2002). "The use and effectiveness of audio in *Halo*: Game music evolved." *Music4Games* (www.music4games.net/Features_Display.aspx?id=24).

Omernick, M. (2004). *Creating the art of the game.* New Riders Games.

Oram, A. (Ed.) (2001). *Peer-to-peer.* O'Reilly & Associates.

Patow, C.A. (December 2005). "Medical simulation makes medical education better & safer." *Health Management Technology*.

Peck, M. (January 2005). "Air Force's latest video game targets potential recruits." *National Defense*.

Pepastaek, J. "The PlayStation Gamemaker: Disassembling Net Yaroze" *Gamespot* (www.gamespot.com/features/vgs/psx/yaroze).

Pham, A. (October 20, 2008). "Mom, I Want to Major in Video Games." *Los Angeles Times* (www.latimes.com/business/la-fi-gamesschools20-2008oct20,1,1900670.story).

PHP Quality Assurance Team. "Handling Bug Reports?" *PHP-QAT* (qa.php.net/handling-bugs.php).

Piaget, J. (2000). *The psychology of the child.* Basic Books.

Piaget, J. (2007). *The child's conception of the world.* Jason Aronson.

Pohflepp, S. (January 2007). "Before and after Darwin." *We Make Money Not Art* (www.we-make-money-not -art.com/archives/009261.php).

Poole, S. (2004). *Trigger happy: Videogames and the entertainment revolution.* Arcade Publishing.

Prensky, M. (2006). *Don't bother me, Mom: I'm learning!* Paragon House.

Rabin, S. (2009). *Introduction to game development.* Concept Media.

Ramirez, J. (July 2006). "The new ad game." *Newsweek*.

Rheingold, H. (1991). *Virtual reality.* Touchstone.

Rheingold, H. (2000). *Tools for thought: The history and future of mind-expanding technology.* MIT Press.

Robbins, S.P. (2001). *Organizational behavior (9th ed).* Prentice-Hall, Inc.

Rogers, E.M. (1995). *Diffusion of innovations.* Free Press.

Rollings, A. & Morris, D. (2003). *Game architecture & design: A new edition.* New Riders.

Rollings, A. & Adams, E. (2003). *Andrew Rollings & Ernest Adams on game design.* New Riders.

Rouse, R. (2001) *Game design: Theory & practice (2nd ed).* Wordware Publishing.

Salen, K. & Zimmerman, E. (2003). *Rules of play.* MIT Press.

Sanchanta, M. (2006 January). "Japanese game aids U.S. war on obesity: Gym class in West Virginia to use an interactive dance console." *Financial Times*.

Sanger, G.A. [a.k.a. "The Fat Man"]. (2003). *The Fat Man on game audio.* New Riders.

Saltzman, M. (July 23, 1999). "Secrets of the Sages: Level Design." *Gamasutra* (www.gamasutra.com/view/feature/3360/secrets_of_the_sages_level_design.php).

Saunders, K. & Novak, J. (2007). *Game development essentials: Game interface design.* Cengage Delmar.

Schell, J. (2008). *The art of game design: A book of lenses.* Morgan Kaufmann.

Schildt, H. (2006). *Java: A beginner's guide (4th ed).* McGraw-Hill Osborne Media.

Schomaker, W. (September 2001). "Cosmic models match reality." *Astronomy*.

Sellers, J. (2001). *Arcade fever.* Running Press.

Shaffer, D.W. (2006). *How computer games help children learn.* Palgrave Macmillan.

Standage, T. (1999). *The Victorian Internet.* New York: Berkley Publishing Group.

Strauss, W. & Howe, N. (1992). *Generations.* Perennial.

Strauss, W. & Howe, N. (1993). *13th gen: Abort, retry, ignore, fail?* Vintage Books.

Strauss, W. & Howe, N. (1998). *The fourth turning.* Broadway Books.

Strauss, W. & Howe, N. (2000). *Millennials rising: The next great generation.* Vintage Books.

Strauss, W., Howe, N. & Markiewicz, P. (2006). *Millennials & the pop culture.* LifeCourse Associates.

Stroustrup, B. (2000). *The C++ programming language (3rd ed).* Addison-Wesley.

Szinger, J. (1993-2006). "On Composing Interactive Music." *Zing Man Productions* (www.zingman.com/spew/CompIntMusic.html).

Trotter, A. (November 2005). "Despite allure, using digital games for learning seen as no easy task." *Education Week.*

Tufte, E.R. (1983). *The visual display of quantitative information.* Graphics Press.

Tufte, E.R. (1990). *Envisioning information.* Graphics Press.

Tufte, E.R. (1997). *Visual explanations.* Graphics Press.

Tufte, E.R. (2006). *Beautiful evidence.* Graphics Press.

Turkle, S. (1997). *Life on the screen: Identity in the age of the Internet.* Touchstone.

Van Duyne, D.K. et al. (2003). *The design of sites.* Addison-Wesley.

Ventrice, T. (May 26, 2009). "The four perspectives of game design: Insight from the mobile fringe." *Gamasutra* (www.gamasutra.com/view/feature/4036/the_four_perspectives_of_game_.php?page=1)

Vogler, C. (1998). *The writer's journey: Mythic structure for writers. (2nd ed).* Michael Wiese Productions.

Weems, MD. (October 5, 2008). "10 Steps to Becoming a Video Game Tester." *Bright Hub* (www.brighthub.com/video-games/pc/articles/9819.aspx).

Welch, J. & Welch, S. (2005). *Winning.* HarperCollins Publishers.

Weizenbaum, J. (1984). *Computer power and human reason.* Penguin Books.

Wilcox, J. (2007). *Voiceovers: Techniques & Tactics for Success.* Allworth Press.

Williams, J.D. (1954). *The compleat strategyst: Being a primer on the theory of the games of strategy.* McGraw-Hill.

Wolf, J.P. & Perron, B. (Eds.). (2003). *Video game theory reader.* Routledge.

Wong, G. (November 2006). "Educators explore 'Second Life' online." *CNN.com* (www.cnn.com/2006/TECH/11/13/second.life.university/index.html).

Wysocki, R.K. (2006). *Effective project management (4th ed).* John Wiley & Sons.

Yuzwa, E. (2006). *Game programming in C++: Start to Finish.* Charles River Media.